People Power

People Power

Unarmed Resistance and Global Solidarity

Edited by
HOWARD CLARK

PLUTO PRESS
www.plutobooks.com

First published 2009 by Pluto Press
345 Archway Road, London N6 5AA and
175 Fifth Avenue, New York, NY 10010

www.plutobooks.com

Distributed in the United States of America exclusively by
Palgrave Macmillan, a division of St. Martin's Press LLC,
175 Fifth Avenue, New York, NY 10010

British Library Cataloguing in Publication Data
A catalogue record for this book is available from the British Library

ISBN   978 0 7453 2902 4   Hardback
ISBN   978 0 7453 2901 7   Paperback

Library of Congress Cataloging in Publication Data applied for

10 9 8 7 6 5 4 3 2 1

Designed and produced for Pluto Press by
Chase Publishing Services Ltd, Sidmouth, England
Typeset from disk by Stanford DTP Services, Northampton, England
Printed and bound in the European Union by
CPI Antony Rowe, Chippenham and Eastbourne

CONTENTS

Section III: Bases of Solidarity: Shared Identities, Interests and Beliefs

Section IV: Controversies in Transnational Action

LIST OF PHOTOGRAPHS, FIGURES AND TABLES

Photographs

Figures

Tables

ACKNOWLEDGEMENTS

This book grew out of an international seminar, Unarmed Resistance: The Transnational Factor, organised at the Centre for Peace and Reconciliation Studies, Coventry University, in July 2006. I am grateful to the Centre and its staff, Alan Hunter and Carol Rank, and especially its founding director, Andrew Rigby, for their support during this project and to Mousumi De for her work during and Charles Harlock for his work after the seminar. Jørgen Johansen and Christine Schweitzer, both researching their doctorates at the Centre, were involved in the early framing of the project. It is greatly to the credit of this Centre (founded in 1999) that it takes questions of nonviolent struggle and solidarity so seriously.

The Joseph Rowntree Charitable Trust deserve thanks not only for funding this seminar but for its supportive attitude towards applied research on nonviolence and its recognition of the need for meeting grounds between activism and research.

Naturally, I wish to thank all of the contributors to the book – some have been very patient in waiting for their paper to emerge in print, some have accepted considerable cuts in length, while one – Janet Cherry – has been wrestling with a situation unfolding as she wrote. I also wish to thank all those who participated in making the 2006 seminar such a rich event, including those who have not contributed to this book but whose presentations can be found on the website of the Centre for Peace and Reconciliation Studies or at www.civilresistance.info/urtf. One of these people needs to be singled out for special thanks. Without April Carter, I don't know when this book would have seen the light of day. She has been a marvellous source of advice and encouragement, commenting on every contribution, editing several, firing off reminders when they were needed, and in general keeping this project on track. It is not to underestimate the assiduous help I received from my other editorial consultant, Andrew Rigby, to acknowledge that his best contribution was to suggest April for this role. I am very grateful to them both.

Many of the contributors to this book have some connection with either War Resisters' International or with *Peace News*, now published monthly – a reflection on the continued stimulation I receive from these sources. I cannot thank everybody whose brains I picked but in addition to those mentioned elsewhere I would like to thank Michael Beer of Nonviolence International and Majken Søremsen.

I am very grateful to Robert Coles, Lou Dematteis and Gary Fields for contributing their photos, and to Mil Rai at *Peace News*, Ken Simons at *Peace Magazine* and Steve York at York-Zimmerman for help with picture research.

It has been a pleasure to cooperate with David Castle and his colleagues at Pluto Press, and on-the-ball copyeditor Matthew Seal. Long may such committed publishers thrive!

It is unusual to acknowledge computer software, but then most people do not use software that is itself an example of transnational solidarity in action. For nearly five years I have been using Ubuntu GNU-linux, an operating system that depends on the linux community whose solidarity allows non-geeks like me to resist Windows and the thrall of Microsoft. ('Ubuntu' is itself a concept much beloved of Desmond Tutu of humanity towards all.)

The close family always seem to come last in Acknowledgements, and sometimes they might feel that's the case in life too. My children Ismael and Violeta enjoy meeting visitors from other countries and have fond memories of their two terms in Coventry, but they do wish that I didn't spend quite so much time on my computer. Yolanda, thank you for so much – your work in Objeción Fiscal (war tax resistance) has always seemed to me a model of transnational solidarity, promoting social transformation at home combined with unconditional commitment to counterparts elsewhere.

ABBREVIATIONS

AARI	All-Africa Rights Initiative
AEI	Albert Einstein Institution
AI	Amnesty International
ANC	African National Congress (South Africa)
ASCOBA	Association of Communitarian Councils and Organisations of Bajo Atrato (Colombia)
ASEAN	Association of Southeast Asian Nations
ATTAC	Association pour la Taxation des Transactions Financières pour l'Aide aux Citoyens (Association for the Taxation of Financial Transactions for the Aid of Citizens)
BPT	Balkan Peace Team (1994–2001)
CAL	Coalition of African Lesbians
CANVAS	Centre for Applied NonViolent Action and Strategies (Belgrade)
CASI	Campaign Against Sanctions on Iraq
CAVIDA	Comunidades de Autodeterminación, Vida y Dignidad (Communities for Self-determination, Life and Dignity – Cacarica, Colombia)
CBO	Community-Based Organisation
CCCH	Coordinating Committee on the Cessation of Hostilities (Mindanao, Philippines)
CHIRRA	Chitungwiza Residents and Ratepayers Association (Zimbabwe)
CHRA	Combined Harare Residents Association (Zimbabwe)
CINEP	Centro de Investigación y Educación Popular (Centre for Research and Popular Education – Colombia)
CO	Conscientious Objection/Objector to military service
COSATU	Congress of South African Trade Unions
CPT	Christian Peacemaker Teams
CRPP	Committee Representing the People's Parliament (Burma)
DfID	Department for International Development (UK)
DVB	Democratic Voice of Burma
EAPPI	Ecumenical Accompaniment Programme in Palestine and Israel
ECHR	European Court of Human Rights
FARC	Fuerzas Armadas Revolucionarias de Colombia
FRY	Federal Republic of Yugoslavia

GALZ	Gays and Lesbians of Zimbabwe
GAM	Grupo de Apoyo Mutuo (Guatemala)
HIVOS	Humanistisch Instituut voor Ontwikkelingssamenwerking (Humanist Institute for Development Cooperation – Netherlands)
HRW	Human Rights Watch
IAMI	Istanbul Anti-militarist Initiative
IANSA	International Action Network on Small Arms
ICNC	International Center on Nonviolent Conflict
ICOM	International Conscientious Objectors' Meeting
IDF	Israeli Defence Forces
IFoR	International Fellowship of Reconciliation
IGLHRC	International Gay and Lesbian Human Rights Commission
ILGA	International Lesbian and Gay Association
ILO	International Labour Organisation
ISM	International Solidarity Movement
IWPS	International Women's Peace Service
LGBT	Lesbian Gay Bisexual Transsexual
LPG	Liberalisation, Privatisation and Globalisation
LTTE	Liberation Tigers of Tamil Eelam ('Tamil Tigers' – Sri Lanka)
MAI	Multilateral Agreement on Investment
MAP	Movement Action Plan
MDC	Movement for Democratic Change (Zimbabwe)
MILF	Moro Islamic Liberation Front (Mindanao, Philippines)
MNLF	Moro National Liberation Front (Mindanao, Philippines)
MST	Movimento dos Trabalhadores Rurais Sem Terra (Movement of Landless Farm Workers – Brazil)
NAFTA	North American Free Trade Association
NATO	North Atlantic Treaty Organisation
NCA	National Constitutional Assembly (Zimbabwe)
NGO	Non-Governmental Organisation
NLD	National League for Democracy (Burma)
NP	Nonviolent Peaceforce (NPSL – Nonviolent Peaceforce Sri Lanka)
OECD	Organisation for Economic Cooperation and Development
OSCE	Organisation for Security and Development in Europe
Otpor	Resist (Serbia)
PBI	Peace Brigades International
PTUZ	Progressive Teachers Union of Zimbabwe
PvH	Phillips van Heusen
R2P	Responsibility to Protect
SACP	South African Communist Party
SADC	Southern African Development Community

SKD	Savaş Karşıtları Derneği (War Resisters' Association, Turkey)
SLORC	State Law and Order Restoration Council (military junta in Burma/Myanmar 1988–97, renamed SPDC)
SMUG	Sexual Minorities of Uganda
SPDC	State Peace and Development Council (Burma/Myanmar)
UDF	United Democratic Front (South Africa)
UN	United Nations
UNHCR	United Nations High Commissioner for Refugees
UNICEF	United Nations Children's Fund
UNV	United Nations Volunteers
USIP	US Institute of Peace
VitW	Voices in the Wilderness
WiB	Women in Black
WILPF	Women's International League for Peace and Freedom
WOZA	Women of Zimbabwe Arise (MOZA – Men of Zimbabwe Arise)
WPB	World Peace Brigade (1961–64)
WRI	War Resisters' International
WSF	World Social Forum
WTO	World Trade Organisation
YIDEZ	Youth Initiative for Democracy in Zimbabwe
ZANU-PF	Zimbabwe African Union-Patriotic Front
ZCTU	Zimbabwe Congress of Trade Unions
ZIMTA	Zimbabwe Teachers Association
ZINASU	Zimbabwe National Students Union
ŽuC	Žene u Crnom protiv Rata (Women in Black against War – Serbia)

INTRODUCTION

Howard Clark

Throughout the world, people's movements are taking action to take control of their lives, to unseat undemocratic regimes, to resist global forces, to protect their livelihood, communities or even their lives, to defend the environment, or to assert their right to self-determination. While in the past movements often resorted to guerrilla warfare, and some still do, today's struggles frequently rely less on weapons than on unarmed forms of action – protests including mass demonstrations and strikes, counter-information (be that about election results or environmental impact), and the construction of alternatives.

Increasingly such movements seek international support, not just from governments or intergovernmental organisations but from networks of active citizens. They look to amplify their voice with the help of activists in other countries. Moreover, there are increasing numbers of transnational networks and advocacy groups set up to address global issues and offering various forms of training. Transnational action aims to strengthen the 'counter-power' of a local movement resisting state or corporate domination.

An outline of this book

This book arises from the contributors' involvement in various forms of transnational nonviolent action. The authors are activists and researchers seeking to enhance the effectiveness of transnational solidarity yet also being aware of its pitfalls and concerned to discuss principles of engagement. Pitfalls? Every group working across borders tends to publicise its achievements. However, they also need to learn from mistakes – either their own or those of others – especially as transnational work requires learning about other cultures and other ways of thinking and doing. Visit any of the world's more publicised sites of resistance or conflict, and we often encounter well-intentioned outsiders who do one or more of the following:

- raise expectations they cannot meet;
- offer funding for what they want to see done rather than what a local movement has decided needs to be done;

1

- mount projects to serve their own organisational needs rather than the people they are claiming to benefit;
- lobby international bodies for what they think is possible to achieve rather than for the demands formulated by those directly affected by an issue; or
- presume to speak in the name of people to whom they have not even listened – international 'leaders' who 'would not recognise a grass root if they trod on it'.

The contributors to this book are less concerned to criticise the shortcomings of others than to elucidate the principles on which they themselves work. Therefore the starting point for the book is not the transnational, but the local. The prime movers for change are not those abroad who offer economic support or training, nor those who try to bring issues to the attention of international policy-makers, nor even those who come to the country to contribute what they can to the struggle and share some of the risks facing local activists. This should all be subordinate to the work of people trying to change their own situation.

In this spirit, **Section I** of this book is devoted to accounts of five movements of unarmed resistance that incorporate distinct transnational elements but firmly place the resistance in its local context. Illustrating the global nature of unarmed resistance, examples are drawn from Africa, Asia, Europe and Latin America, covering struggles for peace and social justice as well as resistance to anti-democratic regimes. Resistance in the West is also important, not only in tackling the global dimension of power structures or providing a basis for solidarity with struggles elsewhere. However, the focus of this book is primarily on the relationships of solidarity with non-Western movements.

The experiences analysed in **Section I** are mainly since 2000 and in most cases are ongoing. Despite some local gains, most are not out-and-out success stories. Success is never as simple as 'winning'. In the context of protracted struggle for fundamental changes, it is also gaining support, expanding networks, opening new spaces for resistance, keeping hopes alive and limiting what power-holders or aggressors can get away with. 'Victory' also has its limits: the one movement studied here that has achieved its main goal – a movement that is rightly celebrated for its panache and that inspired emulation in other countries, a movement that achieved what war could not, namely the unseating of Slobodan Milošević in Serbia in 2000 – can be criticised for its failure to build a different Serbia.

Section II of the book switches focus to a form of activity mainly associated with peace movements – citizens' international nonviolent intervention at the site of a conflict. This includes the work of peace teams – including Peace Brigades International (PBI) and the more recently formed Nonviolent Peaceforce (NP) – who offer 'protection' to local civil society actors in conflict zones. It also includes the more defiant activities of the International Solidarity Movement, a

Photograph 1 The Spirit of Humanity, one of the Free Gaza Boats. On board is Free Gaza organiser and ISM co-founder, Huwaida Arraf. Free Gaza boats successfully ran the Israeli blockade several times between August 2008 and January 2009, although one – the SS *Dignity* – was rammed by an Israeli Navy boat. (Free Gaza)

Palestinian-led initiative that invites foreign activists to take part in nonviolent action in Palestine, and Voices in the Wilderness, which from 1995 onwards until the US-led invasion in 2003 broke the sanctions that were punishing all Iraqis for the crimes of their government and elite.

Section III investigates the functioning of various forms of solidarity based on shared identities, interests and beliefs in mobilising solidarity. There is no denying the impact of the internet on transnational activism, but strong networks need something additional to information-sharing, something that motivates people to take action – a sense of affinity, and awareness of a common bond. Therefore this section studies the role of networks based on gender, anti-militarism and sexual orientation, reports on solidarity action by diaspora groups and by workers, and discusses the role of the global justice movement with a particular focus on the World Social Forum.

Section IV addresses two related controversies that flow from the type of agenda that those purporting to support particular movements might have. Contributions – on funding (Jørgen Johansen) and training (George Lakey) – respond to accusations that even independent unofficial bodies offering solidarity may in effect be promoting Western governmental or corporate interests.

The remainder of this Introduction has three parts: the first introduces concepts of unarmed resistance and the development of resistance movements; the second discusses some of the issues arising from recent pro-democracy struggles; while the third sets the context for the enormous expansion in 'transnational activism' in recent years.

Unarmed resistance, 'people power' and nonviolent struggle

The choice of terms

I hesitated about referring to 'people power' – a term introduced when mass people's action brought down President Marcos in the Philippines in 1986. Subsequently 'people power' has often been used to talk about the downfall of governments and especially to protests against rigged elections. This is rather more limited than the frankly utopian concept 'power of the people' that I have often advocated, based on people taking control of their own lives. However, the term becomes more problematic in that 'people power' has frequently been used to described the mass mobilisation of one section of 'the people' against another: without going further back than 2008, we see examples of this in Kenya after the elections and in Thailand with the occupation of government house in Bangkok.[1] Ultimately I accepted the publisher's suggestion to use 'people power' in the spirit of reclaiming it so that it includes struggles that do not stop short with changing who rules, but which aim to bring about more complete social transformations than we have yet seen.

I preferred 'unarmed resistance' in the current context for three reasons:

- It is more accurate in situations where there is a threat of violence, a measure of counter-violence (such as stone-throwing), or where a movement has an armed wing but adopts 'unarmed' methods in many circumstances as do the Zapatistas in Chiapas, Mexico, and the Palestinians.
- It is a descriptive term, free of other associations.
- It is more inclusive, indeed includes 'nonviolent struggle'.

The term 'nonviolence' here is reserved specifically for movements that reject the use of violence and whose overall strategic framework is of ensuring that justice/human rights/democracy prevails rather than of destroying the antagonist.

'Unarmed resistance' encompasses a wide range of methods. Gene Sharp, who since the 1950s has dedicated himself to researching nonviolent action, has listed 198 nonviolent action methods, but suggests that there are 'scores' more (Sharp 1973). Almost every struggle invents – or perhaps thinks it has invented – new methods. Public methods range from quiet constructive action to direct confrontation, from spectacular stunts by small groups to massive popular demonstrations, from withdrawal of support through a boycott or strike or simply staying at home to occupying land or buildings. To these could be added a host of 'unobtrusive' actions that help maintain morale and construct the networks that underpin movements of resistance in repressive situations (Scott 1985, 1990; Johnston 2005).

The 'power' of nonviolent unarmed action is twofold:

First, **the power of refusal.** Many advocates of nonviolence argue that in the final analysis a regime cannot function without the cooperation – willing or constrained – of at least key sectors of the population. Therefore actual or threatened non-cooperation – by refusal to carry out orders, by strikes, etc. – is in many circumstances the most powerful weapon of resistance. Moreover, maintaining a stance of nonviolence can increase the effectiveness of this action by highlighting the violence – and therefore illegitimacy – of a regime or institution, thereby encouraging self-questioning among its support base or among 'third parties'.

Secondly, **the 'empowerment' of acting together.** At a minimum 'popular empowerment' means strengthening people's sense that they can make a difference, that there are alternatives to resigning themselves to the status quo. Particular elements of this power include:

- the power of communication in its many forms and in many directions, including counter-information;
- the power to organise, to reach out and link with people and other groups;
- the power to disrupt and defy; and
- the power simply to do things differently and show an alternative.

The beginnings of resistance

The term 'resistance' suggests disobedience, refusal and withdrawal, and non-institutional forms of struggle. This, as we shall see, is not the complete picture. Social movement scholars have suggested a distinction between 'contained' and 'transgressive' action (McAdam, Tarrow and Tilly 2001: 7). Forms of action that were once powerful and disruptive – such as strikes, civil disobedience, refusal to perform military service – in some societies have become 'contained', matters of routine. On the other hand, in the context of a closed society, a simple declaration – 'saying the unsayable' – can 'transgress' unwritten limits.

In their study of 'courageous resistance', Thalhammer et al. (2007) look at the internal and external factors conducive to 'ordinary people' making a courageous response to injustice. They term the internal factors *preconditions* – the resister's value system, previous experience and resources – while they group the external factors into *networks* and *context*, context being crucial to the success of any resistance campaign. Although Thalhammer et al. focus mainly on 'other-oriented' or 'altruistic' resisters, their observations are also relevant to 'self-activity' – such as when people struggle to defend their own rights and livelihoods.

Some other studies put more emphasis on the build-up of resistance through 'unobtrusive' activities. James Scott uses the term 'hidden transcript' – 'subaltern' social narratives running counter to the dominant 'official' reality: these might be stubbornly maintained for generations, as Scott shows in his studies of peasant resistance (Scott 1985, 1990). Hank Johnston, who has studied speech acts in authoritarian regimes (Franco's Spain, Pinochet's Chile and the Soviet bloc), refers to a range of informal speech acts in places from bars to kitchens as 'minimal collective action' and 'nascent resistance' (Johnston 2005). He describes an interplay between private and public spheres in expanding 'free spaces' and mounting sporadic protest events, as 'networks of dissent' grow on the quiet through officially-condoned associations, such as churches and clubs. This can escalate into more public action, but still with limited risk: 'hit-and-run protests', extending from graffiti and flag-flying to using funerals and other permitted assemblies, can embarrass officialdom.

Michael Randle's writing (Alternative Defence Commission 1983; Randle 1994) highlights the role of 'semi-resistance' especially in circumstances of occupation or severe repression. In addition to disguised non-cooperation (doing deliberately shoddy work, 'misunderstanding' orders), this includes public but low-risk activities that maintain the morale and unity of a resisting population while signalling dissent. Singing together was so important in Estonia that its independence struggle (1988–91) is sometimes referred to as 'the singing revolution'. Activities such as switching off lights (see below) and also the banging of pots and pans (*cacerolazos*) might catch on in very distinct situations.[2]

Mahatma Gandhi too saw a place for low-risk activities in the context of India's freedom struggle. For instance, he would call a low-risk action – such as a *hartal*, closing shops for a day – to test a community's readiness for a higher-risk, more confrontational action. More central to his approach, however, was the role of constructive action. Gandhi's 'constructive programme' was based in everyday activities to transform daily life. This combined personal practices – such as wearing *khadi* (homespun cloth) and 'bread labour' (doing some physical work for the general good, for instance, spinning, growing food, cleaning up toilets and rubbish) – and collective efforts to eliminate discrimination and ignorance and so to strengthen community self-reliance. This could also be viewed as building what might now be called an 'infrastructure' of resistance – the social networks necessary to mount campaigns and the attitudes necessary to withstand both provocation and repression.

Researchers on strategic nonviolence in the tradition of Gene Sharp emphasise the importance of 'grand strategy' in planning nonviolent resistance. Movements of resistance are defeated, they suggest, not just because of overwhelming odds, but through lack of a strategy that identifies realistic goals, how to build up their own strength, where to make alliances and how to weaken their opponent's power base.[3] Certainly such a plan, as well as increasing the effectiveness of many campaigns, would help outside groups decide on what they can contribute. However, there are also many incalculables in movement development.

One of these concerns the impact of heavy-handed acts of repression. Repression might quell popular agitation for a time, as has happened in Burma (see Section I), but it can also prove a catalyst, 'backfiring' against power-holders. As Brian Martin argues (see Section II), power-holders use various tactics to neutralise the impact of 'backfire', and movements in turn need to develop their own counter-measures to ensure that repression does indeed backfire, including functions to be carried out by transnational groups. Luis Enrique Eguren (see Section II) suggests that transnational groups can help emerging movements by introducing greater predictability into the state's reaction – limiting the scope for and increasing the costs of repression. These strategic calculations, however, still face the unknown: how will the public react to the emerging movement?

Many movements come into existence without knowing what they can achieve. Especially in the early days, every action is an experiment – testing the ground. In 1998 when Otpor began spraying graffiti in Belgrade, few could have imagined the impact they would have in the next two years (see below and Section I). In order to grow and develop, movements have to be capable of improvisation, adapting to changing contexts and widening horizons.

Not only protest but also constructive action can sometimes exceed all expectations. In 1976 Wangari Maathai proposed that Kenya's National Council of Women should organise tree-planting to address various economic problems. This was not even oppositional activity – at first they counted on cooperation with the government's forestry commission. However, it led to the foundation of the Green Belt movement, which by the 1990s had not only planted millions of trees but was in the forefront of national campaigns against corruption and for multi-party democracy. Maathai herself, beaten and jailed at various times, has emerged as a leading spokeswoman in the world campaign to cancel 'third world' debt, a Nobel Peace Prize-winner and a government minister.

Where the 'transnational' fits

The forms taken by transnational solidarity should depend on local movement strategy, and in particular on the phases in the development of that movement. In the 'nascent' or 'pre-movement' phase of resistance, transnational actors have played a role referred to by some social movements scholars as 'movement mid-wives'.[4]

A 'movement mid-wife' concretely might offer connections with related movements or with specific expertise, training both in nonviolence and in response to other needs, and various forms of 'accompaniment', including perhaps the 'protective' accompaniment of a physical presence or 'accompaniment' in a wider sense of general support in their strategy development (examples are discussed in Section II).

As a group or movement grows, there are several motives in seeking international allies – leverage on a corporation, protection against repression, access to resources (contacts, expertise, funds) or the most basic sense of solidarity, of standing shoulder-to-shoulder in a common cause. Local movements also have to be aware, however, of the agenda of those transnational groups that might be interested in working with them. At times such groups, rather than seeking to offer solidarity based on the local movement's agenda, want to find an NGO willing to be an 'implementing partner' for a programme conceived by outsiders. Then if a local group questions the outsiders' assumptions, instead of listening and reconsidering their plan, a well-funded outside agency might simply look for – or even create – another more amenable NGO. When activists complain of the 'NGO-isation' of a local movement, they are often referring to this pattern of imposition. To withstand it, and to insist that 'partnerships' are relationships based on common joint strategising, a local movement needs strategic clarity, good coordination and the confidence to set its own terms for solidarity.

Resistance for what?

Historically, unarmed resistance has been waged primarily against colonialism and for self-determination, or by the excluded and oppressed to attain rights and economic justice. Both remain major themes, and increasingly are pursued with a transnational focus. As will be discussed later in this Introduction, the sphere of transnational activism has expanded enormously. The varieties of action for peace, for human and civil rights (of women, or workers, of 'minorities', of indigenous groups) and for economic justice have proliferated, while concerns previously confined to science fiction have come to the fore – the protection of the planet itself and of particular species.

Issues of democracy at a national level also give rise to unarmed resistance, especially dictatorship, authoritarianism, electoral fraud and other forms of corruption, where the cry continues to be heard that 'outside agitators' or 'enemy agents' are 'interfering' in the affairs of a sovereign state.

Pro-democracy struggles

Even in states with multi-party elections, nonviolent movements often challenge what passes for democracy – rival parties alternating in government while maintaining social injustice, privileging business interests, pursuing the same foreign and defence policies, and making decisions in secret. Historically, therefore, nonviolent action has applied democratic principles beyond the narrow political sphere, using extra-constitutional means of action and advocating more participatory forms of democracy.

Pro-democracy struggle is certainly not necessarily a struggle for regime change. The 1980s pro-democracy movements in the 'Socialist' bloc of East and Central Europe were 'self-limiting' – seeking to expand democracy, for instance, through establishing free trade unions, without seeking to overturn the government. Many – probably most – movement activists were taken by surprise in 1989 when political power came within their reach.

A number of countries have seen anti-corruption campaigns that steer clear of party politics, aiming to change public policy rather than the government. The goal of the remarkable Turkish Citizens Initiative 'One Minute of Darkness for Constant Light' was to instigate government investigation into complicity with organised crime and to remove parliamentary immunity on this. Its high point and major coordinated action was a massive switching off of lights in an estimated 30 million households at 9pm during a two-week spell in February 1997 (Akay 2003). One result was Turkey's most far-reaching investigation and the trial of a number of leaders of crime syndicates. Another was a continuing role for the Citizens Initiative network – in coordinating civic responses after the December 1998 earthquake and using the lights-out tactic again in 2003 against proposed Turkish cooperation with the US invasion of Iraq.

One of the most striking recent campaigns for democracy took place in Nepal. In April 2006, mass strikes and demonstrations forced King Gyanendra to reinstate parliament (which he had dissolved in 2002). The 2008 elections produced the parliament most representative yet of Nepal's diversity, including a third women, which then promptly and almost unanimously abolished the monarchy. A previous 'people's power' episode in 1990 had succeeded in limiting the powers of the monarchy, only to be undermined by the inefficiency and corruption of the subsequent parliamentary government, which in turn led the Maoist Communist Party of Nepal to launch guerrilla warfare in the countryside in 1996. The unusual feature of the April 2006 movement was that the Maoists decided to join with the mainstream democratic parties, and ordinary members of the public, in an unarmed struggle for democratic reform (Vanaik 2008; International Crisis Group 2008). After ending their People's War and entering into constitutional politics, the Maoists emerged as the largest parliamentary party and the ruling coalition appointed a Maoist prime minister.[5]

The centre of discussion on pro-democracy struggles since 2000 has tended to be the 'electoral revolutions'. Elections – the occasions when governments seek to relegitimate themselves – have become moments for a showdown. People who previously have passively endured government criminality have not only voted but taken to the streets to overcome electoral fraud and nonviolently enforce 'the people's will'.

The 'coloured' revolutions of Serbia (2000), Georgia (2003), Ukraine (2004) and Kyrgyzstan (2005) took place in countries noted for their corruption.[6] The democratic opposition united in a coalition, energised in particular by inventive youth activists, and prepared strategies of nonviolent resistance in case the government sought to stay in power by force. In the event, each government stepped down in the face of mass extra-constitutional action. Yet, while formal political power changed hands, the subsequent progress towards democratisation has been disappointing, especially from the point of view of 'civil society' (as distinct from political parties) (see Ivana Franović in Section I).

Various states – especially but not only post-Soviet states – were alarmed by the success of these events, presenting this 'wave of democratisation' as being the work of Western 'democracy promotion' agencies (see Jørgen Johansen in Section IV). However, as participant accounts and the academic literature bear out, it was not so much outside encouragement or support that spread the idea of 'electoral revolution' as the contagion of an idea, an image, a methodology.[7] Be that as it may, there has been a severe clampdown on civil society activity in Russia itself and Belarus, while in Uzbekistan unarmed opposition has been attacked as a front for 'terrorism'.[8] More generally, and not least in the West, the 'war against terror' has provided a pretext for states to 'criminalise' social movements – expanding powers of arbitrary detention, curbing rights of assembly, placing civil organisations under surveillance and restricting opportunities for cross-border cooperation.

Disquiet over the level of Western support for opposition coalitions in Serbia and the post-Soviet countries has spilled over into criticism of the contacts between Serbia's Otpor and counterparts in several post-Soviet countries. It is only natural that youth movements engaged in struggles for democracy should enjoy the interchange of ideas, experiences and perspectives. Nevertheless, trainers from Otpor – and others who are offering training and advice to opposition movements – have been accused of being tools of Western imperialism. This issue is addressed further in Section IV.

The International Center on Nonviolent Conflict (ICNC) is now lobbying for 'the right to help' nonviolent democratic movements. This is already implicit in international humanitarian law, and theoretically should have been strengthened by the adoption of the doctrine of 'Responsibility to Protect' (R2P).[9] This maintains that when a state persecutes or fails to protect a section of its own population, this protection becomes an international responsibility. However, R2P – while urging support for civil society initiatives on 'conflict prevention' – stops short of advocating support for groups waging nonviolent conflict to defend their rights.

Transnational activism

Transnational activism itself is not new, nor even is the concept of 'global citizenship'. Various forms of international solidarity action – including demonstrations, strikes and boycotts – featured in many campaigns in the first half of the twentieth century, and indeed earlier (anti-slavery, workers' struggles, women's movements). However, the enormous growth in number of transnational NGOs in the second half of the twentieth century has led observers to suggest there has appeared 'a new force in international politics ... transforming global norms and practices' (Khagram, Riker and Sikkink 2002: 4). The changes can be seen at various levels – the sheer proliferation of transnational advocacy, the spread of networks and the 'density' of their connections, and the outcome in significant changes in international standards.

Forty years 'sans frontières'

My own activism stretches back for forty years. Looking back to 1968, it is not to discuss events that were formative for my 18-year-old self but to draw attention to the range of initiatives that gained impetus in that atmosphere:

- the second wave of women's liberation arrived;
- Friends of the Earth was founded, soon followed by Greenpeace;
- the critique of 'development' and 'development aid' led to the launch of pro-'third world' groups (including in Britain the magazine *The New Internationalist* – the first to accuse Nestlé of causing baby deaths) and the opening of the first 'world' shops and fair trade networks;
- in 1969 Survival International was set up as a response to the threat to indigenous peoples;
- the Stonewall riots in San Francisco triggered the launch of the gay liberation movement;
- the experience of the Nigerian Civil War led to the establishment of Médecins sans Frontières in 1971 – the first of the 'sans Frontières' groups whose very name asserts that human needs should override state boundaries; and
- the phrase 'Think Globally, Act Locally' was coined.

In each of the areas mentioned, there have subsequently been significant 'norm shifts', especially since the end of the Cold War, that have been reflected in constitutional changes (indigenous rights in Colombia, gay rights in South Africa) and international conventions. 'Top-down' action can certainly advance an issue, such as when the UN – often in response to campaign groups – convenes a conference, declares an international year of concern or dedicates a particular day to an issue. However, the main motor for these changes has been citizens' action around the world.

Global campaigns

A central transnational experience in the second half of the twentieth century was the momentous struggle against apartheid. The global anti-apartheid movement (a movement of citizens that also counted on the support of various governments) did not invent many new methods, but brought together a powerful repertoire of 'people's sanctions' – not least in its anti-corporate campaigning where institutions (universities, churches, trade unions, municipalities) were enlisted into boycott and disinvestment campaigns.

Apartheid was such a monstrous system that it demanded precedent-setting responses. An example from my work with war resisters is that for the first time the UN called on citizens to refuse to fight for their country, a precedent that led to conscientious objection becoming a ground for asylum first for South Africans and then more widely. Today various peoples – most obviously but by no means only the Palestinians – liken their situation to apartheid in order to appeal to the precedents set in the anti-apartheid struggle.

Other campaigns have also proved formative in the spread of transnational activism on a range of issues. Rights-based campaigns – be they for human rights in general or to support particular groups denied their rights – have strengthened human rights instruments, including global and regional conventions and supranational tribunals. Feminism, peace and ecology are also perspectives that cut across national frameworks. In many respects women's movements are among the most highly developed transnational networks. Women's networks have mounted powerful campaigns on various rights, against specific abuses such as human trafficking or genital mutilation, and in solidarity with women trying to change oppressive cultural practices, such as the network Women Living Under Muslim Laws. Women's movements also insist that issues of peace and disarmament, responses to conflict, and economic and environmental struggles, should be seen as feminist issues. Solidarity with women workers has been a strong thread in campaigns against the exploitation of 'cheap labour' by multinational corporations and their subcontractors. Meanwhile the spread of a concept such as 'livelihood struggle' – that addresses the survival needs of a community in both economic and environmental terms – often entails recognising the local leadership role played by women who hold families and communities together.

Transnational campaigns have targeted international institutions, states and corporations, or sometimes a combination of the three. Whether or not they have succeeded in attaining particular demands, overall they have built up the capacity for citizens groups to react transnationally on a range of issues and also have changed the terms of debate over a number of internationally agreed standards.

Campaigns against specific instances of logging, mining, genetic engineering and mega-projects such as big dams have also changed the official terms of reference. While the campaign against the Narmada dams in India did not stop their construction, it did succeed in changing the policy of certain governments towards such projects and convinced the World Bank to withdraw and then sponsor an independent World Dam Commission to lay down standards for the future (Kothari 2002: 238).

Certain concerted transnational campaigns directly address a global issue: the Campaign to Ban Land Mines and the Jubilee 2000 campaign for debt cancellation were outstanding examples (Donnelly 2002; Randle 2004). Less known perhaps but equally significant was the defeat of the Multilateral Agreement on Investment (MAI), one of the successful campaigns against expanding the 'freedom' of corporations (see below). Currently the global campaign on climate change embraces many different perspectives and actors, but benefits from the connections forged in earlier campaigns.

Anti-corporate campaigns such as the Nestlé boycott (for marketing baby formula as superior to mother's milk), various campaigns against Shell (over dumping the Brent Spar oil storage buoy in the North Sea,[10] in support of the Ogonis in Nigeria or the U'wa in Colombia), the anti-sweatshop campaigns aimed particularly against designer garment manufacturers such as Nike – these have all pressured corporations to rethink their positions on corporate responsibility, encouraged too in 1999 by the Global Compact promoting 'corporate social responsibility' launched by then UN Secretary-General Kofi Annan.

Such changes of attitude testify to the impact of campaigns, although it should also be recognised that corporations rarely acknowledge that they heed boycotters or that their profits are affected. Moreover, when corporations use 'social responsibility' as part of their public relations, making 'statements of intention' and offering codes of self-regulation, their change of strategy actually sets back campaigns for more fundamental change, for international monitoring and global enforcement. This critique has been made in detail in relation to sweatshops (Seidman 2007), logging (World Rainforest Movement 2008) and mining (Moody 2007 and at www.minesandcommunities.org). More widely the term 'Greenwash' has been coined, defined by CorpWatch (www.corpwatch.org) as 'socially and environmentally destructive corporations, attempting to preserve and expand their markets or power by posing as friends of the environment'. This is now so widespread that CorpWatch makes bi-monthly 'Greenwash' awards to corporations 'that put more money, time and energy into slick PR campaigns aimed at promoting their eco-friendly images, than they do to actually protecting the environment', while in Britain in 2008 the *Guardian* newspaper has given ecological campaigner Fred Pearce a 'Greenwash' column.

Throughout all these campaigns and the connected multiplication of monitoring groups, transnational citizen's networks have been expanding their capacity to contest global institutions and multinational corporations. A central part of this capacity is counter-information.

Counter-information

Credible information is central to the moral authority of citizens groups, and a host of groups are currently monitoring issues of transnational concern. Amnesty International (AI), founded in 1961, in many ways set the standard for impartial information and popularised one pattern for campaigning – local groups 'adopting' particular prisoners or cases and following them. Since the Worldwatch Institute was founded in 1974 – mainly monitoring environmental issues – the Watch idea has spread. Moscow Helsinki Watch was set up by Soviet citizens to check implementation of the Helsinki Accords of 1976, and in turn inspired the US Helsinki Watch, which grew into the multi-national Human Rights Watch.

This monitoring is vital in strengthening the case of advocacy groups, in showing either the inadequacy of existing standards or failure to comply with them. It also can help maintain activist networks in a state of preparedness, aware – or able to update themselves quickly – about how the situations that concern them are developing and better able to respond quickly as the need arises.

The world-wide web has revolutionised the scene for activists. It can be unstoppable when someone leaks information that power-holders want to hide. An outstanding example is the defeat of the Multilateral Agreement on Investment (MAI), a treaty to limit the powers of local authorities apropos foreign investors. Somebody leaked the draft agreement, and soon it was freely available – together with expert analysis.[11]

As a powerful tool for mobilisation, the web offers new variations of established forms of protest (letter-writing, petitions, graffiti and otherwise doctoring images) but on a new scale and with a new rapidity. The web played an important role in the 'electoral revolutions', but in terms of national communication rather than transnational protest. Repressive regimes have probably less to fear from transnational web protests than have multinational corporations. Perhaps the junta in Burma can simply ignore the 375,000 people around the world who quickly registered as 'fans' of Facebook's 'Support the Monks' Protest in Burma' site in October 2007, or it can try to block internet access inside the country.

A multinational corporation, on the other hand, cannot prevent circulation of damaging information or images. For McDonald's, the nightmare of their decision to prosecute the McLibel Two was compounded as the number of visitors to the McSpotlight website soared to more than a million a month.[12] Nike's refusal to accept an internet order for a personalised shoe carrying the word 'sweatshop', and the subsequent correspondence with the campaigner who had this bright idea, was broadcast far and wide on the web (Stolle and Micheletti 2005).

Counter-information and the internet are seen as crucial elements in the effectiveness of transnational advocacy networks, and in particular in achieving what has been termed 'the boomerang effect' (Keck and Sikkink 1998).

'The boomerang effect'

Keck and Sikkink's graphic image of the flight of the boomerang is now widely used by social movement scholars in discussing the function of transnational solidarity. When a local campaign is not making headway (either because of repression or through lack of social response), then it throws a boomerang towards the rest of the world. In particular, this might involve 'naming and shaming' the target of its campaign with the idea that the boomerang will return, hitting its target with international pressure, be that from the metropolitan home base of a corporation or the international allies of a regime or through transnational citizens' mobilisation. The way that Greenpeace International orchestrates international pressure provides a particularly clear example of the boomerang effect. Local groups approach Greenpeace to take up their cause. If Greenpeace makes it a priority, then the campaign is likely to combine various levels and styles of action:

- lobbying high-level bodies, bringing court cases and presenting scientific evidence to expert tribunals;
- media campaigns including direct action, stunts and 'culture-jamming' (Greenpeace claims the credit for putting the $ in E$$O);
- mobilising its membership in mass letter-writing, petitions, 'cyberactions' and consumer action.

Because Greenpeace has such a comprehensive campaigning repertoire, it is possible to see the 'boomerang effect' concentrated in the activity of one NGO. However, more frequently, it takes somewhat more diffuse forms – involving chains of connections and coalitions of groups, including both NGOs and movements, or through a rapid internet mobilisation. The flight of the boomerang might pass through NGOs and activist constituencies, media, government departments and intergovernmental institutions before returning to make a difference at the point from where it was thrown.

If the 'boomerang effect' provides a useful image, it also illustrates some problems of transnational solidarity. The social movement scholar Sidney Tarrow notes that the boomerang works best when thrown upwards (in terms of global hierarchies of power) rather than horizontally towards parallel campaigns equally distant from metropolitan power centres. Moreover, 'as the locus of decision-making move[s] upward', that is as the boomerang reaches the most distant point in its flight, those in the locality most directly affected tend to have less say (Tarrow 2005: 157–9). In short, a coalition that originates as an act of solidarity reproduces some features of global power relationships.

Returning to Greenpeace, the NGO has been the object of activist criticism for three decades – ever since the Vancouver Greenpeace Foundation established Greenpeace International to supersede the decentralised network of autonomous groups inspired by the original concept. In terms of campaign planning, Greenpeace's approach is coherent with pros and cons open to debate. An entertaining book by one of its outstanding campaign directors (Rose 2005) shows that Greenpeace consciously presents itself as a David perpetually championing the planet against a range of Goliaths. It needs to be seen as a 'protagonist' if it is to maintain its considerable Western support base (2.8 million members worldwide, according to its webpage). It concentrates on easy-to-understand popular messages and also chooses various 'easy targets' (Rose's 'low hanging fruit') to balance some of the 'hard nuts' it also tries to crack.

Greenpeace rarely tries to connect campaign issues: a partial exception is made in the case of indigenous peoples – the communities often most directly threatened by environmental destruction. But Greenpeace is wary of supporting environmental campaigns linked with demands for self-determination, and it is rare to find Greenpeace referring to women's or trade union rights. As one of the groups likely to advise campaigns to 'reframe' their message, Greenpeace would prefer to steer local campaigners away from contentious issues of where social power lies or what constitutes social justice into the comparatively safer waters of environmental impact. In sum, Greenpeace generally seeks results less in terms of local community empowerment than in changing the policies of the power-holders.

Accusations of Greenpeace 'taking over' from local campaigners, or behaving more like a 'green Svengali' than a 'movement mid-wife' in helping local campaigners reframe issues, should not be accepted uncritically – some Greenpeace campaigners have been exemplary in respecting local movements. However, what is true – not just for Greenpeace but more generally for metropolitan groups who play a part in producing the 'boomerang effect' – is that such advocacy groups are tempted to behave in ways that eventually are resented by the local campaigns that are supposedly 'beneficiaries'. Gaining 'leverage' should conceptually be a form of community empowerment, but in practice there is often a tension between these emphases. This is seen most clearly when there arises a disparity between what local movements demand and what is lobbied for by advocates near the seats of global power – an issue raised by Andreas Speck in Section III.

Several commentators on North American solidarity campaigns with *maquiladora* (subcontracted workers) in Central America make related criticisms. Seidman takes issue with what she sees as the 'human rights' approach of mobilising concern through presenting sweatshop workers and others as mere 'victims' rather than as a force trying to organise themselves (Seidman 2007). Dominguez and Quintero (2008), studying Mexican *maquiladora* workers' alliances with North American groups, note the paternalism of Canadian and especially US partners, and argue that Northern support for the process of 'NGO-isation' created divisions because local NGOs are not representative of, still less accountable to, the workers themselves. Armbruster-Sandoval, studying four cases of cooperation on anti-sweatshop campaigns, finds the boomerang concept useful, but suggests that, in over-emphasising the role of transnational advocacy, it 'unconsciously marginalises (mostly "women of colour") garment workers from narratives of resistance while privileging white, First-World, middle-class activists and consumers' (Armbruster-Sandoval 2005a: 467).

Furthermore, because of the global mobility of capital, 'victory' against a corporation tends to be temporary. A corporation might concede workers' demands for 'employment with dignity' only to close the plant as soon as they have developed a cheaper source of labour as did Phillips van Heusen (PvH). In 1997 PvH workers in Guatemala won a six-year struggle for collective bargaining rights, considered a model of cross-border organising at the time. Yet 15 months later PvH closed the factory (Armbruster-Sandoval 2005b: 31). Armbruster-Sandoval suggests that in the final analysis what is necessary is not a boomerang but a struggle to transform global power relations such as we find in the global justice movement (see below).

This book contains several accounts where 'boomerang' has played a role. In Colombia, the army units who killed members of the peace community of San Jose de Apartadó (Section I) now face prosecution, partly thanks to international pressure, while Congress has denied US military aid to that particular brigade of the Colombian army. Peace Brigades International (PBI) (Section II) in Colombia can also be seen as part of a boomerang mechanism, producing authoritative eyewitness accounts of human rights violations. Other examples of 'boomerang effect' are examined in Section III: workers refusing to ship arms to Zimbabwe, Indian diaspora groups in Canada convincing Alcan to abandon a mining project in Orissa, while the European Court of Justice and UN bodies have condemned Turkey's treatment of conscientious objectors to military service. Although these are 'outcomes' of transnational solidarity, the relationships of solidarity are not just instruments to achieve such results. Rather they reflect a deeper commitment.

In Section III, we look at various networks that can and do fulfil boomerang functions in terms of leverage and access to resources but which are based on some sense of commonality/solidarity beyond the particular issue in question. One of these networks, and perhaps the one readers most readily associate with the term 'transnational activism', is the global justice movement.

The global justice movement

The movement that emerged as a response to capitalist globalisation and 'neoliberalism' has since played a major role in anti-war mobilisation, most notably with the biggest day of protest the world has yet seen – 15 February 2003.

The movement's identity is quite malleable. There are many for whom it is an expression of an attitude now popularised by the Zapatistas but historically inherent in anarchism and feminism: 'changing the world without taking power'. Yet somehow many of the same people fail to be embarrassed by and even participate in the uncritical lionisation of politicians such as Brazil's Lula and Venezuela's Chávez.

Participants in some of the big events – either the counter-summits such as Seattle (1999), Prague (2000), Cancun and Genoa (2003), or the World Social Forums (see Stellan Vinthagen in Section III) – view themselves as part of a 'movement of movements' responding to many facets of the global power system. Various commentators refer to this as a 'counter-hegemonic mobilisation', offering movements a critical alternative frame to the existing world system, including capitalist globalisation, the 'war on terror' and other planetary threats. It is this *convergence* that gives the moment its freshness and transformatory character – the encounter between perspectives that are different yet have enough in common to intersect and enrich each other. Yet while the movement is strong on critique and on vision, it is weak on strategy.

It is clearly much more difficult to devise effective strategies against a global power system than it is to tackle its 'worst excesses'. Bill Moyer devised his Movement Action Plan (MAP) model to help social movement activists address issues of strategy, and in particular to recognise their achievements and not lose heart over setbacks. One of several points that distinguishes his approach to campaigning is that Moyer urged movements not only 'to advocate reforms to redress symptoms of social problems, but to promote a paradigm shift, a change in the larger worldview that causes and maintains the problem', ultimately to insist on social change rather than the minimal reforms that power-holders would prefer to concede (Moyer et al. 2001: 71).

To some extent, through its combinations of issues and perspectives from different parts of the world, the global justice movement adds this element of 'paradigm shift' to existing campaigns. Therefore, instead of seeing the desire of activists to 'embrace diversity' as a source of strategic weakness, it can be a strength, as Tarrow has argued: 'Global justice is an effective frame for domestic contention because it facilitates the condensation of many distinct targets in the same protest campaign ... Global justice has proven an excellent frame-bridging symbol.' Nevertheless, continues Tarrow, the global justice movement (and other transnational coalitions) still faces the strategic challenge: how to 'construct a template that is both relevant to local issues and resonates with the broader theme of global justice' (Tarrow 2005: 74–5).

Realising the potential of global movements for transformation depends on maintaining or constructing relationships and networks of solidarity with both vertical and horizontal axes. If movements look vertically for transnational leverage, then they should be advised to look horizontally for inspiration and mutual learning, as discussed in Chesterfield Samba's contribution on lesbian and gay organising in Africa (Section III) and Cynthia Cockburn's work on Women in Black (Cockburn 2007 and Section III of this book).

This book is published at a time when the global justice movement is in one of its less optimistic phases – some even suspect it is coming to the end of its life-cycle. The reality is, as the late Bill Moyer would have pointed out, in the excitement of the take-off stage of the movement, unrealistic expectations are generated leading to disappointment and loss of momentum. The appropriate response is for activists to recognise what they are doing well, to strengthen their structures and in this case deepen the relationships of transnational solidarity, not seeking short-term results as much as grounding the movement for the long haul.

Notes

1. The 'yellow revolution' in Bangkok (yellow to identify with the royal family) sees the People's Alliance for Democracy, representing Thailand's urban elite, arguing to limit the voting power of Thailand's rural poor.
2. Although *cacerolazos* are now associated with protest against the Pinochet dictatorship in Chile and more recently in Argentina, it seems that the first ones were actually right-wing protests against the Allende government in Chile.
3. In addition to Sharp himself, leading exponents of this approach are Ackerman and Kruegler (1993), Helvey (2004) and most recently the material being produced in Belgrade by former members of Otpor (www.canvasopedia.org). They pay particular attention to ending authoritarian rule. Another approach, exemplified by Bill Moyer's Movement Action Plan, is based on analysing campaigns on social issues (Moyer et al. 2001). For further reading on how groups use nonviolence training to develop strategy, see Carter, Clark and Randle (2006), Section I at www.civilresistance.info.
4. For instance, Pagnucco and McCarthy (1999) suggest that the Latin American network Servicio Paz y Justicia operated in this way in the 1980s and 1990s, as did the US Fellowship of Reconciliation in the 1940s and 1950s in assisting the birth of the US civil rights movement.
5. At the time of writing, there remains an impasse over proposals to integrate Maoist guerrillas into the state security forces.

6. The example of Kyrgyzstan is somewhat distinct, not only because of the initial widespread looting – to which 'civil society' volunteers responded by joining street patrols – but also the role of family and business ties in the change of power.

7. On the support offered by Russia on the one hand to the regime, and Western official or quasi-official bodies on the other to the opposition in the Ukraine, and for an assessment of how far external intervention was significant, see Wilson (2005).

8. The most extreme single event was in Uzbekistan – the Andijan massacre of May 2005 in which state forces killed hundreds of unarmed citizens in a predominantly Muslim town. Although this followed the Tashkent bombings of 1999, and although the trigger incident was an armed group raiding police and military armouries and then releasing 23 imprisoned business leaders, it should be noted that this followed weeks of peaceful protest for the release of business leaders whose real crime seems to have been to mount a Muslim 'constructive programme' – creating employment, funding a hospital and schools (Human Rights Watch 2005).

9. *The Responsibility to Protect* report was commissioned by the Canadian government and produced in 2001 by the International Commission on Intervention and State Sovereignty. It has subsequently been adopted as a framework by various departments of the UN. When a state is unwilling or unable to protect its citizens from 'avoidable catastrophe', argues R2P, then protection becomes an international responsibility. The R2P doctrine proposes a framework for 'humanitarian' military intervention, but only after progressive engagement such as responding to 'early warnings' (violent clashes or large-scale human rights abuses) with 'conflict prevention' measures and support for civil society. Since 2003, the Canadian and British governments have been funding a campaign to build NGO support for 'R2P' implementation. However, this does not extend to discussing the use of nonviolent means of struggle. The campaign's website is http://www.responsibilitytoprotect.org.

10. Although Greenpeace itself lost some credibility through exaggerating the residues to be dumped.

11. It also helped that the seat of the body negotiating the MAI – the Organisation for Economic Cooperation and Development (OECD) – is in Paris. The MAI negotiations there in 1998 became the focus for mobilisation in France, which resulted in French government withdrawal and the foundation of one of the central networks of the global justice movement, ATTAC (Association pour la taxation des transactions financières pour l'aide aux citoyens).

12. Prosecuted for libel, Dave Morris and Helen Steel succeeded for nearly three years in turning the courtroom into a tribunal on McDonald's – losing the case despite the judge ruling that most of their criticisms of McDonald's were reasonable. See www.mcspotlight.org.

Section I

Resisting Repression, Civil War and Exploitation, 2000–2008: Analyses of Unarmed Struggle

EDITORIAL INTRODUCTION

This section contains accounts of movements against two profoundly anti-democratic regimes – the Serbia of Slobodan Milošević and the Zimbabwe of Robert Mugabe – and the longstanding military junta which, with some personnel changes, has held power in Burma since 1962. In addition, there are two reports on the long-term nonviolent resistance in India and Colombia against threats to livelihood, in India resulting primarily from industrialisation and in Colombia more from the multi-sided armed conflicts in the country, although economic interests are a contributing factor.

The images of nonviolent action in Serbia, in particular the imagination and humour that the student-based group Otpor brought to the campaign, once again demonstrated the infectious power of successful nonviolence – leading to the foundation of groups similar to Otpor such as Kmara in Georgia and Pora in Ukraine, which in 2003 and 2004 respectively played a key role in the 'electoral revolutions' there.

Early in 1996 I attended some of the daily (predominantly student) demonstrations in Belgrade against local election fraud, and in autumn 1998 I attended one of Otpor's early public events. Already Otpor, best known at the time for its graffiti, was arousing the enthusiasm of experienced democratic activists as well as attracting the less welcome attention of the authorities. However, I admit that it did not occur to me that this group could transform itself into a strategic force able to bring together an opposition coalition. Youth groups in Slovakia (1998) and Croatia (1999–2000) were about to play key roles in unseating the parties that had ruled since independence. However, Otpor went a step further by preparing a nonviolent strategy not just to defeat Milošević electorally but then to force the regime to accept the electoral results – this meant undermining Milošević's 'pillars of power'.

The fact that the Milošević regime was brought down without serious violence in no way detracts from its previous ruthlessness, brutality and criminality. Rather it is testimony to the strength of the 'people power' movement, and especially to the importance of preparing for popular mobilisation to enforce the results of the election if Milošević and his cronies again tried to 'steal' the vote. Subsequently many civil society activists in Serbia have been disappointed with the extent of changes in Serbia post-Milošević. One of the points addressed by Danijela Nenadić and Nenad Belčević is the difficulty Otpor had in adapting to the new situation, while Ivana Franović suggests that the limits of reform can be traced back to targeting the man Milošević rather than the political values he represented.

Serbia, Burma and Zimbabwe have been to varying degrees 'pariah' states, subject to various types of international sanctions. However, in terms of inter-governmental pressure, the states most capable of exerting leverage have been those least inclined to do so. Under military rule, Burma – officially Myanmar – has generally pursued an isolationist policy, with few concessions to democracy except in the 1988–90 period. Serbia and Zimbabwe, however, were more 'hybrid' regimes, combining elements of dictatorship with formal democratic institutions, including elections. Apart from a brief interlude at the time of the Dayton agreements, Western governments (with a few exceptions such as Greece) were hostile to Serbia throughout the 1990s, while Russia generally maintained its traditional ties. Zimbabwe, since its suspension from the Commonwealth in 2002, has been increasingly isolated apart from the critical exception of its relationship with neighbouring states, especially South Africa.

In Burma, the nationwide pro-democracy movement coexists with armed opposition to the regime from several ethnic groups. While the 1988 movement forced the regime to accept multi-party elections and – despite the restrictions imposed by the military – succeeded in winning the vote in 1990, it has not managed to end military rule. There remains, however, as Yeshua Moser-Puangsuwan describes, a permanent challenge to the legitimacy of the junta, periodically surfacing as in the protests of 2007.

In Zimbabwe too, despite massive intimidation, the regime lost the vote in March 2008, yet through wholesale violence and a pact accommodating the opposition Movement for Democratic Change (MDC), Robert Mugabe has contrived to stay in power. However, as Janet Cherry suggests, the contest for political power is only one front of resistance: in Zimbabwe, community-based organisations maintain an ongoing resistance either in their locality or their sector that goes beyond the MDC's agenda by seeking not just a change in the pinnacles of power but more far-reaching changes in Zimbabwean society.

India has had its own pro-democracy movement – the movement against Indira Gandhi's State of Emergency 1975–77, which ended the continuous rule of the Congress Party. Since then the complexion of government in India has changed several times, but what remains constant is the political elite's commitment to 'macro-development'. This long-term resistance to 'structural violence', especially mega-industrial projects that have caused massive displacement, is the focus of the chapter on India. Although the movements of resistance are facing urgent threats to people's livelihood, they need a long-term perspective because of the pervasive and globalised nature of the 'macro-forces' they are challenging. The outcomes, suggests Moses Mazgaonkar, are never as simple as success and failure. Moreover the most important form of solidarity in his view is the willingness to learn from the global South and, in our own situations, to break with the consumerism that underpins globalisation.

The population of Colombia too faces threats from global economic forces, but the particular focus for civil resistance has been to create zones of peace, where conflicting armed groups cannot impose their will. Indigenous peoples, displaced people, women and youth have played a leading role in promoting civil resistance, by which they mean the rejection of armed force from whichever quarter it comes. This might imply confrontation with one or more armed groups; it certainly involves trying to construct a way of life free of intimidation. It by no means guarantees their safety – members of peace communities have been killed by government armed forces, paramilitaries and guerrillas – but it is an option for dignity. Mauricio García-Duran notes the invaluable role of transnational solidarity in accompanying these processes of resistance.

1

SERBIA – NONVIOLENT STRUGGLE FOR DEMOCRACY: THE ROLE OF OTPOR

Danijela Nenadić and Nenad Belčević

Otpor (Resistance) played an important role in the overthrow of Slobodan Milošević's regime in Serbia in October 2000. However, there are different views about the nature of Otpor and the importance of its contribution to Milošević's downfall.

For some, Otpor was the revolution – a genuine populist movement successfully mobilising the energies of all those wishing to defeat the regime. Others, however, such as Vladimir Ilić, view Otpor as a tightly knit and centralised political organisation 'with a rather well-developed structure, a relatively secluded leadership, an invisible but efficient hierarchy and internal informal censorship' (Ilić 2001).

As former Otpor activists, our view is that Otpor was one among many actors in bringing down Milošević. It played a crucial role in connecting the opposition political parties with the non-governmental sector, and in motivating people to vote in the September 2000 elections. However, we would not go so far as to argue that it was the most important player.

This chapter examines the origins of Otpor, its organisation and its sources of support before October 2000, its campaigning style and the repression used against it. Otpor was at the time seen as a heroic instigator of resistance, but has subsequently been criticised for getting support in training in nonviolent tactics from outside Serbia, and for foreign sources of funding. The validity of these criticisms is briefly assessed.

After October 2000, Otpor faced the common dilemma of movements that have achieved their proclaimed goals. This analysis therefore touches on Otpor's final transformation into a political party in November 2003, when it contested parliamentary elections and tried unsuccessfully to open a window of opportunity into 'high politics'.

The political context

Serbia faced many problems by the late 1990s. The multi-national Yugoslav federation had disintegrated in economic crisis and war – the republics of Slovenia, Croatia, Bosnia-Hercegovina and Macedonia had gained independence, thus reducing the Federal Republic of Yugoslavia to Serbia and Montenegro – and Montenegro was beginning the process of secession (it declared independence in 2006). The province of Kosovo nominally remained part of the FRY but after NATO's bombings in 1999 was a territory under international mandate. Internationally isolated and the target of international sanctions, Serbia was in a state of economic collapse while the black market and corruption flourished.

In February 1997, Milošević was for the first time forced to bow to democratic pressure. He had tried to annul the municipal elections after the opposition Zajedno coalition won in 14 of the 15 largest municipalities in Serbia. However, after 12 weeks of daily demonstrations, he yielded. Zajedno's victory was short-lived: it could not stay together and Milošević immediately began to reassert control, becoming president not only of Serbia but of the FRY and changing the constitution to extend the permitted term of office. By 1998, at the same time as Serbian police were mounting an offensive against Albanians in Kosovo, Milošević was preparing new authoritarian measures for Serbia itself – especially directed against independent media and against the university and students who had played such a critical role in the daily demonstrations.

The end of the NATO bombings brought with it hope for the opposition parties that this was one defeat too many even for Milošević, but the country seemed to be in a state of apathy and the opposition remained divided and unable to optimise the situation. The picture for Serbian society was indeed bleak, but some opportunities for organised action against the regime were present. It is exactly these small scale opportunities that the young people who formed Otpor saw and decided to exploit and to stand against the regime.

The origins, strategy and organisation of Otpor

Otpor was formed in the autumn of 1998 by a small group of Belgrade students, who had been active in the 1996–97 protests. The students' goal was the ending of Milošević's rule. They formulated three primary demands:

1. free and fair general elections as soon as possible;
2. abolition of the law governing universities and new legal guarantees of autonomy and academic freedom;
3. abolition of the recent media law restricting freedom of expression, and an end to repression of independent media.

They adopted a clenched fist as their symbol, to represent their determination to persist until victory and the commitment to bring about change.

Initially Otpor was viewed as just another student organisation with no real political influence, and neither the regime nor the opposition parties paid much attention to it. By the time the regime realised the strength, impact and significance of Otpor, it was too late to stop the momentum of resistance.

Otpor's approach was to emphasise that above all it embodied an idea of resistance and of taking personal responsibility, and that ideas are impossible to suppress. Members of Otpor presented an example of how to resist the regime: activists were often arrested, beaten up and subjected to all kinds of repression. Otpor, with its clear and simple messages, gained popularity among ordinary citizens who were not only fed up with the regime but also deeply disappointed in the opposition parties.

Throughout its development, Otpor insisted on the idea of nonviolent resistance. Aware of the historic importance of nonviolent strategy in earlier movements, for example, in the US Civil Rights campaign, Otpor members chose nonviolent, or civil, resistance as one aspect of their struggle. They rightly perceived that it is not necessary to invent completely new strategies and tactics, but to make clever use of available models, adjusting them to their own circumstances.

Otpor moved beyond being purely a student movement in February 1999, when it held its first congress in the Belgrade Youth Centre, at the same time as Milošević's ruling Socialist Party held its official congress. Otpor then decided to broaden its membership to include well-known public figures who wanted to support it, and to welcome anyone committed to defeat Milošević. Therefore they mobilised from all sections of society, workers and peasants as well as students and intellectuals, and from across the political spectrum – monarchists and nationalists to republicans, leftists and feminists. Otpor stated that it was aware of the problems of holding together such a diverse coalition – and in the event it would not last beyond the overthrow of Milošević.

Otpor strengthened its organisational structure at the beginning of 2000. At the time it appeared an unusual organisation, with no leader or vertical organisation. This made it difficult to point to any particular individual, and there were no obvious leaders for the police to arrest. Activists claimed that they had an invisible structure, which was constantly changing to prevent infiltration. They also took precautions by using different people for actions and avoiding repetition.

But the absence of obvious leaders did not mean that there were none. It is fair to argue that Otpor's leadership was personified in a small group of those who had the power to decide on the most important things. Moreover, it is quite clear in retrospect that, while Otpor presented an illusion of fluid organisation and ad hoc decisions, in practice it was well organised but decentralised.

Firstly, Otpor created branches throughout the country and made national calls for coordinated action. Every branch, however, was autonomous and could plan how to carry its own actions to fit local circumstances. There was also a clear division of labour: in every town where Otpor was strong there were sections for finance, relations with the press and organising volunteers. However, there was also a governing body of Otpor composed of well-known personalities that coordinated the activities of branches and sections. According to Otpor members there were, however, only two centralised activities: relations with international bodies and international fund-raising.

Recruitment and activism

Starting with a small group of students, Otpor grew to number over 30,000 supporters and activists by September 2000. People who joined had varied motives. Some said they joined owing to 'hatred of the regime', others stressed 'the need to get things going' or they mentioned 'the idea that together young people can bring about the democratisation of Serbia' (Ilić 2001: 41).

Subsequently some Otpor activists have spoken in advertising terms of the importance of 'branding'. Certainly Otpor was skilful at getting media attention, framing the issues and keeping their movement in the public eye. Activists knew how to use the media, and especially the internet, for recruiting new supporters and informing not only domestic but also international opinion. They attracted media attention also by organising symbolic actions demonstrating the situation that existed in Serbia, and they used the media for immediate announcement of arrests and to organise quick responses.

From the outset Otpor organised many different types of activity all over the country, including petitions, distributing leaflets, holding rallies and workshops, street theatre and concerts. Actions were mostly provocative and designed to raise public consciousness, making people aware of the need to change the regime and mobilising them to join the struggle. Sometimes Otpor activities had a theatrical or carnival dimension. At other times protests were more aggressive and posed a direct challenge to the system.

Otpor's most serious campaign centred on the general elections set for 24 September 2000, and attempted to convince everyone that their vote was crucial and could oust Milošević, who had decided to call an early election to the Yugoslav presidency at the same time as the Serbian legislative and local elections. The 18 opposition parties had been persuaded by Otpor to form a coalition, the Democratic Opposition of Serbia, and to nominate one agreed candidate to run against Milošević for the presidency. Otpor promised to mobilise at least 500,000 votes for this opposition candidate.

Photograph 1.1 'He's finished', says the Otpor poster calling for people to vote on 24 September as in the background Milošević walks away. Otpor's output of posters changed the atmosphere in Serbia after the Kosovo war. (CANVAS)

The campaign was called 'He is finished' and activists toured the country. Their message on leaflets was: 'The 24th September is not only election day – but also a very important day in our history. It is YOU who will defeat Milošević on that day. Make sure that you vote, and that your family and friends vote too – and He is finished!' Otpor promoted the formula 'MASSIVE TURNOUT = BALLOT CONTROL = VICTORY'.

It can be argued that Otpor's greatest accomplishment was to persuade people to take part in the elections against a background of apathy and fear, and to persuade them that a peaceful change of regime was possible.

Otpor's analytical centre set out the framework for mobilising the vote through three campaigns:

1. To activate the 'third sector' (non-governmental organisations) to take part in the election campaign;
2. To get as many people as possible to the polls to increase the opposition's chances of success and decrease the effect of government manipulation of elections;
3. The 'He is Finished' campaign designed to hammer home a strong anti-Milošević message that left no possibility for hesitation or compromise.

All three campaigns aimed to increase electoral turnout but were directed to different sectors of the population: the first to the cities (especially first-time voters); the second to the medium-sized towns and the third to the rural population.

How the regime fought Otpor

Milošević and his allies had always feared the role of students, but had previously been able to control them. After the regime realised that Otpor differed from previous student movements, was well organised and rapidly gaining in influence, it decided to strike back. The government then did everything possible to frighten those who were active or supported the movement in an attempt to slow Otpor's growth and increasing popularity. Almost every protest ended with police intervention. The police interrogated a large number of activists about the leadership of the movement, funding and training. They also took photographs of demonstrators or fingerprinted them, opened criminal records, used arrests and detention, or beat up activists. Nearly half of the Otpor activists were detained at some time and ran into problems in their educational or family life.

After activists in Požarevac (the birthplace of Milošević and his wife) had been severely beaten by Milošević's son and his gang for publicly supporting Otpor, regime repression became more brutal and open. The regime and the media under its control accused Otpor activists of being traitors paid by NATO, of being CIA agents and even fascists. The regime then drafted a law on terrorism, which meant that any member of an organisation not registered with the state was vulnerable to sweeping acts of repression, including life imprisonment. Since Otpor was denied recognition by the authorities, it was undoubtedly the main target of this new law. But increased repression, rather than frightening off supporters, backfired. Instead it motivated people (including those previously passive) to offer greater support.

The most obvious example of police brutality and misuse of authority occurred when policemen, armed to the teeth, broke into the offices of the 'It's time' campaign only 15 days before the September 2000 election. They arrested 25 activists and held them for many hours for interrogation by police and state security. In total the number arrested in connection with Otpor reached 1,559 by October 2000. But subsequently members of the Socialist Party have denied any resort to arrests or beatings, and its coalition partner, the Radical Party, has also denied any complicity in repression.

Demystifying Otpor and questions about foreign support

At the time when Otpor was struggling against Milošević no one from the democratic bloc dared raise critical questions about its actions. Otpor activists were seen as 'heroes', politically uncorrupted but smart and determined young people who had finally taken matters into their own hands. To raise critical questions about Otpor then would have undermined people's last hope of overthrowing Milošević after his many years in power. The somewhat idealised picture of Otpor that prevailed during the final struggle against Milošević is now in need of some demystifying.

One of the greatest successes of Otpor was achieved at the international level. What the Serbian public did not know before, and is still one of the most debated questions, is exactly what international connections Otpor managed to establish. Rightly perceiving the need for substantial aid from outside in order to challenge the regime successfully, Otpor developed links with foreign NGOs, which provided them with help. However, while engaged in the struggle against Milošević Otpor insisted that it was the Serbian diaspora all over the world that had helped them with funding. They also emphasised the support of the Greek government – Serbs have always thought of Greeks as friends and the Greek government as one state willing to help Serbia. Since under Milošević many Serbs came to hate the governments of the USA and Western Europe – especially after the NATO bombing in 1999 in support of the Albanians in Kosovo – Otpor's refusal to admit any links with Western governments is understandable. Moreover, the Milošević regime tried hard to smear Otpor activists as foreign hirelings and traitors.

But it is less clear why, after Milošević was toppled, Otpor remained so secretive about the sources of donations and training. Since Otpor insisted on transparency and urged political parties to reveal their sources of income, its own unwillingness to reveal publicly its foreign donors (whether NGOs or foreign governments) was clearly unwise, and enabled opponents to make foreign aid to Otpor a key issue in public debate.

Foreign training and the originality of Otpor's campaigns has also become an issue in recent years. Various media have argued that Otpor did not invent its own strategy and tactics, such as civil disobedience, but borrowed them from previous well-known examples. This is a fundamentally misconceived argument, since movements always seek to learn from their predecessors. What matters is the capacity to learn those lessons and adapt them to their own political situation.

Furthermore, some critics claimed that activists in the movement went through a process of strict training and education in camps organised by the US government. According to this line of argument, the most important seminar was held in Budapest in April 2000, where 30 activists learned how to challenge the system, how to shape their actions, how to overcome fear and how to answer police questions when arrested, etc. Again Otpor initially denied outside training, but soon 'admitted' that they gained help from outside, and incorporated material from the Albert Einstein Institution in their own training manual. After a time Otpor members argued that democratic change would have happened anyway, but without outside help it would have been more difficult.[1] It should also be noted that Otpor's commitment to nonviolent tactics was made before this seminar based on the activists' own experience and analysis of their own situation.

Otpor's success has undoubtedly encouraged the creation of more or less similar organisations and movements in countries under undemocratic regimes in ex-Soviet republics such as Georgia, Ukraine and Belarus. The Albanian organisation Mjaft! (Enough!) mentions on its website that its struggle for democratisation was inspired by Otpor and its activities.

The question of Otpor involvement in creating similar organisations in other countries has not yet been fully clarified. In fact Otpor as an organisation never intended to promote democratisation outside Serbia. But some Otpor members have taken part in seminars and training sessions as an expression of their personal engagement and a way of sharing their personal experiences. Undoubtedly Otpor has been a potent example. Thus during the demonstrations against the regime in Georgia there were flags with the Otpor fist on the streets of Tbilisi, and the message 'He is finished' could be seen in the Serbian language. But Otpor has been primarily an inspiration rather than having a concrete role in forming similar movements or seeking to 'export' its model.

Otpor after Milošević

After the Milošević regime was defeated and elections for the Republican Assembly in December 2000 were over, Otpor had to decide whether it still had a future, and if so what direction it should take. When it held its second congress immediately after the elections, Otpor was widely criticised, even by some of its members, for acting prematurely when time for reconsideration of policy and organisation was needed. One problem was that there were widely varying views among the membership. Some believed Otpor's role was finished and that it should disband. But according to Vladimir Ilić's research only a minority of activists favoured this solution. Other proposals were that Otpor should become a NGO dealing with educational and cultural issues, that it should revert to being a purely student body, or that it should become a political party.

Although there was an ostensibly democratic debate involving a network of 19 regions that consulted with local members, it is not entirely clear who really made the choice between the various options. We believe that it can be argued that Otpor had an ideological nucleus whose voice was dominant from the outset and who managed to impose their vision of the future role of the organisation.

There is general agreement that Otpor ceased to be a movement after 2000, but differing views about its nature at that point. Some argue it was a pressure and lobby group, others (often its closest allies from the anti-Milošević campaign) that it was a NGO. The majority of political parties, both its opponents and some from the democratic bloc, saw Otpor as a clear example of a political organisation competing for political power. They cited the presence of Otpor representatives on the boards of some institutions and its activity in the everyday political life of the country. Until 2003 the majority of Otpor members allowed for the possibility of Otpor transforming into a political party but claimed that it would be unlike any other existing party in Serbia.

In practice Otpor was going in the direction of becoming a political party. Its structure became more formal, with a Central Board composed of representatives of branch offices and an Executive elected by the Central Board. For the first time members got formal membership cards, and members of other political parties were silently excluded from Otpor.

By the end of 2002 80 per cent of the members replied positively in an internal questionnaire to the crucial question 'Should Otpor become a political party'. Most also favoured a social democratic policy. Otpor duly registered as a political party at the end of August 2003. When elections to the Serbian Parliament in December 2003 were announced, Otpor entered the electoral race. The outcome was devastating: Otpor received a mere 1.76 per cent of the votes and attained no seats. There were numerous reasons for this failure: an unclear vision of Otpor as a political party, too short a period to create a new image, the lack of a strong political message in the campaign, an absence of well-known political leaders with whom voters could identify and competition with previous allies.

The result was widespread apathy, a financial crisis and a huge loss of members. Otpor began negotiations with the Democratic Party, and since it was in a weak negotiating position quietly accepted integration into the Democratic Party in September 2004. A small number of Otpor members joined the Democratic Party, but many others joined other parties or returned to the NGO sector. Most ex-activists dropped out of political activity.

Note

1. The Budapest training seminar was led by Robert Helvey, a former US army colonel and consultant of the Albert Einstein Institution, an independent NGO specialising in analysing the theory, strategy and tactics of nonviolent action. It was arranged by the International Republican Institute – one of the 'democracy promotion' institutions set up in 1983 to carry out the work of the US Congress-funded National Endowment for Democracy. This training session took place at a stage where the US and West European governments were actively supporting opposition to Milošević, so suspicion of official US involvement is understandable. [The issues surrounding external training are discussed further by George Lakey in Section IV.]

1A
SERBIA EIGHT YEARS AFTER

Ivana Franović

It is almost eight years since the '5 October', that day in 2000 when we finally ousted Slobodan Milošević. After a decade of protests, demonstrations, acts of resistance and coalition-building, an estimated million people flooded the streets of Belgrade, demanding that Milošević should go. Many of us hoped we could start anew, establish democracy, build sustainable peace and create social justice. I will try to examine briefly what went wrong and why.

Milošević's successors

Milošević was opposed by a coalition (the Democratic Opposition of Serbia) of 18 political parties, ranging from those really committed to democratic change to Milošević's former associates and 'pure' ethnonationalists. This coalition could not agree about anything except that Milošević must go; they had quite different visions of what Serbia should become. Thus it was unrealistic to expect a new government to fully dissociate itself from its predecessor.

Milošević had not only abused his power inside Serbia (through corruption and embezzlement, repression of political opposition and the media, and even assassinations), but also led the country in wars with its closest neighbours, formerly part of Yugoslavia: Slovenia (1991), Croatia (1991–95), Bosnia and Herzegovina (1992–95), Kosovo (1998–99). This Balkan slaughter was characterised by mass ethnic cleansing, torture (usually of civilians) in concentration camps, nearly 3 million refugees and displaced people, the raping of women, razing of towns and burning of villages, besieging of towns with constant shelling, etc. Yet officially Serbia was not at war, although many of its citizens fought – some voluntarily, though most were drafted.

For any new government this internal and external legacy would be a heavy burden and difficult to confront. For the coalition government it was impossible, since some of its members opposed Milošević not for *starting* wars but for *losing* them, for not being a proper ethnonationalist. This faction of the 'nationally aware' or 'patriot workers' (usually referred to as the 'anti-Hague lobby' because they opposed the International Criminal Tribunal for the Former-Yugoslavia) was symbolised by Milošević's successor, the opposition presidential candidate in 2000, Vojislav Kostunica. Although many of us then thought that Kostunica and his small party were blind and impotent ethnonationalists, he was apparently chosen because – given his lack of importance – the Milošević machine had not managed to demonise him as they had other opposition personalities widely perceived as traitors or criminals.

It turned out that Kostunica's circle was not impotent at all, since they effectively prevented, slowed or perverted any kind of reform. Their slogans of 'anti-revanchism' (not to take action that would be perceived as revenge, and prosecutions are a kind of revenge) and 'legalism' (abiding by the laws even though they were Milošević's laws) served to disguise their aim of keeping Milošević's power structure untouched. They resisted any kind of purge, and they did not intend to allow prosecution of those who had committed war crimes and human rights abuses – especially not by the Hague Tribunal. Nor did they want to dismiss Milošević's key people in the security forces, who could ensure that governments remained in power.

The faction of 'reformists' was symbolised by the brain behind and instigator of democratic reforms – Democratic Party leader Zoran Djindjić, who became prime minister. Peace and human rights activists at that time criticised the new government's slowness in making reforms. But we only realised how deep were the divisions between government factions, and how difficult the position of the reformists, when Prime Minister Djindjić was assassinated on 12 March 2003. The assassins were drawn from organised crime and members of special police forces, and have since been convicted. However, the political responsibility for this crime has still not been investigated. A number of human rights and peace activists argue that this murder represented the annihilation of '5 October'.

The main problem

The failure of 5 October is arguably represented by the failure of Serbia to repudiate Milošević's criminal regime. When Milošević died in The Hague, a huge memorial ceremony took place in front of the federal parliament, and several tens of thousands attended. As Vuk Drašković, then minister of foreign affairs, said on BBC News on 18 March 2006: 'A murderer and his crimes were glorified today.' At the same time there was a small protest on the main square in Belgrade, where only a few thousand mainly young people gathered, because people had become tired of protests.

The transition from a criminal regime to democracy in Serbia is impossible while ethnonationalism is the mainstream ideology. Appeals to Serbian ethnonationalism were widely used by Milošević to gain and stay in power, and the ideology was even strengthened after he was 'finished'. Ethnonationalism and democracy are not compatible, especially not in the multi-ethnic state that Serbia is de facto. Even if these new ethnocentrics love to present themselves as democrats, their understanding of democracy is majority rule, and the majority is the sacred nation (*ethnie*). In this ideology diversity means conflict, and the goal is 'national reconciliation', meaning unification of the *ethnie* in one monolithic society. Therefore those who are not nationalists are not patriots, and those who are not patriots must be traitors. This monolithic worldview leaves little space for democracy.

Ethnonationalist ideology feeds on simplistic interpretations of the past. Serbs are the greatest victims of injustice and violence; we were only protecting ourselves and our people; any war crimes committed by 'us' were only righteous revenge for terrible crimes against us previously (even if a few centuries ago); nobody understands us, and everybody is against us; thus we have to stick together.

Is there any hope?

There have been changes. Some criminals are serving their sentences (if not yet the key criminals). The Office of War Crimes prosecutor was established in 2003, although it works under political pressure, and the prosecutor and other employees frequently get threatened. There is also a special court for dealing with organised crime. Attacks and threats against journalists are rarer than during Milošević's time; police do not beat up people on the streets; and if you criticise the authorities you do not usually fear a knock on the door. People also live a bit better, although living standards are still quite low and unemployment very high. Civil society is somewhat developed (although not very, because different groups see others as competitors, rather than as partners); human rights and peace activists are usually viewed as 'traitors', but now it would be hard to ban them.

Milošević's ethnocentric successors have learnt some lessons. They are aware that war-mongering is not popular (although – as the rhetoric when Kosovo proclaimed independence on 17 February 2008 illustrated – they sometimes cannot resist it). Repression is also unpopular, and would risk provoking a new opposition movement. Nor are all those on the Serbian political scene nationalists. But most sometimes use nationalist rhetoric, to avoid being labelled traitors and to secure more votes. Apart from human rights and peace groups, few now confront ethno-nationalist ideology.

In the May 2008 elections almost half the voters voted for ethnonationalists. This is understandable, since they were in general those losing out in this slow transition, who do not see a future for themselves. Ethnonationalist rhetoric sounds caring and protective. Many human rights activists inflame the situation, since they also tend to confuse ideology with actual identity, claiming that 'Serbs' committed atrocities, and should be blamed. Such rhetoric encourages many proud of their national identity to embrace the ethnonationalists. On the other hand, peace activism and attempts to understand people and their beliefs, rather than making enemies out of them, do help.

It is sad that the movement in Serbia that led to 5 October has evaporated. But we might have anticipated that, since the movement was not anti-ethnonationalist. (Even some Otpor activists used nationalist phrases such as 'With God's help, Serb brothers'.) It can be argued that if the movement had taken an anti-nationalist standpoint, it would not have attracted so many people. Perhaps. But I believe that the main mistake was its central goal: to get rid of Milošević, so attacking a person rather than his policies. The lack of a common understanding of why we wanted Milošević to go is the basis of today's problems. I hope that people elsewhere will learn from our experience. And we can only wait for a new movement: a cultural, transformative, essentially nonviolent and anti-ethnonationalist one.

2

BURMA – DIALOGUE WITH THE GENERALS: THE SOUND OF ONE HAND CLAPPING[*1]

Yeshua Moser-Puangsuwan

The reclusive military junta that rules Burma has kept the country out of the international spotlight. It only pops up after the latest tsunami, cyclone or popular protests, most recently in August and September 2007, after which it quietly disappears again from global attention. This country of 54 million is an imagined state. It was assembled piecemeal by the British Empire as East India. It did not previously, and has never since, existed as an entity under the complete control of a single central authority. Burma contains many different ethnic groups within its modern borders of which the numerically largest group is the Burmans and shares borders with Bangladesh, India, Tibet, China, Laos and Thailand.[2]

Nonviolent action in Burma

The starting point for the current democracy/anti-dictatorship movement within Burma was a popular uprising in 1988 that ended the 26-year rule of Ne Win and brought in a military junta, initially called the State Law and Order Restoration Council (SLORC) and later the State Peace and Development Council (SPDC). The 1988 events were themselves influenced by earlier anti-colonial activities, which were widespread in Burma and linked to those of the Congress Party in India to end British rule.

Mahatma Gandhi visited Burma three times, and in March 1929 spoke to a crowd at Shwedagon Pagoda. He said: 'The conditions in Burma, so far as I can see, are much the same [as in British India]. I have therefore the same remedy to

---

* Parts of this chapter were previously published in Yeshua Moser-Puangsuwan et al. (2005) and Yeshua Moser-Puangsuwan, 'Tyrants always fall – always', *Peace News*, Sept.–Nov. 2003.

recommend to both – nonviolent noncooperation.' The uniform of the Burmese anti-colonial activist was the wearing of *pinni*, a local handmade cloth, similar to the *khadi* (homespun) campaign in India. Burmese activists, led by activist monk U Ottawa, mobilised in harmony with the Indian National Congress's boycott and home rule campaigns. Student activist leader Bogyoke Aung San, father of Aung San Suu Kyi, participated in the INC session of 1940, at which Congress adopted the platform of massive civil disobedience in order to precipitate a crisis in continued British rule of India. The Burmese anti-colonial organisation Dobama Asiayone – led by Aung San – adopted the No War Effort campaign of Indian Congress and urged the Burmese not to aid the British war effort.[3]

The 1988 uprising was also influenced by events beyond Burma's borders. In the 1980s popular uprisings took place in other parts of Asia, including the movements against military dictatorship in South Korea in 1984 and 1987, the 'EDSA' Revolution removing Marcos in the Philippines in 1986 and the 1987 Tibetan uprising in Lhasa against Chinese rule.

The spark for the 1988 popular uprising in Burma was when the son of a local political leader assaulted three students in a tea shop in Rangoon, the capital of Burma. When police would not prosecute, other students became indignant. A minor protest by a few students quickly turned into a major confrontation with the police, resulting in dozens of casualties. Police actions – killings, beatings and detentions – outraged the residents of Rangoon. Over the next few days more and more people gathered distributing leaflets and proclaiming, 'We want democracy! Down with the Ne Win regime! Down with the one-party system!' (Lintner 1989). Soon the public demonstrations escalated and spread to other cities, leading in July 1988 to Ne Win's resignation after 26 years in power. During the following months, puppet governments were appointed and dissolved, and opposition to the ruling party of Ne Win strengthened.

The lady of Burma

By chance or fate, that summer Aung San Suu Kyi, the daughter of Burma's independence hero, Bogyoke Aung San, had returned to Burma to care for her ailing mother. She had avoided any overt political role until she was invited to speak at a pro-democracy rally on 26 August 1988 in the Shwedagon Pagoda where Gandhi had spoken almost 60 years earlier. Here, to a massive crowd, she made her first public commitment: 'I could not, as my father's daughter, remain indifferent to all that was going on. This national crisis could, in fact, be called the second struggle for independence' (full text in Aris 1995: 192–8).

Suu Kyi's first political speech demonstrated her powers as an orator. She spoke with authority and conviction, simultaneously answering critics and endearing herself to supporters, weaving historical and contemporary events into a coherent

Photograph 2.1 Monks march in Rangoon; the banner says 'nonviolence – national movement'. (Robert Coles)

discourse while respecting and yet challenging the listener to rise above their current circumstances. Observers credit her with introducing human rights into the political vernacular of the country: it became a constant point of reference in any talk or presentation, and a prerequisite for democratic development (Kreager 1995: 321). Thus the stated aim of the National League for Democracy (NLD), founded shortly after Suu Kyi's first public address, was not elections or an interim government, but the establishment of basic human rights as the foundation for elections (Kreager 1995: 338). At the same time Suu Kyi began to organise civil disobedience for basic rights. She launched a 50-city speaking tour in which hundreds of thousands of people joined her in violating the ban on public meetings. When opposition publications were restricted, she responded that party publications were their main form of communication with the people, a right that could not be arbitrarily removed, and that they would continue to publish (Kreager 1995: 335, 336, 341).

As tension between opposition and authorities increased in 1989, Suu Kyi called off a major demonstration scheduled for the anniversary of her father's assassination as she expected violent repression. 'I realised I would not get hurt … but others would. To carry on would have been irresponsible. If others had got hurt and I remained unhurt, it would have been a responsibility I could not have lived with' (Ang 1998: 66). Following her decision, eleven truckloads of soldiers were placed at her residence and she was locked within it for the next six years (1989–95).

Popular pressure, and the activities of the NLD, led to the transfer of power to the armed forces as the former regime was forced to retire from formal office. Bowing to popular pressure for democracy, the military sought legitimacy through an open election. This, however, was not to be. On 27 May 1990, the NLD took part in Burma's first multi-party elections for 30 years and won over 80 per cent of the parliamentary seats.[4] The military thereafter stalled on allowing a new parliament to sit. The NLD, less its general secretary, Aung San Suu Kyi, who remained under house arrest, met at Gandhi Hall in Rangoon on 29 July 1990 where the NLD adopted the Gandhi Hall Declaration. This reaffirmed that a peaceful transition would require a democratic environment before a democratic government could be formed. Such an environment was impossible unless people enjoyed freedom of expression as a basic right. Honest and open dialogue, affirmed the declaration, was the only way to fulfil the people's aspiration for democracy:

> We hope that solutions will be found by a frank and sincere discussion with good faith and with the object of national reconciliation based on mutual respect between the NLD and the SLORC. ... In holding such talks: (a) frankness, sincerity and natural respect, (b) national reconciliation, (c) practice of peaceful means and (d) general harmony without hard feelings are essential policies which must be observed.

In the early 1990s there were sporadic demonstrations by small groups and courageous individuals. Despite repressive conditions, people within the pro-democracy movement – students, writers, members of political parties and ordinary people within Burma – continued to resist the military regime by nonviolent methods and to call for change. Meanwhile the military junta's insistence that it was simply maintaining law and order was combined with a continual effort to suppress and stifle dissenting views.

The NLD remained under pressure, with many offices forcibly closed and many of its members coerced to resign or flee into exile. Remaining NLD members continued to insist that the authorities immediately release all political prisoners including NLD Vice Chair U Tin U and General Secretary Aung San Suu Kyi; allow the NLD to operate freely; implement the results of the 1990 election; and initiate tripartite dialogue with political parties and ethnic nationalities. Once Suu Kyi was awarded the Nobel Prize for Peace in 1991, the pressure on the regime to release her increased by the year until she was freed from house arrest in 1995. Upon release she declared:

During the years that I spent under house arrest many parts of the world have undergone almost unbelievable change, and all changes for the better were brought about through dialogue. ... Once bitter enemies in South Africa are now working together for the betterment of the people. Why can't we look forward to a similar process? (Aris 1995: 360–1)

Under Order 2/88 of the junta in September 1988, public gatherings of groups of five people or more had been banned. The NLD and other sectors of Burmese society such as student, women, ethnic and worker organisations defied the ban, although usually not openly. Aung San Suu Kyi and other NLD leaders and members persisted in pressing their rights. Twice in 1988 NLD motorcades with Auug San Suu Kyi were blocked from leaving Rangoon to visit other parts of the country, leading to six-day and 13-day roadside protests and hunger strikes. Yet, despite the continuous harassment and temporary bans on the NLD and associated parties, many people maintained their support for the parties elected in 1990 by attending activities at party offices and circulating literature, audio and video tapes of talks. As a result of the people who came daily to visit her at her residence, Suu Kyi began to record weekend talks, which attracted thousands of people and were listened to nationally by an informal network passing on cassette tapes.[5]

Parallel government

In August 1998, the NLD announced its intention to convene parliament in line with the 1990 election results. When elected parliamentarians announced they would directly assume their lawful responsibilities, the regime panicked. Mass arrests of party officials followed. Those who escaped arrest launched the Committee Representing the People's Parliament (CRPP) in September 1998 as a parallel legal authority within the country, and as a direct challenge to the legitimacy of the military junta.

The CRPP consists of 18 members (initially ten), supported by 251 elected representatives from several parties. Following its inauguration, the CRPP annulled all laws promulgated by the military regime after September 1998 and called for the release of all political prisoners. It demanded immediate dialogue between the junta and the NLD, and the convening of the parliament elected in 1990.

Members of the CRPP constantly risk detention. Aye Tha Aung of the Arakan League for Democracy, representing four ethnic political parties in the CRPP, was detained for over two years for violating publication and emergency laws by writing articles on ethnic issues and discussing the framework for a political dialogue with representatives of ethnic groups. Nevertheless, the CRPP continues to make public statements voicing its consistent request for dialogue with the junta and has set up committees to research social and economic issues, preparing future policy. The CRPP also commits itself on international issues, in January 2000 endorsing the Mine Ban Treaty by promising to recommend 'the People's Parliament, when it is convened' to accede to the treaty 'as a matter of immediate national concern'.

The establishment of the CRPP has provided the people of Burma with a concrete alternative to military rule. The junta has not closed the CRPP as an illegal organisation, but instead calls for its dissolution as a condition for dialogue – a reaction confirming that it views the CRPP as a serious challenge and constant reminder of its own lack of legal mandate.

Aung San Suu Kyi was determined to 'practise the freedom' the authorities claimed it allowed the NLD by leaving Rangoon to visit other parts of Burma once more in September 2000. When her motorcade was again blocked by the military, NLD activists set up tents and waited for nine days to continue their tour. This prompted Suu Kyi's second period of house arrest – a period of 19 months, until May 2002. Suu Kyi believes that in 2000 the military junta was intent on crushing the NLD and that what prevented this was the combination of both internal support (the population of Burma, and the democracy activists who continued to be arrested almost every day) and the external support of those nations and international support groups that withdrew recognition.[6] Eventually, under international pressure including from the UN Secretary-General's Special Envoy to Myanmar, the junta was forced to see the wisdom of releasing NLD leaders and some other political prisoners, and agree to begin a dialogue on the future governance of the country.

Supposedly 'free' in 2002, Suu Kyi once again set out to test the generals' words by travelling to different provinces and states of Burma. Wherever her entourage arrived, thousands of people were waiting despite warnings by the junta to ignore the visit. The military and its USDA[7] proxy sometimes blocked entrances into towns or organised aggressive anti-NLD crowds. Daw Suu Kyi thanked her supporters for their discipline:

> When we first came into town, I was so proud of the people because you did not use force or violent means to deal with the protests against us. And I honour your tolerance. People today here have shown what real strength is. Real strength does not involve violence.

Suu Kyi's primary purpose in these visits was not to speak but to listen, to provide a venue for the people to speak for themselves. The people of Burma lost no time in taking advantage of this space. They turned out in hundreds, and then thousands, mostly young people who had not taken part in the 1988 democracy uprising. They turned out not just to listen to Suu Kyi but to speak to her, sometimes until the very late hours of the night. Around the country, Suu Kyi, and the generals, were hearing the same message over and over. Young people complained that they had no educational opportunities, they demanded them and didn't believe they could get them under the current government. Therefore, they wanted the government to change – as quickly as possible. As this unhappy message from the thousands of people of Burma reached the generals, they sought to silence them by restricting Suu Kyi's movements, to deprive the people of their platform. Eventually, on 30 May 2003, the military regime organised a deadly attack on the NLD caravan in Depayin in northern Burma, leaving an unknown number dead, and beating and arresting others. Suu Kyi herself escaped, only to be detained on returning to Rangoon.

Since 2003 Suu Kyi has been under renewed house arrest, the junta offering to release her only if she will forsake human rights campaigning and leave Burma. Suu Kyi for her part has always left the door open for the generals to walk through and depart as friends. She will not, and cannot force them through. They must see the wisdom of doing so, for themselves, and walk through, for 'if the generals want to see transition to democracy take place without massive violence, they have no other choice', she said (Rangoon 2003). This was not a threat but a clear-sighted statement that there is only so much a people can take.

Meanwhile the CRPP continues with its clear policy goals – to release prisoners, to recognise the parties that participated in the 1990 elections, to oppose intimidation and to support freedom of expression.

Action by released political prisoners

In 2006 the military regime released some of the then student leadership of the 1988 demonstrations. Political prisoners for almost two decades, this group found themselves physically free, but now excluded from universities and most professions. Meeting informally in tea shops they began forming a network. Some of the group's more prominent leaders were rearrested but the remaining members launched a nationwide petition calling for a genuine national reconciliation process and the release of an estimated 1,100 political prisoners, including their rearrested colleagues. The group also chose to dress distinctively in white. Members travelled quietly around the country and within a month collected more than half a million public signatures, which were sent to the SPDC and the UN Resident Representative's office in Rangoon. The junta released five of their comrades. This was followed by a multi-religious prayer campaign at which supporters were asked to wear white during candlelit vigils in Buddhist temples, Christian churches, Hindu temples and Muslim mosques. Tens of thousands responded, offering prayers for a peaceful resolution to Burma's political problems, freedom for all political prisoners, and help for victims of natural disasters that had devastated some parts of the country. On Independence Day 2007, the 88 Generation launched the Open Heart campaign. In perhaps

Burma's first letter-writing campaign, people across the country were asked to write letters recording how junta policies affected their lives. The campaign ran for one month during which they hoped to generate 25,000 letters to the SPDC (Lintner 2007).

These activities set the stage for the response to an unforeseen five-fold price rise in petrol by the regime in August 2007. Instead of riding a bus to the funeral of former NLD leader U Kyi Maung, 88 Generation members decided to walk. More than 400 people walked the nine kilometres. By deciding not to take public transport, one of them explained, they were making a statement about the impact high transport costs have on the average Burmese worker. 'We couldn't pay the new bus fares for our large group so the logical solution was to walk instead. ... Most people are facing problems like this now.'[8] Shortly thereafter, many of the leading members of the 88 Generation were rearrested. In early September, a small demonstration by Buddhist monks in a northern Burmese town was violently dispersed. This led immediately to larger demonstrations by Buddhist monks, and eventually nuns and ordinary people. Between mid-August and early October 2007 over 200 demonstrations were reported in 66 cities within all the states and divisions of the country.[9] A severe crackdown, which thanks to Democratic Voice of Burma activists received global media coverage, began in late September 2007. Organisers, anticipating this, had advised demonstrators to disperse and avoid confrontations in order to avoid high numbers of casualties.

Burmese activists continue to demonstrate their non-acceptance of the military junta's rule by individual and small group nonviolent actions. These include individual demonstrations, graffiti, flyers, damage to junta banners (such as those calling for a 'yes' vote in a planned constitutional referendum) and symbolic acts such as wearing *pinni* (as in the anti-colonial movement), which is the de facto uniform of supporters of the NLD.[10]

Diaspora action for change within Burma and global solidarity

Activities aimed at supporting the Burmese pro-democracy movement focus mostly on ensuring that the junta feels the pressure of international opinion. This is accomplished by keeping Burma in the global spotlight as much as possible and by bringing about action by different governments.

External action is undertaken by both the Burmese diaspora and others. Activities by the Burmese diaspora include the creation of political fronts such as the National Coalition of the Union of Burma, which seek political support from foreign governments on various issues related to Burma, including actions at the UN. The Democratic Voice of Burma has provided alternative media by shortwave broadcasts into Burma since 1992, and by satellite television since

2005. It has a cadre of reporters within the country who work as an underground, 'sabotaging' the regime's media clampdown by using modern telecommunications to bring out news. The DVB has worked hard to professionalise its reporting, aiming not only to reveal the truth but also to set the standards and build the capacity for a professional media once it can be established in Burma. Burmese exiles also document human rights abuses and compile lists of political prisoners within the country. They are able to collect and distribute small levels of support to the families of political prisoners.

Citizens of other countries also act in solidarity with the anti-junta struggle, often in cooperation with exiles. Demonstrations or other media events are frequently organised on remembrance days, such as the birthday of Aung San Suu Kyi. US examples include the 2005 Rock Concert for Suu Kyi broadcast by satellite and its subsequent CD, and the 2008 Voices for Burma campaign, which brought together prominent media stars speaking on behalf of Burma and Suu Kyi. Some foreign activists have engaged in street protests within Burma. National solidarity campaigns are strong in Britain and the USA, and exist in several other countries, including Japan, Australia and Canada.

Amnesty International, Human Rights Watch and other international human rights organisations – making policy recommendations to their home governments and presentations at intergovernmental forums – are a particular source of support to local activists within Burma.

These activities have created the environment for another level of international pressure, such as the investigations into forced labour by the International Labour Organisation (which now maintains an in-country presence) and the visits by representatives of the UN Human Rights Council and the UN Secretary-General. Direct intervention in Burma's prisons by the International Committee of the Red Cross took place between 1999 and 2006.[11]

A few Western governments have placed some types of sanctions on Burma and its ruling elite, but as these are not universal they are more symbolic than functional.[12] Thanks to intervention by advocacy groups, courts in the USA and France ordered the UNOCAL and TOTAL companies respectively to pay compensation to survivors of human rights violations committed by the Burmese army in securing the route for the Yadana Gas Pipeline.

Myanmar (Burma) is a member of the Association of Southeast Asian Nations (ASEAN). In the past ASEAN nations have generally shielded Burma from direct pressure, but several – including Malaysia and the Philippines – have called for the release of Aung San Suu Kyi and for the junta to enter into dialogue. Thailand's stand on Burma has changed according to its government, but it has consistently provided sanctuary for people fleeing Burma, and Thai civil society is supportive of Burma's pro-democracy struggle.[13]

Box 2.1 Resistance in Burma and Tibet: A comparison

Tibet and Burma are Asian Buddhist dominant areas ruled by oppressive regimes and known for their nonviolent opposition. Both Burma and Tibet have charismatic Nobel Peace laureates who are respected worldwide as voices of nonviolence in a struggle against tyranny. However, the parallels end there.

The Tibetan struggle has gained global recognition through the Dalai Lama who travels frequently. In contrast Burma's Nobel laureate's movements have been restricted even when she has not been detained or under house arrest (as she has officially for 12 of the last 18 years). She has not left the country in case she would not be allowed to return.

Enormous numbers of people in Europe, the Americas, and other parts of Asia, including mainland China, have shown a growing interest in Tibetan forms of Buddhism and in preserving Tibetan culture. There is no comparable interest in Burmese forms of Buddhism, and Burma's past and current isolationist policies have resulted in a lack of knowledge about Burmese culture.

The Tibetan government-in-exile has various departments and provides services to the Tibetan diaspora, particularly in South Asia. The Burmese exiles come from a variety of ethnic groups, and a lack of consensus among them has prevented the formation of a government-in-exile with broad support or services.[1]

The Tibetan government-in-exile's diplomatic wing has de facto embassies abroad that represent the Tibetan voice, and a global network of solidarity groups. The Burmese have not been able to mobilise any such coordinated political offensive.

In Tibet, there is no organised armed resistance, and the previous guerrilla organisation was disbanded by the Dalai Lama.[2] In Burma, not only the nonviolent opposition exists, but also 30 or more armed groups.

Burma has a recognised nonviolent opposition within the country, the National League for Democracy, but there is no recognised opposition within Chinese-occupied Tibet.

International solidarity and support for the Tibetan cause has benefited from the clear leadership framework of the Tibetans and the nonviolent resistance they espouse.

The lack of coherence within the Burmese exiles and presence of an armed struggle have caused difficulties for supporters abroad. In many cases foreign solidarity activists know what they are against (the military regime), but not necessarily what they are for (other than the slogan Democracy).

Notes
1. Two entities exist – the National Coalition Government of the Union of Burma and the National Coalition of the Union of Burma – but have no physical home and no ministries that provide services to the Burmese diaspora. They function as political fronts lobbying against the regime.
2. The Four Rivers, Six Ranges guerrilla army made up of ethnic Tibetans was trained and armed by the US as part of the Cold War. Their logistical and matériel support from the US ceased after Nixon's 1972 visit to China.

Notes

1. The junta changed the name of Burma to Myanmar in 1989. The political opposition and many ethnic groups still defiantly use 'Burma', as does this chapter except in referring to the State Peace and Development Council/State Law and Order Restoration Council (SPDC/SLORC).
2. The Myanmar Government's website (www.myanmar.gov.mm) states that there are eight ethnic races [sic] comprised of 135 distinct ethnic groups. Ethnic Burmans are believed to have migrated from current-day Yunnan. Their language is linked with Tibetan, as are the languages of several other major ethnic groups within the country.
3. Despite Aung San's role in organising mass nonviolent protest against British rule, he later changed his tactics, and was trained in guerrilla warfare by the Japanese under whom he fought the British before changing sides to fight the Japanese with the British. He was assassinated as he formed the first cabinet for a post-independence Burma (Rajshekhar 2006, especially Chapters 2 and 3).
4. Parties mobilised by ethnic minority groups also won seats in the 1990 election, the Shan Nationalities League for Democracy taking 23 seats and the Arakan League for Democracy (ALD) 11. With 19 other ethnic-based parties, these formed the United Nationalities League for Democracy (UNLD), which collectively won 66 seats. The UNLD continues to work closely with the NLD.
5. Staying with a family in Mandalay in 1996, I found them listening to a tape of one of Suu Kyi's gateside talks. They said that the tapes circulated among homes in the community, and that the next family in line to receive it was that of a policeman.
6. Author's notes, meeting of Nobel Peace Laureate Jody Williams with Aung San Suu Kyi in her home, Rangoon, February 2003 (hereafter Rangoon 2003).
7. Union Solidarity Development Alliance, the mass mobilisation vehicle of the military regime. Civil servants and students are required to be members. It organises anti-NLD demonstrations and pro-junta rallies.
8. Democratic Voice of Burma, *Activists March against Fuel Rise*, 20 August 2007.
9. ALTSEAN, *Saffron Revolution Update*, 15 October 2007.
10. For a more complete list of the variety of nonviolent actions undertaken by activists in Burma, see Moser-Puangsuwan et al. 2005, Chapters 2 and 3.
11. In mid-2006, the junta required the ICRC to be accompanied on their prison visits – a violation of ICRC's protocols. The ICRC refused, and prisons visits and assistance have not yet resumed.
12. For a more complete list of the variety of solidarity actions undertaken by exiled Burmese and internationally, see Moser-Puangsuwan et al. 2005, Chapter 4.
13. Thailand's policy has vacillated from more to less welcoming. A recent military government was more welcoming than the civilian governments preceding and following it. Apart from the occasional police raid, exiled Burmese are allowed to carry out nonviolent activities. Every major ethnic group with a political organisation maintains offices in Thailand, as does the National Council of the Union of Burma.

3

ZIMBABWE – UNARMED RESISTANCE, CIVIL SOCIETY AND LIMITS OF INTERNATIONAL SOLIDARITY

*Janet Cherry**

Zimbabwe plunged into a severe economic and political crisis in 2008 – a crisis that has been developing since 2000, when President Robert Mugabe's attempt to extend his presidential power was defeated in a referendum, and 'veterans' of the liberation struggle began to seize land owned by white farmers. Since 2000 there has been mounting internal opposition to the ZANU-PF regime of Mugabe, expressed through the creation of the opposition party, the Movement for Democratic Change (MDC), which has regularly contested elections despite governmental vote-rigging, and also through widespread resistance by many sectors of society.

Those resisting inside Zimbabwe have received little support from African leaders, who have been reluctant to join ex-colonial powers in condemning a leader of the Zimbabwe liberation struggle – Thabo Mbeki of South Africa in particular refused to put public pressure on Mugabe, but has tried to broker deals behind the scenes. By 2008, however, other prominent South Africans were challenging Mugabe's legitimacy and civil society groups, especially South African trade unions, began to express militant solidarity with the opposition (see Section III, Chapter 16).

This chapter focuses less on the electoral politics and elite negotiations that capture the attention of the international media than on the spectrum of activity – which is political at another level – that continues as the crisis deepens. It

* The author wishes to thank all the members of CHRA, CHIRRA, WOZA, GAPWUZ, PTUZ, YIDEZ, ZINASU, MDC and others she has worked with and consulted over the past year and a half, and especially those who responded with inputs and criticisms to the first draft of this chapter – Ray Majongwe, Mike Davies, Jenni Williams and Paul Shambira.

Photograph 3.1 Just across the border in South Africa, Zimbabwean hot air balloon activists prepare to interrupt Robert Mugabe's hugely expensive birthday celebrations before the 2008 elections. Apparently, fearing an incident with South Africa, Mugabe refrained from ordering the balloon to be shot down. (Sokwanele)

examines how different sectors of society have been organising to meet the crisis and offer ongoing resistance. It then goes on to consider the relationship between civil society organisations and the opposition political party, the MDC, and the problems of that relationship. Finally, it explores the growing expressions of transnational civil society solidarity in South Africa and internationally. But the limits of such solidarity indicate the crucial importance of self-organising in countries like Zimbabwe.

The scale of the crisis

Since 2000 economic conditions in Zimbabwe, which had been reasonably prosperous in the 1990s, became increasingly dire: spiralling inflation, reaching

2.2 million per cent in July 2008, and continuing to escalate; there were very few jobs, and serious shortages of food and basic goods. Zimbabwe has increasingly relied on food aid from abroad, which the government has openly tried to control to reward its own supporters and penalise supporters of the opposition. In June 2008 it closed down all aid organisations, including CARE International, which were distributing food at hospitals and other institutions.

Facing economic desperation and political oppression, millions of Zimbabweans have become refugees – a mass exodus turning this into a regional crisis, dramatised in May 2008 when poor South Africans in Gauteng province rioted against what they saw as preferential treatment for Zimbabwean refugees, killing 65 of them and driving 20,000 from their temporary homes.

The political as well as the economic crisis in Zimbabwe came to a head in the first half of 2008. Many believed that the 29 March 'combined' election (for the legislature, presidency and local government) would result at last in an irrefutable assertion by the majority of citizens that Mugabe must go. This election saw the opposition MDC gaining a clear, if narrow, majority of seats in the legislature; and good monitoring made it hard for the ruling ZANU-PF to deny it had lost.

Anticipation of change turned to anxiety as the Electoral Commission delayed announcing the results, and finally called for a run-off for the presidency as none of the candidates had received 50 per cent of the vote. While the MDC initially agreed to contest the run-off, brutal attacks on MDC activists escalated, until the MDC presidential candidate, Morgan Tsvangirai, withdrew because the election would be neither free nor fair. Ignoring international criticism of intimidation, coercion and election fraud, Mugabe went ahead and claimed he had been re-elected on 27 June. Analysts have with hindsight uncovered evidence that a 'junta' of security force leaders took effective control in March 2008 to ensure that Mugabe would not be removed (Malone 2008; Timberg 2008).

Despite economic hardship, food shortages, forced removals, bullying and torture by the government, Zimbabweans are not responding as 'victims'. There is evidence of a vibrant and increasingly united civil society: that sphere of social organisation between the state and the individual or family.

Civil society: NGOs

Civil society is often associated with non-governmental organisations (NGOs). There are certainly many NGOs in Zimbabwe: some do advocacy and education work around human rights, media freedom and elections; others offer legal or humanitarian aid. The Zimbabwe Coalition on Debt and Development raises awareness of issues on HIV/AIDS, international debt and economic alternatives. NGOs are by their nature fairly small, professionalised and resource-driven. Despite the importance of their work, relying too heavily on NGOs can be a serious weakness. Activists point to the 'commercialisation of the movement': international funding to local NGOs results in activists becoming professionals. In a context of economic meltdown, it is understandable that supporters demand material rewards for taking part in NGO activities, but this limits the kind of organisation that can take place.

Grassroots civil society

More central to a popular resistance struggle are community-based organisations (CBOs), which represent broad interests. Some, but by no means all, of these mass-based organisations take the form of social movements, linking the specific needs of their members or constituencies to bring pressure for far-reaching social and political change.

The initial impetus for forming such grassroots organisations comes from people's need for representation in their struggles around their daily experiences of oppression or discrimination. Some social groups, however, are better able to organise than others. Social groups that can foster CBOs include: workers in different sectors of the economy; women; students and youth; and urban residents. Zimbabwe is no exception.

Rural areas pose much greater problems for organised resistance. However, even in rural villages, dominated by patronage, patriarchy and control of resources by traditional leaders allied to government officials, there are ways of refusing cooperation with unpopular chiefs who control food distribution and the votes of villagers. Such acts include refusal to pay poll tax to a chief, boycotting a headman's 'food for work' programme and social ostracism – in rural areas a powerful tool – through boycotts of a funeral, or attending the funeral but refusing to eat the food provided by the family of the deceased. It is very difficult for villagers to vote in secret, given high levels of intimidation. For example, in the June 2008 presidential run-off election (boycotted by MDC supporters) villagers had to 'prove' that they had voted for Mugabe by showing the blue ink on their thumbs used to identify those who had voted. Opponents of the illegitimate ballot in some cases obtained 'alternative' sources of the same coloured ink to avoid reprisals by the ZANU-PF militia.

Workers organise

The trade union movement in Zimbabwe represents only a small sector of society. Only a minority are in formal employment in an economy that is more than 50 per cent rural and subsistence-based. Organised workers are divided between the official state-controlled trade unions and the independent Zimbabwe Congress of Trade Unions (ZCTU). The ZCTU has been at the forefront of opposition to the rule of ZANU-PF in Zimbabwe, and took the initiative in forming the MDC. However, in a collapsed economy, where there is little employment in the formal sector, and most people are functioning in the subsistence economy or in grey zones of the informal sector, the tactics of traditional trade union resistance are substantially undermined.

Hence affiliates of ZCTU are desperately trying to protect their membership at 'factory floor' level, while at the same time playing a key role in resistance to Mugabe's regime. One example is the Progressive Teachers Union of Zimbabwe (PTUZ), which has been fighting for years to improve the working conditions of teachers. Teachers are paid so badly, and so seldom, that they cannot afford to send their own children to school. In 2007 alone, 5,000 teachers left Zimbabwe for South Africa, where most end up working as gardeners or construction workers. Those who remain in Zimbabwe and continue to organise are subject to extreme repression – the arrest and assault of charismatic PTUZ leader and poet Raymond Majongwe is just one example. Nevertheless, teachers continue to seek ways to offer education, and to work with both students and parents to maintain their rights.

While PTUZ is known as a militant minority union (in opposition to the 'official' union Zimbabwe Teachers Association – ZIMTA), its support is greater than appears on paper. As conditions for all teachers steadily worsen, the prospects of united action increase. In early 2008, an extensive teachers' strike demanding better pay saw PTUZ joined by the pro-government ZIMTA. By March, other civil servants including health workers and local government officials had also joined the strike, engaging in go-slow actions if not total work stoppages (see www.libcom.org, 5 March 2008; www.kubatana.net).

The poorest sector of workers – farm workers on commercial farms – have been represented for more than ten years by the General Agricultural and Plantation Workers Union of Zimbabwe (GAPWUZ). This body promoted the national farmworkers' strike in 1997 and the wage negotiations of 2000, both succeeding in raises wages. It also exerted pressure in 2006 for an alternative council for wage negotiations between employers and workers. The union has employed a range of tactics: negotiations, publicising the plight of farmworkers, acts of protest and persuasion, acts of noncooperation such as the withholding of labour, and interventions such as roadblocks. In one instance, farm workers engaged in a 'work to rule' – refusing to carry machinery and implements from the workshop, reducing working hours.

The farm invasions by 'war veterans' to drive out white farmers – that began in 2000 but have continued spasmodically – were in some cases resisted peacefully by farm workers, through locking gates, blocking roads and staying on the farms where their employment was at least secure. In most cases, however, workers and their families lost both their jobs and their homes, weakening their economic position in terms of bargaining power, as well as leading to social insecurity and hunger.

The impact on the urban population of government economic and fiscal mismanagement has been severe. Yet this crisis has not been met with passive acceptance. The MDC and ZCTU have responded with frequent calls for a general strike. However, the dangers of this form of action are now well understood: from explosions of anger in the form of looting and destruction of property (as has happened before in Zimbabwe and elsewhere) to failure simply because so few members of the workforce are in formal employment. So the general strike tactic has to be used very selectively. Even a very disciplined use of methods of non-cooperation is limited in this environment: the withholding of labour in a context of low formal employment makes little sense; the withholding of buying power when there is no food on the shelves makes no sense at all. Other forms of non-cooperation are still possible, though, depending on what outcome is envisaged. Teachers leaving the education system without putting alternatives in place will lead to the collapse of the system, from which it will take years to recover.

Urban community resistance

Urban civil society is thus in a weak position to withdraw labour or buying power. However, there are other forms of civil resistance used by urban-based groups such as Bulawayo Agenda, the Combined Harare Residents Association (CHRA) and the Chitungwiza Residents and Ratepayers Association (CHIRRA). CHRA is a democratic association representing residents in various neighbourhoods. It effectively challenges the legitimacy of the government-appointed council and its inefficient rule of the capital city by initiating campaigns around water shortages, electricity cuts, lack of rubbish removal and poor public health services. CHIRRA and CHRA have been particularly vocal in their opposition to the water rates charged by the recently 'privatised' Zimbabwe National Water Authority. Privatisation has severely compromised water and sewerage services to poor urban residents, with some high-density Harare suburbs suffering repeated water shortages and cut-offs. CHIRRA effectively challenged an increase in water rates in 2006, and a threatened water rates strike was enough to get the increase reversed. CHIRRA obtained another victory when the council sold property to their own management in an act of blatant corruption; in this instance CHIRRA took the case to the High Court, where the sale was reversed.

Other positive and participatory forms of citizen action have taken place, such as 'clean-up campaigns', which engage residents in positive action and put pressure on local government for delivery of services. But such actions raise interesting issues. Do they empower ordinary people and potentially create a situation of 'dual power', or do they weaken pressure on the state by 'letting it off the hook'? Such dilemmas have been faced by civil movements elsewhere.

The interesting possibility arises, however, of people in Harare, Bulawayo, Mutare and Chitungwiza (the four largest urban centres), which saw an overwhelming majority of MDC councillors elected in March 2008, simply taking control of local government. How possible is this? After the election crisis, which stretched through April to the end of June 2008, and continues after the disastrous 'run-off' presidential election, newly elected councillors and parliamentarians were unable to take up their offices. The ongoing violence against opposition members led many to flee their homes and sometimes their country, causing a complete impasse in governance. In Chitungwiza, although the overwhelming majority of councillors elected in March were MDC representatives, there was a brutal attack on four MDC councillors' houses on 19 June. Four MDC youths guarding the house of a councillor in detention were themselves abducted and killed by ZANU-PF youths and state security force members; their bodies were found the following morning.

Since then, however, some councillors in these cities have taken office, opening the way for creative ideas for cooperative governance, for civic associations to work together with urban councils for improved service delivery and to hold councils to account to prevent corruption.

Protest and mobilising women

Certain sectors of civil society in Zimbabwe, notably women and tertiary students, have engaged in very creative forms of organised protest. Other acts of protest are individual and spontaneous, showing how desperate people are for their grievances to be heard. To give a few examples: an action by women who dressed in white and soiled their white garments with tomato sauce, protesting that they cannot afford sanitary pads; a man who took off his clothes in an act of symbolic disrobing, saying that his ancestors had told him that things were wrong in the country; activists who wrote the name of the political leader on a dress, put the dress on a dog, and let the dog run around.

Protest alone, however, has never resulted in a change of power, let alone a fundamental transformation of society. Those activists who have engaged consistently in disciplined, well-organised and creative protest are now challenged to go beyond protest and seek ways of creating alternative institutions. From alternative education classes to local women's cooperatives for production of food and bartering of goods, the challenge is to go further than day-to-day survival and put into place social structures that can empower ordinary people in a more long-term sense, not just to survive the current crisis but to establish a sustainable local economy.

Ordinary women have been among the most vocal and organised groups in Zimbabwean civil society. Women of Zimbabwe Arise (WOZA) was formed in 2003 as a women's civic movement to:

- provide women from all walks of life with a united voice to speak out on issues affecting their day-to-day lives;
- empower female leadership that will lead community involvement in pressing for solutions to the current crisis;
- encourage women to stand up for their rights and freedoms; and
- lobby and advocate on those issues affecting women and their families (http://wozazimbabwe.org).

After organising creative protests and listening to thousands of ordinary people to draw up a 'people's charter', WOZA built its support base to the point where men wished to be involved, hence the formation of MOZA, the male equivalent of WOZA, and the amalgamation into one organisation, WOZA/MOZA.

The 'Power to the People' campaign in 2007 involved a day of action in Bulawayo where hundreds of WOZA members peacefully demonstrated at shops and businesses, calling for affordable food and an end to special sales to cronies and the security services. Men from MOZA then marched to a hypermarket making the same demands.

On 28 May 2008, 14 WOZA members marched to the Zambian embassy in Harare, calling on Zambia (as chair of the Southern African Development Community – SADC) to take urgent action to end the violence. They were held in prison under harsh conditions and charged with 'distributing materials likely to cause a breach of the peace' (Amnesty International, 3 June 2008).

Other groups and national alliances

Other sectors of society are mobilised through representative organisations: youth through YIDEZ (Youth Initiative for Democracy in Zimbabwe) and tertiary students through ZINASU. In the economic sphere, given the importance of the informal sector, the Zimbabwe Cross-Border Traders Association has played an increasingly significant role in representing this constituency of thousands of small traders bringing goods and currency into Zimbabwe from South Africa and Botswana. Religious constituencies – primarily mainstream Christian denominations – are organised into powerful church lobbies, notably the Christian Alliance. Even gay and lesbian rights activists have made strides recently, working under the most difficult of conditions (see Section III, Chapter 13). There are also other 'voices' that do not claim to represent a constituency, but use various means of media and protest to articulate dissatisfaction with the status quo. These include

Sokwanele/Zwakana and resource networks such as Kubatana.net, which have an electronic/internet presence, as well as engage in grassroots actions to spread their message: the open hand – symbolising 'stop!' or 'Enough!' – printed on the hides of cattle in rural areas is one such action.

Attempts have also been made to form national alliances, campaigns and forums that represent a broad spectrum of civil society – the campaign for a new constitution resulted in a semi-permanent organisation called the National Constitutional Assembly (NCA). For some time the NCA has taken the lead in organising civil society around national political demands for a new constitution. Its branches in most parts of the country have organised demonstrations putting forward civil society's demands for an acceptable settlement. The Save Zimbabwe Campaign similarly continues to distribute information about the situation and lobby for support. A civil society forum convened in 2007 brought together a wide range of groups to adopt a common vision and platform of action for change. The problem is that, to date, none of these groups has successfully unified all strands of opposition, civil and political, into a sustained challenge to the regime.

This point is illustrated by the meeting of the National All Stakeholders Constitutional Conference held on 29 September 2007 in Bulawayo. Here, over 900 representatives of 24 civil society organisations met to consider the outcome of the SADC mediation between ZANU-PF and the MDC. The conference rejected outright the proposed constitutional Amendment 18, which was seen as a betrayal by civil society as, among other things, it was understood to allow Mugabe to 'hand-pick' his successor, and argued strongly that the voice of civil society should be heard before any such constitutional 'deals' were accepted. Despite this, the MDC accepted various compromises allowing the elections in March 2008 to go ahead. Civil society organisations then met in February at a People's Convention and agreed to participate in the election campaign, despite feeling ignored by the MDC on the issue of Amendment 18.

The real test of this civil society unity, and its influence on the opposition MDC, came with the March–June elections in 2008.

The March and June elections and civil society responses

The MDC, as an opposition party, has inherent limitations, despite its appellation as a movement and its background in the militant labour movement, the ZCTU. As a political party, its actions focus of necessity around the winning (or not) of elections. It has thus far proven unable to provide a broader political leadership that incorporates civil society and unites it in a common strategy to bring about the required political change.

The MDC did make significant gains in the March 2008 elections (for the presidency, legislature and local councils). Critically, it was able to put into place systems for monitoring and collecting election results as they were posted up at polling stations, an important advance achieved by the opposition in pre-election negotiations. For the first time, MDC's rigorous and public parallel count meant that the ruling ZANU-PF could not simply announce their victory, but was forced into a protracted vote recount. As tension mounted, while the final count was awaited for a month, the opposition managed to maintain impressive nonviolent discipline. There were rumours of a general uprising, of sabotage of strategic installations and of impending widespread violence. None of this happened despite great frustration. Civil society groups initiated a 'Make Our Vote Count' campaign in mid-April through peaceful nonviolent social action, and after many weeks the MDC called for a one-day general strike. The strike won limited support, and did not come close to paralysing the country.

While the WOZA protests as part of this campaign were well organised, as usual, the leadership were quickly arrested; Jenni Williams and Magodongu Mahlangu were held for six weeks before being released on bail; over 1,500 MDC activists were still in police custody on 15 July. The problem was, as in previous stolen elections, that there was no 'grand strategy' of response for the MDC to act in concert with civil society groups. Activists say that in February 2008, civil society groups agreed at the People's Convention to support the MDC in the election campaign, although many were not convinced that it could win, given the regime's record of 'stealing' elections. Some activists were surprised that the MDC did so well in the first-round election, welcoming this expression of the desire for real change among the majority of the population. The problem was that they had no 'plan B', if the election failed or was stolen. The suppression of both civil society and political opposition in the period between the elections made a united response that much harder to coordinate. It is easy to talk about a mass uprising to defend a stolen vote; much harder to do.

What is the role of civil society in such highly charged situations? There are parallels with South Africa in the decade of mass mobilisation, the 1980s. Groups of South African students, youth, women and workers, having organised on a sectoral level around issues affecting them, came together in a powerful united front – the United Democratic Front (UDF) – to contest national government policies. Perhaps it was a blessing in disguise that the leadership of the main liberation movement, the African National Congress (ANC), was then in exile – this allowed for the development of a truly mass-based opposition to the apartheid government. Civil society became highly politicised and highly polarised – some would argue rendering it not a 'true' civil society. After the ANC was demo-cratically elected in 1994, a 'normalising' of the distinction between political and civil society occurred. Ordinary citizens were expected to participate in politics through voting (for the ANC); and civil society organisations would continue to look after their specific or sectoral interests as workers, teachers, women and so on – which they do.

Perhaps the full extent of this separation between political parties and civil society is reflected in the response of South African democrats to the current crisis in Zimbabwe. ANC loyalists have been unable to respond decisively, because their leadership has enjoined them not to 'interfere' in party politics in Zimbabwe. However, the labour federation COSATU, the most powerful expression of organised civil society in South Africa, has criticised Mugabe and taken the most significant solidarity actions in support of its labour ally, the ZCTU. While the voice of human rights advocates, liberal (Democratic Alliance) opposition members and church leaders is important, it does not substitute for broad-based civil society action – as can be seen in the example of the dockworkers refusing to unload Chinese arms destined for Mugabe's government (see Section III, Chapter 16).

International civil society solidarity

COSATU endorsed the view of ZCTU that the 27 June presidential election was a declaration of war on the people of Zimbabwe, and resolved to mobilise a blockade in Limpopo province (the northern province of South Africa that borders Zimbabwe) to remind 'the now illegal and illegitimate government that Zimbabwe is not an island and that they do need the cooperation of neighbours like South Africa to survive'. COSATU further called on all its other provincial structures, civil society organisations, the ANC and South African Communist Party (SACP) to hold rallies in solidarity with the people of Zimbabwe during June and July, and urged workers throughout Africa and the world to isolate Mugabe and show solidarity with Zimbabwean workers.

These statements were significant as they indicated that the tide had turned in South Africa among the most powerful allies of the ANC, namely COSATU and the SACP. As tensions within the ruling ANC increased, ANC President Jacob Zuma was also forced to take a clear position on Zimbabwe – which put more pressure on his rival Mbeki to broker a solution to the impasse.

Despite these calls, and additional calls for South Africa and other neighbours to cut off power supply if the election was stolen, after the illegitimate presidential election the UN Security Council was unable to implement even limited sanctions targeted against particular Zimbabwe government members, as the resolution was vetoed by China and Russia. While international governments struggle to get consensus on the appropriate response to Mugabe's continued rule, international, continental and regional NGOs and civil society groups have launched solidarity campaigns and made demands in support of Zimbabwean civil society.

Both in Zimbabwe and internationally, civil society groups have also responded with campaigns against the regime. Electronic means such as blogging and text messaging, as well as short wave radio, have been crucial for Zimbabwean activists to distribute information about repression both between themselves and to the outside world. There are also instances where proactive campaigns of pressure have been initiated using the same technologies. One example was the WOZA 'telephone campaign', distributing the phone numbers of Zimbabwean political and security leaders, and calling on the public to phone these individuals, demanding that the repression come to an end. It is of course hard to measure the impact of such efforts, but they surely contribute to the understanding among those in power that they cannot act with impunity. Threats of being taken to the International Criminal Court have also been considered. Another campaign coordinated by the 'This is Zimbabwe' blog involved writing letters to a German company supplying paper for the printing of Zimbabwean banknotes. After the international media took up the story, it was reported that the company concerned announced that it would stop selling to the Zimbabwe government (Shankman 2008).

While only certain African governments have, even now, been prepared to condemn Mugabe outright, civil society groups in Southern Africa have been more outspoken. The SADC Council of NGOs, the Southern African Trade Union Coordinating Council and the Fellowship of Christian Councils in Southern Africa called on their governments on 3 July 2008 to declare the Zimbabwe presidential run-off election illegitimate and to send a peacekeeping force to the country. The statement also demanded that Zimbabwean police and armed forces should be confined to barracks and that ZANU-PF's youth militia and war veterans organisation should be disbanded – demands in line with those of the MDC.

A campaign of solidarity with the people of Zimbabwe was launched by African and international civil society organisations, such as CIVICUS, Amnesty International and the Global Call for Action Against Poverty, on 12 July 2008. The campaign began with a 'symbolic ballot' at the Human Rights Watch offices in Johannesburg, and called for a 'continent-wide' grassroots campaign to allow 'African voices to speak out against injustice in Zimbabwe' (PANA, Lusaka, 11 July 2008).

The outcome (so far) of the struggle with Mugabe

The sophisticated reign of terror against the opposition re-established between 29 March and 27 June 2008 meant that levels of fear rose to such an extent that the kind of civil society action mentioned above has been hard to sustain. Some activists are feeling desperate; and there is no doubt that MDC leadership has engaged in talks about a possible unity government because they understood this desperation and the necessity of finding some resolution. Yet civil society leaders in Zimbabwe are resolute that there can be no satisfactory political resolution between elites, and that their involvement in the negotiation process is essential to achieving a thoroughgoing democratisation process.

Looking further ahead, if there is a transitional government, civil society groups are concerned that ZANU-PF will retain control over the security forces and resist their restructuring. Nevertheless they hope that even a 'messy compromise' would allow them to rebuild their structures and mobilise their constituencies around a range of issues: the adoption of a new constitution; transitional justice mechanisms; rebuilding of the economy; restructuring of the education sector; and effective and accountable local government.

WOZA spokeswoman Jenni Williams, having recently been released from jail, issued a statement emphasising the demand for civil society participation in the mediation process, and supporting the demands of Southern African and international civil society organisations. Her statement reflected the views not only of WOZA/MOZA and its membership of some 60,000 grassroots citizens, but was also agreed to by a broader coalition of civil society groups under the auspices of the People's Convention. The demands included the representation of civil society in the talks; that a Government of National Unity was unacceptable, and that the way forward was through a transitional authority that was inclusive and headed by a neutral body or person; and that this transitional body had a mandate to address economic crisis as well as the drafting of a new 'people driven' constitution. Only then could a referendum and truly free elections be held.

Zimbabwean civil society activists considered a 'campaign of civil disobedience' to ensure that the above demands were met during the negotiation process. COSATU and Zimbabwean civil society groups demonstrated at the SADC summit in Johannesburg in mid-August 2008, demanding that the SADC refuse to recognise Mugabe as a legitimate president.

On 15 September 2008, MDC and ZANU-PF leaders signed a power-sharing deal negotiated by former South African President Thabo Mbeki on behalf of the SADC. The deal provided for Mugabe to retain his position as president, while MDC leader Tsvangirai was given the position of prime minister. While it was hailed by international powers as the beginning of a new phase in Zimbabwe's history, civil society organisations in Zimbabwe were sceptical. Their scepticism was borne out in the failure of the party leadership to reach agreement on the division of positions in the new cabinet, especially those relating to control of the security forces. There were rumours that some ZANU-PF leaders were unhappy with the sharing of power and threatened a coup; Mugabe himself apologised to his party for the 'humiliation' of sharing power with the opposition. On 29 September ZCTU announced its rejection of the deal as an 'elitist pact between powerful politicians [which] pays little regard to the wishes of workers or the electorate' (Nyamhangambiri 2008). The same day WOZA conducted protests demanding that a new government be formed immediately to begin addressing the economic crisis facing ordinary Zimbabweans. A group called FPEP demanded greater women's representation in the new government. Meanwhile, continued spiralling inflation led to government measures allowing Zimbabwean citizens to use foreign currency; and international organisations warned that the worst harvest in living memory was bound to lead to desperate hunger for 5 million Zimbabweans in the next six months.

Mugabe's promise that a government would be formed by 3 October was not realised, and the MDC called for SADC to intervene once again to ensure that the provisions of the 'power-sharing deal' were honoured. A ZINASU student protest was brutally broken up by riot police on 14 October, and WOZA leaders Jenni Williams and Magodongo Mahlangu were arrested yet again at a WOZA protest on 16 October demanding the formation of a new government and the provision of relief to the hungry. It is clear to both Zimbabweans and concerned observers that unless there is some stability in government, the economic crisis will continue and the humanitarian crisis will escalate.

4

COLOMBIA – NONVIOLENT MOVEMENT FOR PEACE AND INTERNATIONAL SOLIDARITY

Mauricio García-Duran

The protracted conflict in Colombia is sometimes described as a war against the civilian population. Rather than confront each other directly, the 'armed actors' tend to attack the real or supposed social base of 'the enemy'. Therefore the civilian population is constantly exposed to reprisals by one armed group or another – be they the forces of the state, the guerrillas, the paramilitaries, narco-traffickers or urban militia. The armed conflict itself directly claimed nearly 60,000 lives from 1990 to 2005, two-thirds of them murdered civilians. However, the national homicide rate tripled – with targets often being worker or community leaders – to a peak of nearly 30,000 assassinations a year, one of the highest totals in the world. Each year between 200,000 and 400,000 people have been displaced – mainly women, children and the elderly. In each area of the country, the conflict has a particular character – according to the degree of central control, the economic interests at play and ethnic composition.

In the face of this, there have arisen peace initiatives at every level of society – from the displaced themselves to the political elite. However, demanding peace is not the same as making a commitment to nonviolence. The state has always claimed a monopoly on 'legitimate' violence and, the Uribe government, in line with other advocates of the global 'war on terrorism', treats those who reject all arms as part of 'the enemy'. On the other side are those who refuse to criticise guerrilla violence, seeing it as necessary for social transformation even though the idealism of the 1960s 'liberation struggle' has been superseded by practices of forced recruitment, kidnapping, extortion and narco-trafficking. However, there are also many – most prominently women and indigenous leaders – who explicitly opt for nonviolence, rejecting all types of war and violence. As one woman leader put it:

Is there a just war? No, for us, no war is just: not religious war, nor ethnic or nationalist wars, nor any war on behalf of anything. We speak from the perspective of what happens to us, women, during the war. For example, when women became a war booty in Pueblo Nuevo (Turbo – Urabá); they are a booty for everyone, a means of retaliation against the other parties. And when that happens, we think that there is not a just war in our country. (Personal interview, Piedad Morales, 30 April 2003)

The term 'civil resistance' hardly existed in Colombia until 2000. Then, between 2000 and 2005, it became popular in the media and among people working for peace because of the proliferation of actions of civil resistance against the armed actors.[1] The concept was understood in the Colombian context as a form of civil and nonviolent defence. But it also took on two other meanings. First, it included every social initiative expressing rejection of violence. Thus many collective actions (marches, demonstrations, even meetings) began to be called 'actions of civil resistance'. Some of these initiatives have been led by mayors of towns and cities with the vision of civil resistance as, in the words of Luis Eduardo Garzon, then mayor of Bogotá, 'a reaction to any act of violence' (*El Tiempo*, 28 August 2004).

Second, the concept was used to refer to communal efforts to protect life, including addressing forms of violence not caused by the armed conflict, such as the structural violence of poverty and discrimination against women (Villarreal and Ríos 2006: 162). As in the case of indigenous peoples:

Nowadays, the indigenous peoples are not worried by the development of the war, but [by] what is going to happen in the post-war period. ... The indigenous peoples are directly or indirectly involved in this war, and what they are doing is to prepare the children with the ancestral diets (food security) to resist the battering of the war, because their aim is to survive and resist these years of war. That is the reason why the indigenous people from Cauca have civil resistance; that is how we, indigenous people, resist the war. It is a survival mechanism of some peoples. (Interview with Armando Valbuena Goauriyú, in Sandoval 2004: vol. 2/64)

In a context of armed conflict any action for peace includes some level of resistance. However, broadening the concept of civil resistance can be misleading, especially when considering different contexts: it is not the same to face an armed actor as to promote a productive project.

Peace mobilisation[2]

The 1990s saw an increasingly diverse repertoire of peace action. Datapaz, the database on peace actions kept by CINEP (Centre for Research and Popular

Education), registers 15 distinct forms of collective action, grouped under five general headings.[3] (See Figure 4.1.)

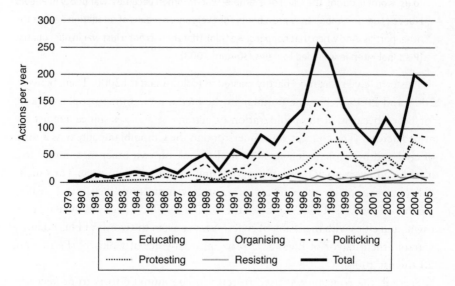

Figure 4.1   Collective action for peace in Colombia, by strategies (1978–2005)

Strategy 1 – Educating

This includes: 'forums, congresses, and seminars', 'educational programmes and campaigns', 'cultural and sporting events', 'religious celebrations' and 'peace awards and honours'. Together, these initiatives represent 50.1 per cent of all collective action for peace that took place between 1978 and 2005.

Strategy 2 – [Self-] Organising

Building organisations and networks to promote peace. Although this only accounts for 3.6 per cent of all activity in the 28 years studied, it has been crucial in lending substance to peace mobilisation.

Strategy 3 – Politicking

Participating in elections and referendums (particularly at the local level), building social consensus and seeking alternative solutions through dialogue/ negotiations. Together, these three types of initiatives represent 10.1 per cent of all collective action.

Strategy 4 – Protesting

Mobilising people against violence and to demand peace. This includes: 'marches and demonstrations', 'strikes and shutdowns' and 'occupations and blockades'.

These are traditional forms of action common in social movements. Together they represent 31.5 per cent of all collective action for peace between 1978 and 2005.

Strategy 5 – Resisting

This expresses a more proactive attitude to the armed actors and embraces three types of initiatives: (a) declarations of neutrality and peace zones; (b) actions of civil resistance, which account for 4.7 per cent of all collective action for peace developed, and (c) processes of organisation and communitarian resistance, including both massive mobilisations, such as the Mandate for Peace and the 'No More' Marches, and local efforts to build more democratic and peaceful alternatives.

Peace mobilisation in Colombia has a low 'propensity for contentiousness' – rarely using tactics that imply the use of force and confrontation. Most activities (60 per cent) show a low level of confrontation with authorities and other social actors; 37 per cent an intermediate level, and only 3 per cent a high level. But even in those with high levels of confrontation, only four peace events registered in Datapaz (of 2,079 events in 28 years) involved the use of violence – one occurred in Coconoco (Cauca) on 31 December 2001 when guerrillas killed a student leader leading a peace march against the guerrilla offensive; and in May 2002 in Cantagallo (Bolivar), a group of citizens reacted to a paramilitary attempt to kill a municipal worker by attacking the paramilitaries with sticks, stones and machetes, killing one of them.

A wide mobilising infrastructure for resistance and peace

One consequence of the growing peace mobilisation has been the emergence of a large and diverse organisational structure. Table 4.1 shows part of this complexity, but far from covers the whole infrastructure for peace. One indicator of its breadth is that in seven years there have been no fewer than 1,180 nominations for the annual National Peace Prize.

The most prominent organisations linked with civil resistance are those involved in what can be called 'peacebuilding from below', addressing the degradation of the armed conflict, looking to protect the population and undertaking communitarian projects to address some of the social consequences of protracted violence.

Some communities undertaking resistance are:

- indigenous communities struggling for their identity and autonomy, supported by projects such as Proyecto Nasa and Proyecto Global de Jambaló;[4]
- the peace communities formed by displaced people, like San José de Apartadó, San Francisco de Asís, Nuestra Señora del Carmen, Natividad de María, and others;

Table 4.1   Civic peace initiatives: Thematic and geographical approach[*]

Types	National Initiatives	Regional Initiatives	Local Initiatives
Protection, defence and resistance to violence	Citizen's Mandate for Peace; The 'No More' Movement; Peaceful Route of Women; Conscientious Objectors Group	Bajo Atrato Peace Communities (San Francisco de Asís, Nuestra Señora del Carmen and Natividad de María); Indigenous Communities projects in Cauca; Integral peasant association of the Atrato – ACIA; 53 women initiatives in Nariño, Cauca and Chocó	Carare and Opón Peasants Association; San José de Apartadó Peace Community; Self-Determination, Life and Dignity Communities (Cacarica, Dabeiba and Balsita); Women in Black; Murindo Committee of All United for Life and Peace
Peace and conflict resolution education	Children's Movement for Peace; Youth Network for Peace; Peace Week (REDEPAZ); National Pilgrimage for Life, Justice and Peace (Bishops Conference); Movement for NonViolence in Colombia	School of Peace and Co-existence (Peace Programme); Montes de María Communication Collective; Network for Community Justice and Treatment of Conflicts (Justapaz)	100 Territories of Peace (or Municipalities of Peace); 100 Experiences of Participation (Redepaz)
Deepening democracy	Strengthening of Marginalised Sectors (Peace Planet); Monitoring of Plan Colombia (Peace Colombia); Citizens' Working Groups for an Agenda for Peace (Indepaz); School for the Development of Democratic Leadership (Long Live Citizenship); Initiative of Colombian Women for Peace	Departmental Constituent Assemblies of Antioquia, Tolima and Nariño; Constituent Assembly and Peace Laboratory of Eastern Antioquia; Governors of the South's Consensus for Peace	Public consultation in Aguachica; Constituent Assemblies of Mogotes, Tarso, San Luis, Micoahumado, Samaniego, Floridablanca, Sonsón, Guatapé and Granada; Community Peace Assemblies of Argelia, El Olival, El Hato and Tibu; Pensilvania Vivid Community
Dialogue and negotiation	National Peace Council; National Conciliation Commission; National Network of Mayors for Peace; Civilian Facilitation Commission with ELN; Ideas for Peace Foundation; Peace Observatory	14 Departmental Councils for Peace; Association of Municipalities of Alto Ariari	Municipal Peace Councils
Peace and development	Network of Peace and Development Programmes	19 Peace and Development Programmes (four of them as peace 'laboratories')	
Networks and coordinating bodies	REDEPAZ; Permanent Assembly of Civil Society for Peace; National Network (and Alliance) of Women for Peace; University Network for Peace; Businessmen for Peace; Media for Peace	24 Departmental Working Groups for Peace; Solidarity Network (Twin Towns, Visible Links)	Municipal Working Groups for Peace (around 150 in the whole country)

* Compiled by the author with the help of Fernando Sarmiento and Carlos Fernandez; published in García-Durán 2004.

- the communities that demanded and negotiated respect from the armed actors, like the Carare-Opón Peasants Association and the Murindó Committee All United for Life and Peace.

In addition, there are different groups of women, flagging their opposition to all forms of violence, like Mujeres de Negro (Women in Black) and the La Ruta Pacifica de Mujeres (Peaceful Route of Women), and the growing number of projects and organisations in Nariño, Cauca and Chocó. Finally, it includes the network of conscientious objectors supporting young men resisting conscription to the armed forces.

Maybe the most important result of these initiatives in such a context of protracted conflict has been the possibility to empower people/communities, making them able to resist violence and to develop their own initiatives for peace, showing an 'increased capacity to interact constructively across the lines of conflict' (Lederach 2005: 97). In other words, these are concrete ways for different social sectors to recover from the damage of violence and to show wider possibilities for restoring the social fabric.

Evolution of resistance as a strategy in peace mobilisation

Initiatives for resistance appeared rather late in the process of peace mobilisation in Colombia (see Figure 4.2) They reflect paradoxical feelings: 'fatigue' with the armed conflict but also a gradual overcoming of fear of the armed actors – there came a moment when people demanded respect and not to be involved in the armed conflict, and they found the strength to do so.

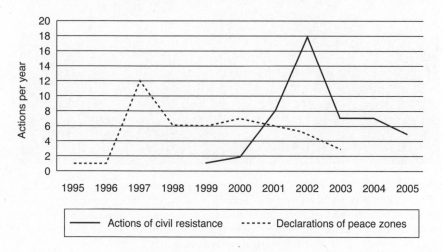

Figure 4.2   Dynamic of Strategy 5: Resisting (1995–2005)

Declarations of peace [or neutral] zones

Between 1995 and 1998 there were three different types of declaration. First, the population of some zones declared themselves 'neutral' in the armed conflict, such as Punta de Piedra in Urabá, Murindó, Zaragoza and above all the indigenous organisation in Antioquia. For the 'indigenous governors' of Urabá, being neutral is

> that we do not accept being recruited by any armed force. Not the army, nor the guerrilla, nor the paramilitaries will find any information on us. ... We will keep protecting our rights, working to strengthen our organizations without being involved in the armed conflict. We support a civic, democratic, pluralistic and participative society. (Gobernadores Indígenas de Urabá 1997: 24)

Second, groups of forcibly displaced people in the Urabá region declared themselves peace communities, aiming to disengage from the armed conflict and make possible a return to their place of origin. The first such community, founded in 1997, was San José de Apartadó, with others following supported both by various Catholic Church bodies and with international cooperation. They began returning to their areas of origin and developing diverse types of projects.

Photograph 4.1 The Peace Community at San José de Apartadó, established in 1997. Community members commit themselves to participate in community work, to oppose injustice and impunity for crimes, to refuse to take a direct or indirect part in war or to bear arms, and to avoid distorting information or offering it to one side.
(Ruben Dario Pardo Santamaria)

Third, municipalities declared themselves 'peace territories', demanding respect for the civilian population living there. Among them were Puerto Wilches, Villavicencio, Corinto, Aguachica, Tulúa, Ungía, Medellín and Samaniego. The majority of them occurred as part of the campaign 'One Hundred Peace Municipalities' promoted by Redepaz.

These declarations of 'peace zones' are by no means universally respected by the armed actors. Far from exempting the residents from violence, declaring for peace can even be a source of harassment. Against a backcloth of driving people off their land in the course of the armed conflict or to make way for more lucrative business, armed actors on all sides target 'leaders', including teachers and others doing basic development work. At times the state security forces insist on establishing police stations or military barracks in the zones, and President Uribe's 'democratic security' policy does not accept the 'neutrality' of peace communities, indigenous groups or others who reject all armed force. The paramilitaries seek to intimidate residents while FARC guerrillas also encroach into the demilitarised zones. The most prominent peace community, San José de Apartadó, has been hard hit by the armed actors: around 10 per cent of its members – some 150 people – have been killed, mainly by paramilitaries, often acting in collusion with state security forces, and around 20 by the FARC.

Actions of civil resistance

Between 2000 and 2005 the actions of civil resistance emerged with considerable force: 34 of the 48 actions registered in Datapaz. Some involved face-to-face confrontation between an armed actor (the guerrillas or paramilitaries) and the population, normally around an attack or kidnapping. Others opposed violence without directly interacting with the perpetrators: for instance, protest events such as voluntary blackouts or *cacerolazos* (people in the street banging pots and pans). These were explicit expressions of resistance to armed actors, mainly against guerrilla groups, although there were three cases directed against paramilitary groups. Normally these were nonviolent, although in four cases there were violent confrontations with fatalities, three with paramilitaries and one with the guerrillas (interview with Carlos Rosero, in Sandoval 2004: 2/56). Indigenous people have played a leading role in these initiatives.

There have also been acts of civil resistance at the level of local government, such as the mayor in Bogotá. Cases where the unarmed civilian population has gone out to face armed groups – particularly the guerrillas to demand the release of kidnapped 'hostages' – have had most media impact and publicity.

Resisting as a communitarian process

Behind an event of civil resistance there often lies a long process of community work and organising, especially in the case of indigenous people and African-Colombians.

> The war is not going to finish in the next few years. ... It is necessary to strengthen the capacity for resistance of all social sectors ... to create the right conditions to survive, and in some cases, under very difficult conditions, take the communities away from the impact of war. (Interview with Armando Valbuena Goauriyú, in Sandoval 2004: 2/63)

The communities assert their neutrality in relation to the conflict and demand autonomy from any armed group: they do not want to get involved in the dynamics of war.

> In this recent time where the conflict has escalated, and got worse, there are indigenous communities that clearly say we cut ourselves off from the armed actors, we are not aligned with anyone. They do not go through our territory, etc. It is like a strong position of autonomy and active neutrality. (León 2004)

Initiatives of civil resistance and international solidarity

The international work of Colombian peace activists does not consist only in informing the rest of the world about the Colombian context but also in expanding certain concepts: for instance, Luis Eduardo Guerra, a leader of the Peace Community of San José de Apartadó, complained of the tendency of human rights organisations to treat conscientious objection to military service as an individual right without recognising the collective refusal of a whole community.[5]

International solidarity has been crucial for the development of unarmed resistance in Colombia. It would have been hard to sustain without this help. The experience of the Bajo Atrato since 1996 serves to illustrate the overall pattern of international solidarity.[6] The following forms of international nonviolent intervention have taken place:

Local actions, campaigns and lobbying

In different countries, particularly France, Italy, Spain and the Netherlands, groups have campaigned in solidarity with the peace communities. In France, a platform of NGOs and a network of local committees raised awareness about the situation of the communities and generated different types of social and political support:

- activities for raising awareness of the situation: conferences, festivals, etc.;
- publishing leaflets and books;

- annual delegations visiting the communities;
- lobbying their governments and the European Union to put pressure on the Colombian government;
- organising tours of representatives of the communities and NGOs working with them;
- denouncing human rights violations and other abuses against the communities;
- finding 'fair trade' distributors for products grown in peace communities; and
- disseminating information about peace communities in situations of armed conflict elsewhere.

This social and political support has helped sustain the communities. One consequence was that the peace communities of the Bajo Atrato were awarded with the Human Rights Prize of the French government in 1998. Another has been in restraining abuses by armed actors and those with economic interests in the region by making them feel that they are under international observation. The US Congress's (temporary) suspension of military aid in 2005 was a reaction to the murder of a leader and seven members of the Peace Community of San José de Apartadó in February that year, and there can be little doubt that the Colombian government's decision in 2008 finally to prosecute soldiers of the XVII Battalion for that massacre was also the result of lobbying in the USA.

Witness and accompaniment

The presence of international volunteers with the peace communities has been an important contribution, bringing some protection and security. Both the armed forces and the illegal armed actors have normally refrained from violence against the communities in presence of these witnesses. At the same time, this presence encouraged the members of the communities to develop inner strength. In the Bajo Atrato, in addition to the presence of PBI, there have been volunteers from France and Spain, some of them working as part of CINEP's team in the region.

Humanitarian assistance

For displaced people seeking to resettle after declaring a peace community, humanitarian support is vital, particularly at the moment of return. This came more from international governments, agencies and NGOs than from the Colombian government. One important challenge for this humanitarian aid was to coordinate the different institutions, agencies and NGOs for the delivery of the aid, in order to have wider coverage and better and timely distribution.

Funding

International funding has been crucial. The peace communities and the organisations working with them have received money from governments (France, Spain, the Netherlands and the EU), international organisations (such as the Red Cross), international NGOs and agencies (Secours Catholique, Oxfam, Swiss Aid, etc.). But in addition, there is some help coming from the grassroots level in Europe. For example, the French solidarity committees have developed fund-raising activities in each locality. Previously, international aid supported the communities by funding the institutions through organisations working with them. Now, however, the relationship is more direct, as in the case of ASCOBA (Association of Communitarian Councils and Organisations of Bajo Atrato).

Conclusions

The dynamics of peace mobilisation in Colombia have shown the way in which people living in a context of protracted armed conflict can develop different ways of resistance – and essentially nonviolent resistance – to violence. Above all for the 'peace zones', international solidarity and support is crucial. They have shown enormous resilience, but ultimately remain fragile unless they are backed by others in a dynamic of globalising solidarity for a just, lasting and sustainable peace.

Notes

1. Datapaz registered 48 actions of this type between 1999 and 2005, 18 of them in 2002. These not only imply a rejection of the military activities of an armed actor, but nonviolent confrontation between civilians and combatants. Two examples from Cauca: on 12 December 2002, residents of Bolivar repelled the FARC for the third time. Early in the morning, on hearing rifle shots at official and police buildings, pyjama-clad residents went out chanting to the rhythm of the *chirimia* (a regional folk music) that FARC were not welcome. Many publicly prayed the *novena* (nine days) of Christmas. The guerrillas had to withdraw, furious with the population. A second example is in a *resguardo* (protected area, rather than a reservation) for the Pioya people in Caldono, when FARC took a Swiss missionary hostage. The *indigenas* surrounded them, leaving the abductors no option but to release the victim.
2. See García-Duran (2006) for a detailed analysis of peace mobilisation in Colombia.
3. To the four strategies of 'educating', 'politicking', 'protesting' and 'organising' used by Lofland (1993) and Mushaben (1986), Datapaz adds 'resisting' – the population resisting armed actors.
4. These are two projects founded in the 1980s to strengthen indigenous self-organisation in the Cauca region. 'Nasa' is the preferred name for Colombia's second most numerous ethnic group, often called Paéz.

5. Quoted after the assassination of Luis Eduardo Guerra in an open letter (28 February 2005) on behalf of two Ecuadoran human rights groups, http://www.mediosparalapaz. org/index.php?idcategoria=1973&resaltar=objeci%F3n+de+conciencia [accessed 10 October 2008].

6. I thank Eduardo Vega and Claire Lunay for discussion on this section.

5

INDIA – MACRO VIOLENCE, MICRO RESISTANCE: DEVELOPMENT VIOLENCE AND UNARMED GRASSROOTS RESISTANCE

Moses (Anand) Mazgaonkar

Background and context

India is considered a newly industrialising and developing country that is being encouraged to catch up with the developed West. Gujarat state has led the way in implementing this 'globalising' agenda over the past 15 years. As a result there are rising investments in hazardous chemical industries that:

- are natural resource-intensive;
- have little employment potential; and
- cause mass displacement and dispossession of large communities practising traditional vocations.

While uncritical policy-makers and economists like to circulate the growth-story, there is a tragic unfolding reality that most people sold on the idea of 'globalisation' either deliberately choose not to, or naively cannot, see. That reality is:

- growing inequality is the quickest social process and the biggest unreported story;
- 'high' economic growth is coupled with declining human well-being, including decreasing per capita food availability;
- there are fast cars, a few excellent expressways, underground metro rail and a choice of airlines on the one hand, and failing public transport and other public services on the other;

- the glare from the spectacle of city beautification, high-tech urban infrastructure construction and flashy glass towers that rise overnight, blinds people to the slums and ghettos being razed to the ground making millions homeless (the last few years have seen massive demolition drives in every major city of the country);
- the privatisation of education, health services and public food distribution services;
- the profits from privatisation of public resources and national properties such as roads, water, electricity, coasts and ports, forests and lands, are promised to corporations via concession agreements and special rights while their costs and losses are underwritten by public funds; and
- laws have been and are being changed to bring about LPG (Liberalisation, Privatisation and Globalisation), including the creation of special economic zones that are deemed 'foreign territories' to circumvent the operation of labour and other laws.

Impacts

Development-induced displacement uproots more people than any tsunami, cyclone or earthquake. For the common people, development most often can be distilled down to the 'D's of Displacement, Dispossession, Disempowerment, De-skilling, Destruction of natural resources and Dehumanisation. The development ideology brooks no dissent and rides roughshod over communities, cultures, traditional occupations and lifestyles. It would be too lengthy to detail every instance of development-induced violence, so I shall just cite a few examples:

- dams and other development projects have displaced anything between 25 and 50 million people in the last 50 years;[1]
- uranium mining in the eastern predominantly tribal state of Jharkhand causes genetic defects among the families of mineworkers, and the authorities simply refuse to acknowledge the problem, while cities enjoy the benefits of nuclear power;
- in the eastern state of Orissa, 13 indigenous people trying to protect their lands from acquisition for a steel manufacturer were killed by the administration/police/corporation nexus. Their private parts were mutilated during post mortem to teach the indigenous people a lesson (this is not the only instance of violence and killing in the state);
- ports and coast-based export-oriented industrialisation is displacing and dis-employing fisherpeople across the country (the leader of the movement against the port in Gujarat died of police torture);[2]

- for the farmers in the southern states of Andhra Pradesh, Kerala, the western state of Maharashtra and the northern state of Punjab, the reality of globalising export-oriented agriculture has prompted mass suicides (the official national statistics are 86,922 farmer suicides during the years 2001–05); and
- factory workers are either forced to go without pay for months, or are losing their jobs owing to changing technology and shifting production facilities.[3]

This is the state of the indigenous (Adivasis), farmers, pasturalists, fisherpeople and factory workers – the primary producers in India's high growth economy. The map of '21st century', information technology-driven, high-tech, 'developed' India is blotched with the blood of the poor toiling majority. The result of mass suffering: about 15–20 per cent of the mainly urban middle class 'have never had it so good'.

The flavour of the times is:

- to be a satellite and service economy revolving around and dependent on others, a far cry from Gandhi's emphasis on *swadeshi*/self-reliance;
- pay and use: only those with the means have the right and access to services;
- universalisation of middle-class norms, lifestyle, aspirations and the selling of dreams;
- paying public lip service to such buzz-words as 'sustainable development', 'participation', 'human rights' and 'justice', while those at the wrong end of the line live and experience a vastly different reality;
- a clinical lack of sensitivity to the growing violence and iniquity that characterises our society; and
- while the violence of the system is denied or ignored, any self-defence actions leads to people being demonised as 'anti-national', 'anti-development', Maoists or Naxalites.

The tragedy is that the forces unleashed by these processes pit one set of victims/poor people against another: the drought-affected versus the displaced, the unemployed versus internal migrants, farmers versus factory workers and so on. People end up fighting for a share of the same small pie. This is in contrast to the criminally wasteful use of natural resources that sustains the lifestyle of a small privileged sector of the population. First a scarcity is engineered, then the 'brilliant' solution of privatising resources in order to streamline their distribution is invented!

The details here may be drawn from India, but this story resonates throughout the world. This applies as much to the Ogonis of Nigeria, the Mapuche of Chile, the people of Cochabamba, Bolivia and the indigenous of the Philippines. People everywhere witness their resources being appropriated in the name of more 'efficient management', 'choice', 'liberty'. The irony is that our public discourse seems to get smarter, the language more refined. Consequently we are mystified by cleverly changing language disguising a constant reality. We are made to hear a language that conceals rather than communicates.

Resistance for survival

The assault on traditional occupations affects a large number of communities across India. Those that resist are met with state force. But not all communities resist. Lacking education and awareness of the machinations of corporate deceit and state pressure, many are 'persuaded' (cheated) to part with their land and their homes. Some are seduced by the promise that they too will be able to share in the profits that will accrue from such 'development'. A study of how different affected communities react to violation of their right to life and livelihood is very instructive. Four examples cited in the following paragraphs pertain to Gujarat, where there has been an active campaign for raising awareness and trying to organise people to resist.

Movement against Umargoan Port in Gujarat

As part of its infrastructure development efforts, the government of Gujarat planned a mega-port in South Gujarat with Unocal, a US-based energy corporation. The port project claimed it would generate employment and boost exports. The loss of livelihoods for local fisherpeople and the resultant impact on a population of up to 50,000 was never mentioned. Peaceful protests of the fisher communities were rewarded with arrests and torture leading to the death of one of their leaders. If the government thought that this would smother the movement, it was not to be. Public outrage and resultant solidarity, media attention, and the reaction of the government, contributed to the movement gaining strength.

The government tried to instil fear by such means as filing false cases against activists and ordering menacing movements of police in the area over an extended period. The nonviolent tools people took recourse to were prayer and protest meetings, village to village foot marches, media outreach, getting prominent people to visit the area to express their solidarity (particularly former military officers as the murdered leader had been a former military officer), and setting up a people's commission of inquiry (because the government initially refused to set up an official commission).

A significant challenge faced by any movement confronting the development juggernaut is the loss of people who are either cowed or bought. This has the potential to do enormous damage except in a nonviolent movement where planning and decisions are a transparent process, where resistance is a conscious decision, and where the willingness to undergo suffering is a primary resolve.

Participation in resistance has a liberating effect. People learn to overcome fear, they come to deal better with state power that otherwise commands awe. Every movement develops its own songs, literature and resources. The success of a movement ought to be measured from the bonds it creates among the activists even if it fails in the long run.

The semi-literate fisherpeople who spend a good proportion of their time out at sea have managed to hold off port construction for over six years now. Women played a major role from the start and at every stage: they engineered the breakthrough from the spell of fear.

Adivasi (Indigenous) forest lands struggle

Indigenous people, with their unique culture and oral history, have generally lived in harmony with nature. Often they were resettled in forest villages as a labour force for the timber trade – first for the shipping industry, then for the construction of railways and then to meet the expanding urban demands. They were only wage labourers but they ended up being held responsible for the destruction of India's forests. They had never demanded nor possessed title-deeds to the lands on which they settled, and as a consequence state governments have sought to evict them from their properties and deny them access to their forests – justifying this as a necessary measure to reverse the trend of environmental destruction, a trend caused by overconsumption, development and urbanisation. According to Government Planning Commission estimates 60 per cent of all those displaced by development projects have been Adivasis, though they constitute only 8 per cent of the total population.

The latest threat of eviction from their traditionally cultivated lands came in the year 2002. Tribal houses were destroyed in many places, and criminal cases filed against them in addition to the usual harassment perpetrated by the Forest Department. Activist groups and NGOs got together as they realised there was a pattern in what was unfolding. There was a transnational dimension to what was happening to them. In order for India to fulfil international agreements to achieve 33 per cent of land under forest cover, Adivasis were expected to sacrifice their home lands.

However, a decentralised but coordinated movement across different states in the country over the last three years has prevented them from being dispossessed of their lands. The resistance has consisted of village-level meetings, demonstrations, holding non-official public hearings, court interventions and lobbying with

Photograph 5.1   Adivasis (tribal peoples) march for land rights
(Michael Mazgaonkar/Paryavaran Surakshi Samiti).

the government. Fortunately or otherwise, politicians have to fight elections. Enough pressure was exercised on the government to require them to draft a new law giving people formal titles for lands traditionally belonging to their ancestors. The fight continues, and the draft law is expected to be passed in the coming months.

Campaign against industrial pollution and mining

As a forerunner in industrialising India Gujarat is subject to a plethora of environmental problems that are conveniently overlooked as a 'minor' cost of 'progress'. The state specialises in all manner of chemical production, every river is polluted with effluent, groundwater is severely contaminated, hazardous solid wastes lie indiscriminately strewn across the 275 industrial hubs/estates located within the state, and there are serious occupational and community health problems that the state authorities refuse to acknowledge.

The aim of organising people on this issue was to challenge the state policy of specialising in hazardous chemicals, especially as Gujarat is a water-scarce state. Raising the various environmental and health issues should have resulted in a critical look at the policy. What was achieved, however, were mere 'technical fixes' of effluent treatment and waste disposal, shifting the problem out of sight through some compensatory measures and a public relations offensive by the government.

The problem in trying to mobilise people around the issue is that the industrial workers who are exposed to these occupational health problems are often migrants and economic refugees willing to put up with a great deal, and as such reluctant to threaten their employment. The affected local communities do not organise because they do not have it in them to challenge state policy, and would rather find a way around the problem, escape it rather than fight it.

The fight to save land and village commons

In trying to outdo itself in globalising and liberalising, the government of Gujarat introduces ever-new schemes and incentives for potential investors and industries. To promote corporate farming the government decided to turn over grazing lands and village common property resources for industrial agriculture. The different communities that make a living from these common property resources were deemed 'non-contributors' to the official gross domestic product and therefore dispensable. These include goat, sheep and cattle herders, those who live by making charcoal from local shrubs and plants, and others who engage in small-time sand mining for a living. 'Save our Lands' is a campaign to protect the livelihoods of these marginal communities. The government had to agree to distribute its excess landholdings among the landless.

The outcomes of these four battles cannot be viewed in simple binary terms of success or failure. It is meant to be a process. Yet the positives and the negatives have varied. There was some measure of achievement in the first two cases, as well as in the fourth case, whereas the third example should go down as 'no substantial achievement'.

Lessons

Lessons learnt from each of these campaigns have been very educative. One can itemise them as follows:

1. These battles were not only against state power but also against the dominant global ideology of liberalisation, privatisation and globalisation, and therefore against the cultural violence sweeping the world.
2. A battle against state power is a challenge, and success stories are few and far between. The common people engaged in their daily struggle for survival do not have the time or energy to fight for change. They are often gullible. Their tendency is to seek an escape from problems rather than confront them. Therefore activists, NGOs and thinkers act as advocates for the victims, without commensurate support from the affected. Activists can either be enablers and facilitators, or come to occupy leadership roles and decide for the affected. This has its own dynamics because they are 'outsiders' who do

not suffer the plight of the victims and therefore cannot fully identify with them. Consequently there is the danger of preaching without practice.

3. In India, a real effective movement takes off only when a traditional community identity is involved, where people live and work together, share together the risks and hazards of survival – as in the case of the fisherpeople and Adivasis. The odds are that migrants who constitute a disparate group thrown together in response to survival needs will not organise, as they do not constitute a community with a shared past or an anticipated shared future.

4. Resistance, in order to be sustainable, has to be indigenous to the affected community. No amount of outside support will sustain it in the long run. It will in any case not be empowering if it depends on individual, charismatic, central, outsider leadership.

5. Resistance, in order to be empowering, must necessarily be nonviolent because nonviolence is the only tool that is universally accessible. Nonviolence involves an experiential journey of growth as one tries to bring over opponents to appreciate one's viewpoint rather than defeat them. It can plant the seed for a mutually shared future.

6. The state apparatus and the vested interests that are threatened by people's or people-oriented campaigns waste no time in neutralising the campaigners using fair means and foul – including the law, police, media and every possible tool to brand them as 'anti-development' or 'anti-national' and thereby marginalise the movement.

The above observations relate to 'outsider' roles in local resistance movements, although such external involvement is by fellow-nationals. It is important to expose the role of outsiders who are internationals to the same critical analysis.

The transnational factor

It would be a folly to believe that it is only recently that the transnational factor has come into play. India has experienced colonisation, the industrial revolution and present-day technological revolution. India's freedom struggle was a mass-based movement fought with minimal direct transnational assistance. The effort was also to minimise dependence on financial resources to the barest minimum. All the work was voluntary. The organisational membership fee was a few pennies. By contrast the post-Independence development vision was totally founded on Western financial aid that killed individual initiative, the spirit of sacrifice and the value of participation in the process. As a consequence perceptions, policies and programmes are more often than not funder-driven. In practice it is the funding agencies and foundations who deliberately or otherwise set the agenda. Consequently all attention is focused on material development, physical targets etc. A human-centred, rights-based, social consciousness focus was dispensed with. That is how it has been in the 60 years of official 'development movement'.

Consequently, we have a dinosaur of a development army that is apparently decentralised and autonomous, but conditioned in thinking, with shared goals and objectives, using the same language and style of operating. It is absolutely uncritical of the status quo and it will not challenge the establishment/official line. The development bureaucracy has grown too big and has a vested interest in self-perpetuation. It has the uncanny ability to convert every issue, problem and struggle into a fundable project. That being the rationale of its existence it will simply not disturb the apple cart.

From this perspective the transnational influence is negative to the extent that it is limited to monetary aid, is of an unwieldy scale, self-perpetuating and disconnected from reality.

Other forms of assistance and solidarity

Activists working for peace and justice have always stood for sharing of concerns and globalisation of the movement/s. It is only in the last two decades that the language has been hijacked for use in commerce. In its real sense it would encompass the following:

- solidarity action, moral support;
- sharing of information, analyses and multi-disciplinary expertise;
- lobbying, exerting pressure, holding to account, especially when there is some kind of leverage on any of the players involved; and
- a two-way learning and sharing process.

These are very constructive forms of support and help that play a crucial role in a movement. Any movement has to be a broad alliance between the affected victims, facilitator-enabler activists, media, conscientious intelligentsia-experts and the global solidarity element. Every movement goes through various cycles and phases, it is never up and growing all the time. Experience teaches that the various elements of the alliance have to play more or less prominent roles at different phases in the life-cycle of a movement. Very often a movement needs a boost, especially when it effectively disturbs the status quo and a backlash from the establishment is inevitable. That is when transnational solidarity has to keep the flame burning, to let the perpetrators of injustice/violence know that the world is watching. On the other hand such solidarity makes the movement vulnerable to the charge of serving foreign masters and other illegitimate interests. It must be borne in mind that the establishment/governments/corporation nexus can lay claim to some form of legitimacy and recourse to legal sanction, unlike a resistance movement, which can be depicted as largely 'self-appointed' and thereby lacking in legitimacy.

Unlike transnational solidarity activists, who have the space to engage in symbolic protests, lobbying and letter-writing, those engaged in struggle on the ground face a more direct battle and therefore have a very limited space to operate in and are often subject to grave physical threats.

Finally, it is crucial to recognise that global solidarity should be a two-way process – it should not be just 'one-way' support for resistance movements in 'problem areas' of the third world. Third world movements can help first world movements question their lifestyles, their consumption patterns and the repercussions these have globally.

Alternative globalisation should embody a resounding 'no' to commerce driving all human actions, a 'no' to the subtle and not so subtle systemic violence, a 'no' to displacement and dispossession of the poor and marginalised. It must be based on a call for a human-centred development, involving a search for technologies that promote life in consonance with nature. It must embrace a two-way exchange and learning process that leads to a questioning of myths such as the need for 'development of the poor' and the recognition that it is the poor who not only subsidise the rich but also sustain this planet.

Notes

1. Estimates by various scholars have ranged from 25 to 50 million. There are grounds for believing that the most realistic figure is closer to 50 million.
2. Lt Col. Pratap Save died of police torture because he led the anti-port movement in South Gujarat.
3. *People's Democracy*, XXVIII, No. 44, 31 October 2004, estimates job losses in the manufacturing sector between 1998 and 2000 at 230,000, in agriculture at 70,000 between 1992 and 2000, and in mining at 90,000 between 1994 and 2000.

Section II

Nonviolent Citizens' Intervention Across Borders

EDITORIAL INTRODUCTION

The second half of the twentieth century saw various 'experiments' with transnational nonviolent intervention – cross-border action by citizens. Building on the excellent compilations of Moser-Puangsuwan and Weber (2000) and Schweitzer et al. (2001), this section discusses the work of Peace Brigades International (PBI), the recently formed Nonviolent Peaceforce (NP), the Balkan Peace Team, international projects in Palestine – specifically, the International Solidarity Movement (ISM), Ecumenical Accompaniment Programme in Palestine and Israel (EAPPI) and the International Women's Peace Service (IWPS) – and the sanctions-busting Voices in the Wilderness. The backcloth to these projects is numerous other efforts to make transnational connections between movement groups, conceptually part of a transnational 'chain of nonviolence' (see Afterword). These include:

- short-term delegations and study tours organised by peace, solidarity, human rights and sectoral groups;
- placements of long-term international volunteers in peace projects;
- 'twinning' – not just town to town but peace group to peace group;
- training workshops on themes or in skills;
- involvement of peace groups from conflict zones in global peace networks, including international speaking tours;
- marketing of 'fair trade' or solidarity products produced by peace initiatives.

Projects of nonviolent intervention draw on three main streams of activity. The most obvious is a tradition of protest and solidarity projects, trying to bring a situation closer to home and often carried out in concert with domestic peace campaigns. As well as the attempted incursions into nuclear test zones – at sea (the Golden Rule, Everyman and later Greenpeace boats) and on land (the Sahara Protest Team: see Carter 1977, and later Greenpeace actions in Nevada) – several projects have tried to enter war zones or run military blockades. These include Nonviolent Action in Vietnam (Arrowsmith 1972), Operation Omega to Bangladesh (Hare and Blumberg 1977; Prasad 2005), Witness for Peace in Nicaragua (Griffin-Nolan 1991), the Gulf Peace Team (Burrowes 2000; Bhatia, Drèze and Kelly 2001) and various actions during the war in Bosnia (Schweitzer 2000). Such actions have generally begun with ad hoc groups, although both Greenpeace and Witness for Peace grew into organisations.[1]

A second, more institutionalised stream is that of international voluntary work for peace and reconciliation, a concept pioneered by Service Civil International after the First World War, mainly organising workcamps, and developed further by Eirene in the 1950s, organising long-term placements. There now exist many national schemes of 'volunteers for cooperation and development', often government-funded. The UN Volunteers (UNV) declare a special interest in peace projects, but this has increasingly taken the form of engaging in combined civil–military peace-keeping missions.[2] Since the 1990s various nonviolent groups have tried to establish national schemes building on this second stream but linking with a third stream of activity – that of seeking to develop nonviolent alternatives to armed intervention.

The principal inspiration for this third stream has been Gandhi's vision of a 'peace army', the Shanti Sena (Weber 1996). This envisaged community-based nonviolent activists coming together to mount nonviolent projects in response to conflict, either in their own locality or elsewhere. At the heart of this project lay Gandhian values (nonviolence, the search for truth, the stand for justice), both as a source of credibility for outsiders entering a situation and in shaping the strategies they would pursue. There have been three attempts to 'internationalise' the idea: the World Peace Brigade (WPB – 1961–64), Peace Brigades International (PBI – 1981 onwards) and the Nonviolent Peaceforce (NP – 2002 onwards).

The sheer ambition of the WPB can be seen from its flagship project: a Freedom March from Dar es Salaam into Northern Rhodesia (now Zambia) to coincide with a general strike inside the country. This strategy, devised with Zambia's future President Kenneth Kaunda, relied for its credibility not on the WPB having a solid organisational base – that was exactly what it lacked – but on the moral authority of those around the world who had used nonviolent direct action in the cause of colonial freedom, civil rights and nuclear disarmament. Political progress towards Zambian independence made the march unnecessary and in May 1962, after months of costly preparations, it was called off. The WPB mounted three smaller projects but petered out over the next three years.[3]

WPB emphasised nonviolent confrontation of injustice, in particular encouraging the involvement of public figures in civil disobedience. In contrast PBI and NP present their role as 'opening space' for local actors. They describe themselves as 'non-partisan' – a term open to interpretation but as a minimum indicating not being aligned with any particular group or organisation.[4] PBI long ago abandoned any aspiration to offer a direct alternative on a large scale: its Colombia project

– its largest and longest-running project – has around 50 volunteers working in four teams. While NP still retains the vision of being an alternative to military intervention and seeks to deploy hundreds not just tens of field staff, its proposals to develop a 'rapid deployment capacity' have receded. Both PBI and NP have been more concerned to develop a solid system of organisation, collective decision-making, professional standards of work, and repertoires of activity transferable to other conflicts.

PBI specialises in 'protective accompaniment', that is, travelling with local activists or organisations who have been threatened. In contrast, NP insists that 'protective accompaniment' can effectively be combined with other roles – including facilitating dialogue and remonstrating with non-state armed groups to release people they have kidnapped.[5] NP also offers its 'staff' (eschewing the term 'volunteers') a higher stipend, theoretically in order to enable a wider range of people to join its work, although it should also be noted that this now offers people from most countries in the world an economic incentive to do this work. War Resisters' International (WRI), having initially welcomed NP as an 'experiment', in 2007 decided despite reservations to become a 'supporting organisation', recognising that NP is in its early days and its evolution is not decided.[6]

As international organisations deploying 'non-partisan' teams of selected and trained people committed to at least a year as team members, PBI and NP represent one end of the spectrum in international nonviolent intervention. The other end is the International Solidarity Movement. Motivated by outrage at the Israeli occupation, self-selected activists join protests initiated by Palestinians. Somewhere in between on the spectrum are the Christian Peacemaker Teams, whose predominantly North American teams are willing to engage in nonviolent confrontation and combine organising short-term delegations with maintaining a long-term presence. Founded in 1984, CPT has engaged in projects around the world, including Colombia, Palestine and North America itself. It has around 30 long-term volunteers doing one-year terms, and 150 self-financed 'reservists' who commit themselves for three years, devoting between two weeks and three months a year to participation in CPT projects. Present in the West Bank since 1995, CPT 'works alongside' local activists, sometimes in the background as accompaniers, but often taking the lead, as for instance in launching the Campaign for Secure Dwellings (against house demolitions). It has also been willing to take action against Palestinian bombings (for instance, offering to ride an Israeli bus route). Unfortunately, CPT's fine work in Hebron has received far less publicity than the episode in Iraq in 2005 when four CPT associates were taken hostage, one killed and the others freed after several months by a special military anti-kidnapping unit (Kember 2007).

Participation in projects of nonviolent intervention often leads to further involvement. For some projects, this is essential to their functioning – participants go home and say what they have seen. EAPPI's contract even stipulates that, on returning home, accompaniers should speak to at least 15 meetings. Sometimes new commitments arise in response to the changing situation: activists involved in the Gulf Peace Team (1990–91) founded Voices in the Wilderness. Collectively and personally, nonviolent intervention proves to be a learning experience, which makes continuing evaluation and reflection essential.

Notes

1. In 2008 Witness for Peace recently celebrated its 25th anniversary, still organising US delegations to Latin America although now mainly centred on issues of social justice versus 'Free Trade'.
2. Currently about 40 per cent of UN Volunteers are in this role – some 2,100 people in 19 missions (www.unv.org). The idealism of UNV's website is rather belied in Kosovo, where UNV still has around 250 volunteers, often playing bureaucratic roles connected with local government. The 'stretching' of the concept of volunteer should also be noted: many volunteer schemes now offer a stipend, in the case of UNV more than many volunteers were earning at home.
3. Fuller accounts of the WPB can be found in Moser-Puangsuwan and Weber (2000), Prasad (2005) and Yates and Chester (2006).
4. 'Non-partisanship', it should be noted, is an operational not a political principle: the overall context of the work of 'non-partisan' peace teams is solidarity with the promotion of nonviolence and human rights.
5. PBI does not arrange meetings with guerrilla groups, partly because it lacks leverage on them and partly because a hostile government could wilfully misrepresent this.
6. The reservations were: that 'non-partisanship' and 'professionalism' will lead to NP becoming just one more international NGO working on conflict rather than a radical alternative response; that NP's orientation will be shaped by its need for state funding; and that NP's public reporting is primarily self-promotional (in contrast to PBI's publicising the perspectives of those groups it works with). See http://wri-irg.org/node/3253.

6

MAKING ACCOMPANIMENT EFFECTIVE

*Brian Martin**

Why is accompaniment – sending international teams to support resisters who are under threat – effective? And what can be done to make it more effective?

Liam Mahony and Luis Enrique Eguren (1997), in their study of international accompaniment, say that it works through deterrence: aggressors decide that the negative consequences of bad publicity and international pressure outweigh the advantages of attacking activists. Accompaniment can expand the political space available to activists and limit the actions aggressors can take with what they consider 'acceptable' costs. Other studies of nonviolent intervention (Moser-Puangsuwan and Weber 2000; Müller 2006) include examples of accompaniment with rich detail about actions and their consequences, but give less attention to how it works.

There is, however, another framework for understanding why accompaniment can often be effective, which I call 'backfire' (Martin 2005, 2007). This builds on the insights that can be obtained by exploring the process called political jiu-jitsu. Nonviolence researcher Gene Sharp (1973) studied hundreds of actions and campaigns. He found that when violent attacks were made against peaceful protesters, this could be counterproductive for the attacker, encouraging more people to become activists, generating more support for the protesters from third parties and weakening commitment from some members of the attacker group. This occurred in 1905 in Russia as a result of killings of protesters, in 1930 in India as a result of beatings of protesters, in 1960 in South Africa as a result of a shooting of protesters by police. More recently the jiu-jitsu effect occurred in 1991 in East Timor as a result of a massacre of protesters by Indonesian troops. In each case, police or troops had overwhelming superiority in force. But by exercising it against nonviolent protesters, they actually strengthened their opponents. Like the

* The author wishes to thank April Carter and Tom Weber for helpful comments on drafts.

sport of jiu-jitsu, in which the energy of the opponent is used against them, political jiu-jitsu turns the attacker's violent energy into support for the protesters.

But these famous examples are exceptions to the rule. In most cases, violent attacks on protesters do not produce a jiu-jitsu effect. Why not? Looking at these and other examples shows that attackers predictably use a variety of methods to inhibit outrage from their actions. These methods can conveniently be grouped into five categories discussed below: cover up the action; devalue the target; reinterpret the action; use official channels to give an appearance of justice; and intimidate or bribe people involved. For example, prior to the 1991 Dili massacre, there were other equally serious massacres in East Timor, but these received little attention, mainly because of censorship by the Indonesian government. At Dili, foreign journalists witnessed the killings. Their reports led to international outrage.

The backfire model goes beyond the theory of political jiu-jitsu. The relevant difference here is that backfire focuses on the methods used by perpetrators of injustice to prevent domestic or international outrage in response to violence or repression of resistance, and on the counter-tactics that resisters can use to promote outrage.

The backfire framework can readily be applied to accompaniment. Two injustices are potentially involved. One is whatever local activists are dealing with, such as beatings and threats, extrajudicial killings or environmental destruction. The other is threats to and attacks on the activists. Accompaniment is designed to reduce the danger to activists, allowing them to continue their valuable activities.

1. *Cover-up* is the first method perpetrators use to inhibit outrage: if possible, they carry out killings in secret, out of the public eye. Accompaniment makes this much more difficult. It introduces witnesses, moreover ones well connected with international networks with the potential for publicity, including media coverage, and diplomatic intervention.

2. *Devaluation* of the target is the second method of inhibiting outrage: targets of injustice are called terrorists, criminals, traitors and subversives. They are sometimes slandered, for example being accused of spying or sexual misbehaviour. International accompaniment challenges this devaluation by showing that someone – an independent person, from a valued foreign country – believes the activist is doing worthwhile things. Furthermore, the foreign organisation has picked out this activist as worthy. This validation is a powerful counter to devaluation.

3. *Reinterpretation* is the third method of inhibiting outrage. Government officials might say the activist's concerns are not important, or are being addressed, and that the activist has not been threatened or harassed, or that attacks are due to rogue elements. An international volunteer can help to challenge such

claims by documenting what activists have been doing. The very presence of independent witnesses is powerful testimony that what is at stake is human rights, thus challenging the government's line.

4. *Official channels* are the fourth method of inhibiting outrage. After the Dili massacre, for example, the Indonesian government and military set up inquiries that led to token sentences for a few individuals. Official channels like courts, ombudspersons, expert panels and government agencies give the appearance of offering justice, but in practice they are often biased in favour of perpetrators. As well, they are slow, procedural and expensive. Accompaniment is an alternative to official channels; indeed, it implies official channels are not working.

5. *Intimidation* is the fifth method of inhibiting outrage. Intimidation is a primary tool used against activists. Accompaniment helps counter intimidation: the presence of witnesses gives moral support to activists.

International accompaniment thus responds to every one of the five standard methods by which perpetrators of human rights abuses try to reduce outrage from their actions. This could be illustrated from accompaniment in many different countries; a good example is provided by Guatemala in the 1980s, where Peace Brigades International (PBI) first tried out escorting (Mahony and Eguren 1997: 17–57).

The Guatemalan government was carrying out horrific attacks on opponents. A favoured method was disappearances: activists were taken away, presumably murdered, with no information about what had happened or who was responsible. Disappearances rely on the method of cover-up to reduce outrage, along with intimidation: anyone who protests might be the next to disappear.

But some in Guatemala were willing to protest. In early 1984, Grupo de Apoyo Mutuo (GAM) – Mutual Support Group – was formed. Most of its members were women who had lost family members in government repression. GAM asked for support from PBI. The story of GAM and PBI shows how accompaniment challenges each of the five methods of inhibition:

1. *Cover-up*: while PBI observers were present, no members of GAM were killed. Indeed, the government wanted to get PBI volunteers out of the country, for example by cutting short their visas.

2. *Devaluation*: the government fiercely attacked GAM. For example, Guatemalan ruler General Mejía Victores said it was linked to 'forces of subversion' (Mahony and Eguren 1997: 25, 38). PBI was also denigrated: it was said to be a tool of the US government and to be supporting, indeed manipulating, the subversive organisation GAM (ibid., p. 42).

3. *Reinterpretation*: President Mejía conceived himself as a nationalist who promoted the interests of his country by defending it against subversives (ibid., pp. 30–6). The army even portrayed itself as the victim, not the attacker, saying it was subject to a 'perverse campaign of harassment and persecution by the so-called "GAM" ... in open hostility to the dignity and prestige of the armed forces' (ibid., p. 46).

4. *Official channels*: the army carried out its killings under a façade of parliamentary democracy. But the government would not establish an inquiry into disappearances, despite demands by GAM. The government thus did not rely heavily on official channels to reduce outrage from its actions against the population. But it did in trying to get PBI out of the country, for example in producing a detailed legal argument saying PBI volunteers were not international observers (ibid., p. 42).

5. *Intimidation and bribery*: disappearances were certainly intimidating. Many people were reluctant to join GAM for fear of being tortured and killed. Intimidation was also used against PBI volunteers, for example, when they were stopped by men in cars who threatened them or demanded to see their passports (ibid., pp. 40, 42). PBI volunteers were told, privately, that they would not be expelled from the country if they promised 'there would be no disruptive actions' during a forthcoming election campaign (ibid., p. 43), which can be interpreted as a form of bribery.

In summary, PBI's support of GAM, by challenging the methods used by perpetrators of repression to reduce outrage, reduced the ability of the government to carry out repression without adverse international consequences. After two GAM activists were assassinated, the international pressure on the government was intense: 'If the GAM assassinations were intended to squelch efforts at building international pressure against Guatemala, they had clearly backfired' (ibid., p. 28). PBI's presence helped ensure there were no more such assassinations, and GAM activists recognised it. GAM leader Nineth de García said of PBI, 'Thanks to their presence, I am alive' (ibid.).

Backfire analysis also suggests ways to increase the effectiveness of accompaniment. To counter cover-up, documentation and communication are vital, so having cameras and tape recorders is valuable, as is ready access to international communication. Emergency response networks – people in other countries ready to send messages of concern – are powerful tools in countering cover-up.

The higher the status of the accompaniers, the more effectively they help counter devaluation. Furthermore, exemplary behaviour by volunteers helps validate those accompanied. This is the aim of training.

Countering government lies and rationalisations is an important task. If volunteers have skills in investigation, critical analysis and clear expression in writing and speaking, they can use these to help activists engage more effectively in the struggle over interpretations, and can communicate their own understandings to international audiences.

Often it is better to avoid official channels. Rather than writing a letter to a government official, it is better to write a letter to a newspaper or e-mail list – the government official will probably learn about it as well. Rather than calling for a government inquiry, it is better to write and publish a detailed account of the events, or set up a people's inquiry. Many people believe that official channels should be tried, to give the other side a chance. Often, though, it is better to use a mobilisation strategy.

To counter intimidation, one method is to expose it. Being prepared to document and publicise threats and harassment is vital.

The basic approach is to think about the tactics likely to be used by the aggressor – such as cover-up and devaluation – and to develop one's own tactics accordingly.

7

DEVELOPING STRATEGY FOR ACCOMPANIMENT

Luis Enrique Eguren

International accompaniment[1] (or the engaged presence of international observers) at the site of a conflict is perhaps one of the clearest expressions of support for people engaging in civil resistance. The very fact of the presence of observers or accompaniers is an embodiment of international concern. This chapter reflects on how international accompaniment can support the processes of resistance of civil society and what should be taken into account in assessing its impact.

In this context, international accompaniment refers to deploying teams from other countries whose presence will offer some protection to communities or civil society organisations. This chapter discusses accompaniment by international non-governmental organisations (NGOs), although some of these concepts can be extended to the presence of international observers from intergovernmental organisations, such as the UN.

Changes at the transnational level

Recent decades have seen a striking growth in the number of 'transnational' NGOs and networks. Their impact is hard to measure, but it is difficult to explain changes in international norms concerning human rights or the environment without referring to the role of transnational NGOs and social movements (Sikkink 1993: 411–41). These changing norms can in turn be used to pressure governments to go beyond simply acting in their own security interests. See Figure 7.1.

Resistance and social space

Resistance is a slippery concept. Some societies or sectors of society maintain forms of cultural (or sub-cultural) resistance over generations. However, when a 'hidden'

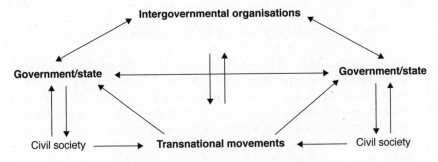

Figure 7.1 Establishing international norms

resistance becomes organised to achieve particular objectives, then the resisters claim a different type of *social space*. They emerge as a social actor, demanding to be noticed. At this moment of emergence, organisations might be especially vulnerable to repression. For example, an organisation of relatives of disappeared people might at the beginning be uncertain, doubtful about their own initiatives, and have few members who can combine their family or professional life with social activism, etc. The accompaniment for this incipient process of resistance has to be flexible and adaptable, yet – as we shall see below – maintain certain necessary baselines. This approach will be very different to the accompaniment of a long-established and experienced social organisation.

Accompaniment may again have a particular role when a movement seeks to expand its social space. This can refer to literal space, as in Colombia when communities of displaced people have asked for accompaniment to protect their attempt to 'return', or to settle in a particular area and establish a peace community. Social space is also metaphorical, as for example when new activities are launched, or are extended to reach social sectors or geographical areas previously not involved.

Even fledgling movements can create the possibility for *inserting* international accompaniment into a situation. More experienced movements can envisage ways in which international accompaniment will enhance their work, and so will develop a joint strategy with transnational NGO accompaniers. Ultimately, at the stage of negotiation between a resistance movement and its government, then there might be room even for the presence of observers from intergovernmental organisations, such as the UN, or regional election observers.

The civil resistance discussed in this chapter is located in 'civil society' and can be seen as 'counter-hegemonic'. 'Civil society' is a sphere distinct from state institutions, yet not absolutely separate, in that there is an interface of multiple connections and influences. Civil resistance is 'counter-hegemonic' because it is fundamental to guaranteeing pluralism, and to seeking the inclusion of marginalised or excluded social sectors. When a government fails to meet its responsibility to

Box 7.1   Symbolically defining space: Cacarica's 'Wire of Life'

In the second half of the 1990s, AfroColombians living in the Bajo Atrato (by the River Atrato in the jungles of north Colombia) were displaced by military and paramilitary groups. These wanted to expel the population and the guerrillas from this area, with the double objective of establishing military control and exploiting the land. The displaced population experienced their *deterritorialisation* for several years in various refuges in rural areas and inner cities. But the support of Colombian organisations, the Catholic church and international organisations made it possible for them first to analyse and learn from their displacement, and then to begin to campaign for an organised return to their lands. Thus, during their displacement a process of *reterritorialisation* was generated, which did not cease on their return. Indeed, they not only maintained organisational structures, but even regrouped themselves into two settlements to resist the constant harassment of the army and paramilitaries.

Processes of *reterritorialisation* offer the resistance opportunities for raising consciousness among individuals, to develop and improve social structures, and also to absorb such concepts as human rights, solidarity and gender equality, and to re-evaluate and re-assert certain traditional or indigenous practices. All this gives new life to the processes of resistance and generates social change. Here too international accompaniment has a role, as its presence is associated with transnational values, and adds a distinctive stamp to the 'political reconfiguration' in the resistance space.

The spaces for resistance, when people have a territory or physical entity, define themselves in different ways. The work of the Communities for Self-Determination, Life and Dignity (CAVIDA) in Cacarica, assisted by national and international accompaniment, has made possible a prolonged process of resistance.[1] One objective is to avoid military and paramilitary access to the settlements. Therefore, among other strategies, the community has built a fence around its settlements, with small wooden posts and three single strands of barbed wire, little more than a metre high. They call this the *malla de vida* (wire of life). It seems too frail an obstacle, in a jungle and in a context of armed conflict where for many months several hundred soldiers surrounded the settlements (outside the fence). Nevertheless, the fence in itself, despite its structural weakness, became a point of reference and contention for the army. Officers and soldiers frequently alluded to it, saying that when ordered to do so, they would enter and remove it. All this, from *outside* the fence.

In other words, the fence entered into their vision, perceived as a reality and a problem, and not as an insignificant detail. The army recognised that within the community (on the other side of the fence) there is an organised process, with national and international accompaniment. The control of access that the fence provides is only symbolic, yet somehow it is also a *representation* of the space for

▶

resistance gained by the community. The fence acquires meaning on being perceived by those outside it, and so feeds and restructures the perception of community space, both of those inside and outside the fence.

It is difficult to achieve the goal of inserting a safe *physical space* in a zone of domination. The people there remain the target of pressure and attacks, and the risk of a new displacement persists. Yet, as one tactic in an ambitious strategy, it offers a symbol of the safe space for which the community is struggling.

Note

1. Accompaniment by Colombian organisations such as, among others, the Comisión Intereclesial de Justicia y Paz and by the international NGO Peace Brigades International. Editor's note: see also contribution by Mauricio García-Duran above (Section I, Chapter 4).

respect all the rights of all its citizens and aligns itself with the interests of a few (one social sector of the country, or the claims of a transnational corporation for example), civil resistance can become a necessary resource against the hegemony of those interests. Slater (1997: 263) refers to social struggles as 'interpretation wars': groups are stigmatised for questioning what is 'given', the habitual social order. International accompaniment confers *credibility* on these groups and reinforces their interpretation.

Resistance frequently take places in a context of conflicts where the force and power of those involved is unbalanced and asymmetric. This is why a general objective for an international presence is transforming the conflict so as to expand or improve the capacity of those resisting to negotiate for their objectives with the authorities (or other actors responsible for aggression and rights violations, such as guerrilla groups). Here two points are essential for accompaniment to be effective:

*   to operate within a clear normative framework, accepted at the international level, such as *the set of international norms on human rights*; and
*   for the civil resistance to maintain its *nonviolent character*.

International observers and accompaniers: strategies and tactics

Missions by intergovernmental organisations such as the UN have political and financial advantages no NGO can command, but also political limitations that do not apply in the same way to NGOs. Despite their limited resources and logistical capacities, it can be easier for NGOs to enter conflict zones. They are often better able to adapt to the local context and to follow an agenda and mandate based on ethical principles and transnational concerns for human rights. Being non-governmental, NGOs do not infringe the sovereignty of a government. Their capacity to dissuade or deter human rights violators depends on the degree of support that they can achieve from international public opinion and from governments. Therefore, the strength of the NGO resides in the level of international awareness about the protection of human rights and movements of resistance, and its capacity to generate *friction* between governments and the public opinion of their countries, or to challenge governments to respect internationally accepted norms (such as human rights).

Accompaniment also augments the power of resisters to act and make a demand visible. Take, for example, the capacity to demonstrate at a governmental building about government neglect of a displaced population. This type of protest requires that the resistance organisation has the space to do it, that is, they are not afraid of the negative consequences of the act. At the same time, carrying out this act expands the space for resistance. If the action is carried out with international accompaniment, the consequences are more predictable – for example, it may be hoped that with accompaniment there probably won't be direct violence and that the follow-up to the accompaniment will prevent individual reprisals against organisers. The more predictable the consequences of an action, the more likely that people will overcome their fear of protesting.

The functioning of deterrence[2]

The protection that international accompaniment can offer is based on the hypothesis that international presence can dissuade or deter violations of norms – including the norm that peaceful protest is legitimate and should be legally allowed – because the potential echo and international impact of violence against resisters increases its political costs.

In order to deter potential aggressors, it is first necessary to inform them of the corresponding *deterrent commitment*: that is, what will be the costs of aggression – such as breaking a norm. If the deterrent commitment is sufficiently high, and if potential aggressors see this and analyse clearly, they will be dissuaded. The deterrent commitment depends, then, on the capacity to inflict costs on the aggressor.

This deterrent commitment should be credible and clear, and strong enough to raise the costs of aggression. It should include ensuring that information (or denunciation) will reach high-level forums, and that it will probably entail clear political and/or economic costs for the aggressor. It is therefore vital for international accompaniment projects to build up their network of contacts – locally, nationally and internationally, with other NGOs but also with local officials and state bodies, and with foreign embassies as well as with strategic media outlets.

Accompaniment does not operate alone. Its deterrent function has to be seen in the political context of other measures with deterrent effects (for example, the production of reports by national or international NGOs, resolutions of the UN, diplomatic or other governmental responses, etc.). This set of deterrents, including observers, can be categorised as 'international pressure'. These factors usually depend on each other. 'Immediate deterrence' – in relation to a specific violation or action – will only function if 'general deterrence' (international pressure) exists. In turn, international pressure itself might well depend on observation on the ground (that is, 'international accompaniment').

Therefore it is crucial to understand that an international presence on the ground is only strong if it can generate the necessary backing from NGOs and international organisations and, in the last analysis, a response from governments. Otherwise, it can only 'witness' rather than protect.

Scenarios of resistance appropriate for international observers

Intervention by international observers is not valid for every scenario of resistance. Because its effectiveness derives from the existence of international norms and the responsibility of states to uphold them, observers offer little protection unless there is a functioning state. Only if the government is the executive authority can it be responsible to other governments for its actions and therefore respond to eventual international pressure. In situations of lawlessness where the state or government cannot play its role (as for example Somalia at the beginning of the 1990s), international accompaniment lacks deterrent power. Nevertheless in most countries where there are resistance movements, the state is established and the government does have executive power.

The presence of observers requires a measure of consent or acceptance by the parties in conflict, and preferably should follow a request for this presence, especially from those who are to be accompanied. Governmental consent can be explicit (such as issuing visas) or implicit (letting observers work). What defines the space for work that governments (or other armed actors) allow observers is the calculation of whether the political cost of expelling them outweighs permitting their presence. Accompaniment groups can influence this calculation through the network of contacts they build up and the image they present of themselves, especially by explaining the principles of their work in terms of internationally agreed norms and by applying their operating principles transparently and consistently.

The degree of effectiveness of international observers partly depends on how those carrying out aggression view their international interests. If the state is responsible for violent repression, then there is a hierarchical ladder of decision-making from the central government through various branches. The deterrent commitment has the power to influence various points on this ladder, including the government itself and its security forces. Parastatal actors (for example, paramilitaries) and non-state actors (for example an organised group of hired assassins working for private interests) appear less susceptible to international pressure, although in reality paramilitary groups and death squads often depend on government collusion, and some non-state groups depend on international patrons.

If a non-state or parastatal aggressor has sufficient control of a geographical area, and the government does not (or cannot) exert its authority, international presence will not be effective. Furthermore, if the aggressor's interests are in opposition to those of the government, they could benefit by attacking international observers, damaging the government's image in other countries. Such issues need analysing when deciding in which scenarios an international observer presence can be effective.

In preparing their strategy, accompaniment organisations need to analyse the geopolitical influences that will most affect the international reaction, and also whether there are reformist elements within the state likely to be responsive to human rights criticisms.

Mere international presence is not sufficient. To be protective, an accompaniment organisation needs to have a specific strategy and a series of activities, such as ensuring the maintenance of the presence, continually building up the network of contacts, regular communication with the authorities and officials at various levels (both domestic and from other countries), publication of analysis and information, etc. And of course, it is essential to remember that the state has a responsibility to protect the human rights of the people in resistance, and that the work of international accompaniment aims to provide a permanent reminder of this to the state itself.

Expected outcomes from transnational accompaniment

The principal areas of impact for accompaniment are the monitoring of norms and protection.[3]

Impact of international presence: Monitoring norms

When they are monitoring a particular negotiated agreement, or more general international norms, observers have the twofold role of: deterring violation of the agreed norm and, if it is violated, documenting and publicising the violations in a way that will unleash a chain of negative consequences for those perpetrating violence, so that in future they will revert to respecting the agreement or the norm.

The observers do not themselves impose these negative consequences, but rather aim to trigger actions by governments or other actors (condemnation at the UN, withdrawal from commercial agreements, sanctions, etc.). In this sense, the observers are witnesses who give legitimacy through their presence to reports and accusations of failure to comply with agreements or human rights violations.

Furthermore, the presence of international observers can be a key factor in the decision-making of governments, highlighting the correct form of action and detailing the range of options available. Observers *frame* the issues: focusing on what is essential, proposing specific lines of action, and creating a common point of reference for government officials, security forces, state bureaucracies, etc. Observers can act as *brokers*, through their presence linking local and international questions, and inhibiting the tendency of governments to formulate strategies from a narrow point of view such as state security.

Impact of transnational presence: Protection

There are key elements in protection. One is to gain *access* to the people engaged in resisting. Another is the *presence alongside the resisters* of third parties, be they compatriots or foreign accompaniers. A third key activity is the search for and dissemination of *information*, using it strategically and applying the moral weight derived from access to the population and places affected. This information should be used in *advocacy* to achieve the necessary action of governments, either in representations through restricted channels or through publication of the facts when governments lack political will.

Advocacy should not replace the information coming from the people affected, but rather transmit it, recognising that the resisters, through their struggle and through affirming their rights, are regaining their humanity and character as persons. It is their lives and experience – transmitted by themselves and by others such as international or local NGOs – that will stimulate resistance by others.

According to international law, those responsible for the protection of citizens are governments (in the first place the government of the country involved, and then other governments) and in certain conflicts armed opposition groups. They have the capacity to use armed force to protect or attack the population and in fact do so. Given this responsibility, the gap between *what ought to happen* (protection of citizens in all circumstances) and *what happens* (civilian resisters become a target for repression) depends on two factors: political will and technical capacity. Any discussion over protection should take both will and capacity into account in analysing how to achieve on-the-ground protection.

There is a permanent tension between a normative framework and political will to act (or to desist from a course of action). No framework can overcome lack of political will. To generate and consolidate the necessary political will, political pressure is necessary. The pressure to make governments recognise norms is important but not sufficient: they should guarantee to put these norms into practice, to monitor their own compliance and to measure its impact.

Therefore, the immediate results that can be expected from international protection are:

- To develop a greater knowledge, capacity and especially will in governments responsible for protection; to make them more accountable and reduce the impunity of those who – whether acting in their own interests or those of third parties – either engage in repression, or fail to carry out their duty of investigation and protection.
- To enlarge the secure space for action by resisters, enabling them to enjoy the rights that had been violated; and to promote a greater capacity and spirit among resisters to take initiatives, devise processes of self-protection and assert their rights.

How to measure the impact of protection

Accompaniment should not be provided solely on the basis of good will, but also on the basis of evaluation, which could use indicators such as:

- to assess how much the government (or other bodies responsible for protection) comply with international norms on protection;
- to assess over time how far other perpetrators of attacks on movements of resistance are reducing this pressure; and
- to assess how far the conditions of life for people are improving in a permanent and sustainable form.

Because decision-making is subject to many influences and is not always based on rational calculation, there is always a grey zone both in assessing risks and in evaluating the effectiveness of protection and the weight of deterrence. One tactic to reduce uncertainty is to establish patterns of action with proven results. Particularly careful analysis is needed when the resistance breaks new ground, or when an armed actor changes its pattern of operations.

Possible negative effects of international accompaniment

The world remains marked by colonial and post-colonial processes and struggles for decolonisation. In many Southern countries, foreigners coming from the North are seen in this light, imposing social and political models, boasting superior technology and having unequal power. However, the interface they offer with local resistance permits building bridges between the local and the transnational based on universal values.

Nevertheless, the key decisions in international politics continue to be made by a number of regional or international powers, and the nationality of those carrying out accompaniment matters because it correlates to their capacity to generate actions by their own governments. To use this capacity of citizens of the North to influence their governments should be understood tactically, as an immediate reality that is evident in transnational social movements. The only exception is when the organisation itself has sufficient political weight to mobilise governmental action.

International accompaniment is a form of resistance that at the appropriate time, together with other types of resistance, can be inserted into an environment of domination. And therefore we have to be aware of the forms of domination within international accompaniment, such as the risk of transmitting cultural clichés or interfering with the local processes of organisation. To prevent all these requires explicit policies specifying how to act in international accompaniment – good intentions and a naive confidence in universal values too often do not translate into concrete preventive action.

Notes

1. Strictly speaking, the more precise term is 'transnational accompaniment'. However, 'international accompaniment' is more widely used.
2. For a fuller analysis of this, see Mahony and Eguren (1997). Editor/translator's note: the term *disuasión* can be rendered either 'dissuasion' or 'deterrence'. Deterrence is used here, following Mahony and Eguren (1997: 85) who refer to dissuasion as a 'more inclusive concept', being – according to Gene Sharp – 'the result of acts or processes which induce an opponent not to carry out a contemplated hostile action. Rational argument, moral appeal, increased cooperation, improved human understanding, distraction, adoption of non-offensive policy and deterrence may all be used to achieve dissuasion' (Sharp 1985: 33). They comment that 'each of these tactics is used at different times by the accompaniment organisation or by the international human rights community that the volunteer indirectly represents'.
3. There exists a third overlapping area, *human security*, not dealt with here. Editor's note: see also Christine Schweitzer's chapter below (Chapter 8).

7A

WITH PEACE BRIGADES INTERNATIONAL IN COLOMBIA

Louise Winstanley

'The plight of civilians trapped in war and misery stands as one of the great challenges of our times' (Mahony 2006: v). This is one of the challenges that drew me to work with Peace Brigades International (PBI), plus the fact that they sought peaceful resolution to conflicts. The three key principles of PBI were ones I considered vital when working in another country in conflict: non-partisanship, nonviolence and non-interference in the internal affairs of countries or the accompanied organisations. PBI appealed to me because it tries to avoid the colonial attitudes often perpetuated by organisations working abroad.

PBI started in 1981. Its aim was to send teams of volunteers to countries where the lives of human rights activists struggling nonviolently to achieve justice were threatened, but only if invited to do so by local NGOs. PBI aims to create an atmosphere in which perpetrators of violence against civilians recognise that there will be a political cost for their abuse. International accompaniment – both physical and political – is to protect the lives and working space of human rights defenders. This international physical presence also aims to provide a safer space for communities to be able to resist the terror tactics that paralyse and stigmatise them.

PBI's accompaniment has evolved over time and according to the country context. For two years (2004–06) I was a PBI volunteer in Colombia. The experiences I describe are repeated across all PBI field teams in one form or another. PBI currently accompanies human rights defenders, community-based organisations (CBOs) and communities in Colombia, Guatemala, Mexico, Nepal and Indonesia. The volunteers make a minimum commitment of one year and work in teams, physically accompanying activists as they go about their daily work. In Colombia, as well as human rights activists and CBOs such as the Organización Femenina Popular, PBI also accompanies peace communities and communities living in zones they themselves have designated 'humanitarian zones'.[1]

PBI is made up of a network of Country Groups in Europe, North America and Australasia. If something happens to those we accompany (usually at a time when they are not being physically accompanied – nobody has yet been killed in the presence of a PBI escort), word is sent out to each of these groups. They then contact their respective foreign ministries and support networks – including made up of politicians, lawyers and human rights activists – with the aim of getting their government to raise the issue with the government concerned. This brings

Photograph 7.1   It looks like an idyllic boat trip but a PBI volunteer is escorting two workers for Justicia y Paz on a risky journey through territory controlled by hostile armed forces. (PBI)

pressure to bear on that government to protect the lives of those threatened and let them continue with their work.

PBI's presence in any country is visible both physically and politically. PBI volunteers wear t-shirts and jackets clearly displaying the PBI logo – and where necessary a flag, for example if travelling by canoe – clearly announcing our presence. Equally we meet regularly with civil and military authorities, embassies, human rights organs and international bodies such as the UN. This raises the visibility of human rights defenders at a national and international level, so increasing the political costs for potential perpetrators of violence. In this way PBI seeks both to protect the working space and the lives of those that we accompany, helping them stay and carry on their work rather than having to go into exile.

One example that will always remain vivid for me was accompanying a human rights lawyer to the scene of an atrocity. Local people suspected that the army was responsible for the atrocity, yet – because this took place in a combat zone – the army itself was the body officially responsible for investigating it. This area had one of the highest rates of extra-judicial executions, many *campesinos* turning up dead, often in another department of the country and presented in the military courts as guerrillas killed in combat.[2]

The lawyer I was accompanying had investigated nearly a hundred cases of extra-judicial killings incriminating army members, to be presented to the Inter-American System of Human Rights. Now he wanted to discover what had happened in this farmhouse where seven members of a family, including one pregnant woman, had been murdered in their beds. To do this he had to walk for several hours in mountainous terrain in an area controlled by the unit of the army that he was accusing in other cases. He had already been denounced in the press by one local army captain as 'the legal arm of the guerrilla'. Without international accompaniment, said the lawyer, it would be very easy for him to 'disappear' and he would not have been able to walk to the farmhouse.

Human rights defenders often travel hours in difficult physical terrain, with the psychological pressure of death threats for the work that they do. At such times the accompaniment of PBI is essential. The people we escort work tirelessly for human rights, to protect communities, to establish the truth of what happened to the disappeared, to bring to justice perpetrators of massacres. Their fight is against impunity and for justice and truth. The threats are designed to terrorise themselves and their families – one lawyer I accompanied received a package through the post: in it was a doll painted with a red cross and a message, 'you have a beautiful daughter take care of her'. Another defender's mother received a wreath with the words 'rest in peace Danilo' dated for the following week. But this is just one part of what I observed: another and motivating part was the commitment felt towards the families of the disappeared or massacred, or to colleagues who had been murdered or disappeared.

The work of PBI is of a small team of volunteers supported by a global network of committed activists. We accompany organisations of human rights defenders, who in turn accompany hundreds of families whose members have been massacred or disappeared, and who also accompany leaders of communities, such as the *Humanitarian Zones* of Jiguamiandó and Curbaradó where people have come together to peacefully reclaim lands from which they were violently displaced. In this way the work of relatively few people is multiplied.

This form of protection works only in some conflict situations, not all. In Colombia I know it is making a difference: in the words of one Colombian human rights advocate,

> I am more aware than ever of the great role you [PBI] have played and the work you do in my country where everyday horror is greater than fiction, just as I am convinced that I owe my life to you and that of my family too. (Osiris Bayter, ex-President, Regional Corporation for the Defence of Human Rights, CREDHOS, Barrancabermeja)

PBI also sees its work as contributing to a worldwide growth of peace activism. What its volunteers learn while accompanying in the field is fed back into the Country Groups on our return, stimulating these groups, bringing first-hand information that provides added motivation. Many volunteers also carry on working in human rights organisations, both in countries where they have been accompanying and in international organisations.

Notes

1. These zones are populated by people who have joined together to remain on or near the collective land, which they were forced to leave.
2. Between July 2002 and June 2007, there were at least 955 cases of extra-judicial executions and 235 cases of involuntary disappearance attributable to the armed forces, according to the report of Coordination Colombia, USA and Europe. The Colombia report for 2005 of the UN High Commission on Human Rights drew attention to the practice that the armed forces could kill, collect the corpse (as evidence) and bury it without registering any name.

8

CIVILIAN PEACEKEEPING: PROVIDING PROTECTION WITHOUT STICKS AND CARROTS?

Christine Schweitzer

Introduction

This chapter focuses on one sector of the broad field of nonviolent intervention that can be called 'nonviolent peacekeeping'. The function of peacekeeping is to prevent or at least lower the level of violence. It is one of three 'approaches to peace', as Johan Galtung (1976) called them. Together with peacemaking and peacebuilding, these three approaches formulate a general theory of achieving or maintaining peace:

> peacemaking aims to change the attitudes of the main protagonists, peacekeeping lowers the level of destructive behaviour, and peacebuilding tries to overcome the contradictions which lie at the root of the conflict. (Miall, Ramsbotham and Woodhouse 1999: 22)

Peacekeeping can be implemented by both military or civilian forces. Authors who are mainly interested in nonviolent intervention have further broadened the concept of peacekeeping to include other, smaller-scale activities such as protective accompaniment of human rights activists threatened by death squads – activities that Schirch (1995: 20–31) calls 'intercessionary peacekeeping'.

The literature on nonviolent peacekeeping is mainly descriptive. The important exception is the work on protective accompaniment by Mahony and Eguren, especially their book on Peace Brigades International (1997). They develop a theory of nonviolent deterrence to explain how protective accompaniment 'works' or does not 'work'. This chapter, drawing on experiences other than PBI, argues that 'deterrence' is not the only mechanism operating in nonviolent peacekeeping, and suggests integrating different approaches into a framework of an escalation of unarmed conflict intervention.

The theory of nonviolent 'deterrence'

The deterrent power of international accompaniment, as proposed by Mahony and Eguren (see Eguren, Chapter 7 above) is that it 'raises the costs' of attacking an accompanied activist. The aim is to affect the chain of command, from decision-makers down, but accompaniment can also give pause to individuals:

> We should not assume that the thugs who pull the trigger are unaffected by international presence. No one wants an unexpected witness around when they are carrying out a crime. The volunteer's presence may have a moral influence on individual perpetrators. It also introduces an uncertainty factor – the attacker does not know what the consequences of this witness will be, so unless he has explicit orders that take the accompaniment into account, he is likely to restrain himself rather than risk getting in trouble with his superior. (Mahony 2004: 8)

Mahony and Eguren (1997) go into detail about assessing the impact of accompaniment on political space, and in their subsequent work (Eguren 2005 and Mahony 2006) have further developed procedures on risk assessment for local activists. The key protagonists in their work remain the local activists – those who are primarily exposed to violence, those who invite accompaniment and who at times jointly plan its strategic use.

Two main criticisms have been made of the nonviolent 'deterrence theory':

1. In many situations, the external governments most likely to apply pressure in response to publicity or lobbying by accompaniment groups are North American or European. This could therefore mean, it is argued, that the tactic uses existing power imbalances, neo-colonial dependencies and patterns of privilege, even to some extent reproducing them (Kinane 2000; Boothe and Smithey 2007).

2. The kind of pressure exerted is usually out of the hands of nonviolent activists, and might sometimes include military threats. In the case of the OSCE's Kosovo Verification Mission, 1998–99, a large unarmed mission was in effect part of a military escalation: it was introduced by threatening military intervention, a NATO 'Extraction Force' stood ready to evacuate them at need, and its denunciation of Serbian atrocities in Kosovo prepared the way for NATO's 1999 military intervention.[1]

Most nonviolent accompaniment organisations are aware of these problems and take steps to mitigate them. This chapter suggests that there is much to be gained from viewing 'protective accompaniment' not just from the perspective of 'deterrence', and to bring it into context with the other strategies to achieve what Mary B. Anderson has called 'peace writ large' (Anderson 2003).

Nonviolent Peaceforce in the Philippines (Mindanao)

Nonviolent Peaceforce (NP) is a young international NGO based in Brussels, founded with the goal of developing unarmed peacekeeping, in the sense of having direct impact on the human security of populations caught in an armed conflict through the presence of large numbers of international trained professionals using purely nonviolent means.[2] It currently has field projects in Sri Lanka and the Philippines, and has completed a project in Guatemala.

In Mindanao, the second largest island in the Philippines, more than 120,000 lives have been lost in a 30-year struggle for independence waged by Muslim groups against the Christian majority in Mindanao. The main guerrilla group, the Moro National Liberation Front (MNLF), signed a peace treaty with the Philippine government in 1996. MNLF leaders joined the government structures in Mindanao, but a splinter from the MNLF, the Moro Islamic Liberation Front (MILF), continued to fight. Eventually, after several ceasefire agreements, fighting more or less stopped, except for violent incidents still occurring in central Mindanao. Negotiations for a comprehensive peace agreement are currently being conducted.

The ceasefire is being monitored by an official mechanism, including both the government and the MILF, which has four elements: the Coordinating Committee on the Cessation of Hostilities (CCCH), Local Monitoring Teams, an International Monitoring Team (staffed mostly by Malaysia), and an Ad hoc Joint Action Group. The CCCH has set up monitoring posts in the conflict areas that are staffed by government and MILF soldiers plus representatives of local civil society initiatives. The extraordinary feature of this set-up is the close involvement of several hundreds of local civil society peacekeepers, mostly working in a voluntary capacity.

These local peace groups invited NP to send an international team to provide support and a protective presence to local groups working to prevent violence. Beneficiaries of the project are vulnerable communities, individuals and civil society groups whose lives and work are threatened by the continuing violence or threat of violence, in particular women and children.

NP sent its first six-person team to Mindanao in May 2007. In their first year, they worked successfully with local groups in helping prevent several incidents triggering full-scale military confrontation. The tasks of NP teams are:

- to enhance the scope and quality of local people's organisations and peace/ human rights advocates;
- to reduce the incidence of violence in the vicinity of NP field sites through unarmed international civilian peacekeeping, thereby aiding in the maintenance of the ceasefire(s);
- to support human rights reporting mechanisms in remote conflict areas and assist/connect local and international advocacy groups who work for peace with justice by responding to people's grievances;
- to localise grassroots conflicts so that they are resolved through dialogue at the lowest level and do not escalate into larger crises;
- to help to set up a system of early warning and early response by local civil society.

In NP's analysis, there is a double mechanism of protection involving its teams. They are providing the 'eye and ear of the world', and being outsiders are able to talk to all sides of the conflict without being seen as partisan. At the same time, their own security is based on the trust given by the local communities and NP's civil society partners. The result is a relationship of mutual support and protection that has the outcome of increasing the impact of joint peacekeeping efforts.

Nonviolent Peaceforce in Sri Lanka

Sri Lanka has suffered serious violence since 1983 when the Tamil Tigers launched a civil war to achieve independence for the Tamils living in the north and east of the country, in order to end alleged discrimination against Tamils by governments representing the Sinhalese majority. A ceasefire signed in 2002 broke down after a few years. When the Tigers split – one faction allying with the government – government troops managed to regain control of large parts of contested territory. All sides have been accused of serious human rights abuses by organisations such as Amnesty International and Human Rights Watch. Impunity, extortion, political killings, disappearances, arbitrary arrests and abductions in which security forces seem to be involved have increased, and are no longer limited to the troubled areas of Sri Lanka but occur in Colombo and the south as well.

NP launched its first project in Sri Lanka in late 2003 at the invitation of and in partnership with local groups, at a time when the ceasefire was expected to lead to a final peace agreement. The project consists of five teams of approximately 25 internationally recruited field team members (in their majority from countries from the Global South), applying unarmed peacekeeping methods such as protective accompaniment, mediation, observing and reporting in volatile areas in the north and east of Sri Lanka. Their objectives are to prevent violence, or at least reduce the level of and potential for violence; to support and improve the safety, confidence and ability of Sri Lankan peacemakers and other civilians to address conflict in nonviolent ways; and to work with Sri Lankans to provide human security and deter resumption of violent conflict.

Aside from accompaniment, presence and monitoring, a major element of the work is linking people to authorities or agencies, to some extent training, and dialogue at the community level (Furnari 2006). Such activities do not fall under 'peacekeeping' if that is defined as a purely dissociative approach. But they are part of a strategy to provide human security. Their goals have been to increase people's well-being by helping them to get access to aid, to solve conflicts that otherwise would probably lead to communal violence and killings, and to help civil society groups cooperate in developing their own activities against violence and human rights violations.

NP staff's security in Sri Lanka is also based on the acceptance and trust by the local community in addition to its international linkages. The source of its impact is being non-partisan outsiders with intimate knowledge of the communities in which they work, and thereby being able to offer at a local level what in a diplomatic context would often be called 'good offices', making a concrete contribution to the health and security of groups at risk (youth at risk of abduction by armed groups, for example).

Balkan Peace Team

The Balkan Peace Team (BPT – 1994–2001) was an international volunteer project set up in response to the wars in the former Yugoslavia from 1991 onwards.[3] BPT had one team in Croatia and another in Serbia and Kosovo.[4] It had a broader mandate than PBI or NP, although it shared the goal of opening space for local actors rather than being one of the countless NGOs in the area following their own agendas and doing their own externally planned projects. Its main focuses were protection and support of dialogue, with protection being more important in Croatia, while support of dialogue at the civil society level had priority in Serbia and Kosovo (Müller 2006; Schweitzer and Clark 2002; Schweitzer 2005). Many BPT activities in Croatia had to do with human security. The teams accompanied local human rights activists in trying to prevent the illegal eviction of Serbs from their flats and monitoring the situation in the areas militarily reintegrated into Croatia in 1995 in order to deter harassment or worse of the remaining Serbs.

BPT was an experiment in combining several roles that other projects tended to keep apart. Unlike many peacebuilding projects, it focused on human security/protection (civil peacekeeping) without rigidly limiting its role to this one aspect. And it allowed itself to get involved in a range of peace-building activities without feeling that doing so it would lose its character or endanger its non partisanship.

The ways in which BPT made a difference included:

- Serving a *preventive* function in regard to potential human rights violations.
- Fulfilling a *mediating* role between local NGOs and international organisations or NGOs. In Croatia, BPT was often called upon because, as an international NGO, it had easier access to other 'internationals' than local activists. Bigger international bodies sometimes paid lip-service to local involvement but rarely took local groups seriously.
- Serving as a *bridge* between local NGOs or private citizens and local authorities in the same way as NP does in Sri Lanka.
- Facilitating *contact* between NGOs from 'different sides'. As internationals, BPT had more freedom of movement between the conflict areas than local NGOs.
- Facilitating *contacts* with international peace networks and acting as on-the-ground support to internationally initiated dialogue projects.
- This placed the organisation in the position to *support 'civil society' dialogue*. Meetings mediated by BPT between activists and students from Serbia proper and Kosovo did not take place abroad (as with most dialogue projects), but with people accompanied by BPT to visit each other in their towns, so giving participants more sense of ownership over the meeting than in an international workshop.
- Carrying out an active *advocacy role*. BPT alerted other international organisations about, for example, the policy of Croatia regarding refugees or occasions when the practices of international bodies were less than helpful.

BPT was able to play these different functions because it was an international project. And in many instances its effectiveness probably can be explained by the deterrence theory. But there is one important modification: The former Yugoslavia was an arena with a multitude of international intervenors, many and the most conspicuous of them being backed by military force. BPT made a point of distancing itself from high-profile international interventions, both on the symbolic level (not using the fancy four-wheel drive white cars favoured by the UN and EU) and on the practical by seeking dialogue rather than invoking the threat of international power. So while it certainly profited from this power, its approach was different from PBI's, and the sources of its influence were partly in how it was distinct from other international organisations.

Additional examples and discussions

Peace-keeping is not confined to 'internationals'

There are more local or national initiatives than tends to be recognised in the international literature. The probably best-known examples are the Pakistani and Indian 'peace armies' as developed by Abdul Ghaffar Khan and Gandhi, and a number of local peace teams or peace monitoring missions that can be found in such different countries as Croatia, Indonesia, Philippines, Sri Lanka and of course India today.[5] Their effectiveness is probably mainly derived from respect in the community, being centred inwards, not outwards to the international world. The focus of the Indian Shanti Sena is and was on convincing those ready to apply violence, and to strengthen the communities to resist that violence, using methods of dialogue, counteracting rumours, physical interpositioning and aid and reconstruction (Weber 1996: 116–17).

Larger-scale unarmed peacekeeping missions rely on local people for security

The Nonviolent Peaceforce Feasibility Study found that larger-scale unarmed peace-keeping missions, mostly governmental, relied on local people for security – albeit to differing degrees.

> Relying on the Bougainville people to ensure the safety of peace monitors reinforces the realisation that peace on Bougainville is the responsibility of the Bougainville people. They are only too aware that, should the safety of the PMG [Peace Monitoring Mission] be placed at risk, there is a very real danger that the peace process will falter. This was emphasised on a number of occasions when Bougainvillians assisted patrols in difficult circumstances. (Foster 1999)

Modes of action of NGOs to provide human security

Looking at how NGOs provide human security, a concept much related to peacekeeping, Slim and Eguren (2004) distinguish five main modes of action:[6]

1. *Denunciation:* publicly pressuring authorities into meeting their obligations and protecting those individuals or groups exposed to abuse.
2. *Persuasion:* further private dialogue to convince authorities to fulfil their obligations and protect those exposed to violations.
3. *Mobilisation:* discreetly sharing information with selected people, bodies or states with the capacity to influence the authorities to fulfil their obligations.
4. *Substitution:* directly providing services or material assistance to the victims of violations.
5. *Support to structures and services:* empowering existing national and/or local structures by helping projects that enable them to carry out their functions to protect individuals and groups.

Methods used include humanitarian assistance, presence and accompaniment, monitoring and human rights reporting, and humanitarian advocacy. Apart from 'substitution', the other 'modes of action' directly refer to the goal of opening space and protecting civil society in resistance. As well as 'deterrence', two other mechanisms are at work: *persuasion*, defined as making authorities act of their own accord, and *substitution*, defined as the NGO acting in place of the authorities.

Conclusion

All these examples show that deterrence is only one factor in nonviolent peacekeeping being effective (compare also Schweitzer et al. 2001). Relationship-building to the local community and trust that is built up to the different actors in conflict is at least as important as having 'international clout'. The identity of the peacekeepers (factors here might be age, gender, country of origin, religion and others), the role they assume in the conflict and whom they represent, local law and tradition (for example, social norms against harming unarmed opponents or of hospitality), and a basic interest of all sides in avoiding further violence are important elements here. If the last criterion is not given, then both armed and unarmed peacekeeping become a lot more difficult or even impossible, as is well recognised also by the UN and other providers of military peacekeeping. The answer from the side of governments is peace 'enforcement' – 'robust' military intervention under Article 7 of the UN Charter (Hillen 2000). The final section of this chapter will discuss if nonviolent actors have similar means of escalating their intervention.

Outlook: the escalation of nonviolent intervention

Escalation of conflict *intervention* does not have the well-developed model of stages that exist for the escalation of actual conflicts, but the general trend is evident: The more difficult a settlement of a conflict becomes, the more force is needed (Miall, Ramsbotham and Woodhouse 1999: 11). In negotiations with international mediators, 'sticks and carrots' up to military threats or eventual military intervention are the tools well exemplified in a number of wars of the last twenty and more years, from the 1991 Iraq war, the wars in Bosnia-Hercegovina 1992–95 and Kosovo 1998–99 to the more current crises in Sudan, North Korea and Iran. In peacekeeping, as mentioned above, 'robust mandates' are the answer preferred by state actors.

For nonviolent action (*not* international intervention) the German researcher Theodor Ebert (1981: 37), building on Gene Sharp's work, has defined three stages of escalation; each stage has both subversive/opposition and constructive elements (see Table 8.1).[7] This escalation is presented in the context of the growing extent to which those ruled withdraw their consent and refuse to obey.

Table 8.1   Theodor Ebert's stages of escalation

Stage of escalation	Subversive action	Constructive action
1.	Protest and persuasion	Presenting alternatives
2.	Legal non-cooperation	Legal innovation
3.	Civil disobedience	Civil usurpation
	Reformative or revolutionary	Reformative or revolutionary

However, even if transnational nonviolent intervention works in alliance with local movements, it does not really include this dimension of withdrawal of cooperation as the ultimate instrument in struggle: because regimes primarily depend on their own subjects. Moreover, withdrawal of cooperation is not directly available to international nonviolent peacekeepers, especially non-governmental groups. Instruments they have available are public blaming and protest, increased support of oppositional groups within the target country, boycotts and nonviolent actions directed at the offending side (such as the recent solidarity movement with the Tibetan struggle, which is using all these instruments).[8] All these may be tools to escalate pressure without resorting to direct physical violence, though there is certainly an element of force inherent in these means (as I would argue there also is in Ebert's and Sharp's models of escalation).

Sharp has commented on transnational intervention that:

> World opinion on the side of the nonviolent group will by itself rarely produce a change in the opponent's policies. Frequently a determined opponent can ignore hostile opinion until and unless it is accompanied by, or leads to, shifts in power relationships, or threatens to do so. (Sharp 1973: 662)

From this it follows that the role of transnational intervention by nonviolent groups is to contribute to a power shift. This has two dimensions: the negative of challenging the legitimacy of the regime – or of all armed groups – through highlighting their human rights violations and so weakening their position internationally; the positive of contributing to popular empowerment, in terms of opening space for local groups and building 'a counter-power', for example, by providing financial and material support or facilitating training on strategic nonviolence.

Measures to confer legitimacy on nonviolent actors in the situation might include connecting local groups to international influential networks and advocacy organisations, facilitating deals with fair trade networks marketing products from peace communities, assisting recognition by organising visits from higher-profile/higher-status delegations (Nobel Prize winners, UN human rights officials, etc.) and invitations to carry out international speaking tours or address international forums, etc.

However, while such a model of contributing to a power shift is comparatively easy (at least in theory) when there is a violent conflict where clearly an oppressor and an oppressed side can be distinguished, things become much more entangled in situations where there are several armed sides engaged in struggle, and civil society clearly marginalised, as it is the case in Sri Lanka.

Notes

1. Kosovo, a former autonomous province of the republic of Serbia, was in the 1990s characterised by the nonviolent struggle of its ethnic Albanian majority against Serbian rule and Kosovo's loss of autonomy. In 1998 armed action triggered atrocities by Serbian security forces and massive displacement of Albanians. Under intense international pressure, a ceasefire was agreed in October 1998 to be 'verified' by the KVM. However, in March 1999 after negotiations to make Kosovo an international protectorate failed, NATO decided to attack FR Yugoslavia.
2. NP is a federation of about 85 member organisations (mostly groups with an explicit nonviolent action or resistance background) from all continents. See www.nonviolentpeaceforce.org for general information and reports of the two projects presented here.
3. The Balkan Peace Team was founded and run by a group of mainly European-based peace organisations, from Austria, France, Germany, the Netherlands, Switzerland and the UK. They included Austrian Peace Service, International Fellowship of Reconciliation, War Resisters' International, Federation for Social Defence (Germany), Brethren Service (US), Peace Brigades International, and MAN – Mouvement pour une alternative nonviolente (France). Its coordinating office was based in Germany.
4. The team in Croatia began in 1994, when a ceasefire was in force between the governments of Croatia and Serbia (and Serbian militias) that left parts of Croatia under Serbian control. In 1995, however, Croatia reoccupied most of this territory, and negotiated the peaceful reintegration of eastern Slavonia after two years of UN interim administration.
5. Further examples include Shanti Sena, Sri Lanka; peace teams set up in eastern Croatia; and the Philippine NGO Bantay Ceasefire monitoring in Mindanao.
6. Human security is distinct from state security. It refers to 'freedom for individuals from basic insecurities caused by gross human rights violations' (A Human Security Doctrine for Europe 2004). It widens the notion of threat to include 'protection of citizens from environmental pollution, transnational terrorism, massive population movements, such infectious diseases as HIV/AIDS and long-term conditions of oppression and deprivation' (Human Security Now 2003: 6).
7. International nonviolent intervention should be distinguished from Sharp's use of the term 'nonviolent intervention', which denotes 'methods that intervene directly to change a given situation' (Sharp 2005: 62).
8. See also Christine Schweitzer, *Strategies of Intervention in Protracted Violent Conflicts by Civil Society Actors: The Example of Interventions in the Violent Conflicts in the Area of Former Yugoslavia, 1990–2004* (forthcoming).

8A
MAKING PEACE PRACTICAL:
WITH NONVIOLENT PEACEFORCE IN SRI LANKA

Rita Webb

Mahatma Gandhi articulated the vision of Shanti Sena, a peace army. I wanted to become a veteran of service in that kind of army, a foot soldier in a mission that might point a way out of the vortex of violence that humanity was spinning into. So I took a two-year leave of absence from my job, a hiatus from my community, and left my husband and family behind to be trained and deployed as an unarmed civilian peacekeeper with Nonviolent Peaceforce's (NP) first peacekeeping project in Sri Lanka.

In 2002 a Norwegian-brokered ceasefire agreement gave NP the opening needed to begin testing out ways in which unarmed civilians from around the world could serve and protect civil society in areas of conflict. Six years on I find myself still in Sri Lanka, with NP now a truly global and growing organisation.[1] NP's goal remains to help reduce and prevent violence so that local peacemakers and ordinary citizens can contribute to lasting peace with justice in their war-torn regions. As our NP literature says, we are learning every day what people of good will from around the world can say *Yes* to, after they've said *No* to war.

In all our field sites in Sri Lanka, we're saying *Yes* to local peacemakers when they ask for our accompaniment to feel safe enough themselves to reach out to families directly affected by conflict-driven violence, perhaps through the killing or disappearance of a family member, or perhaps through the forced conscription of a son or daughter into one of the armed groups. We're saying *Yes* to community-based organisations and local community leaders, who want to build community networks across ethnic divides to reduce the potential for communal violence and prepare nonviolent responses to violence when it does occur. We are saying *Yes* to local, national and international partners who want to collaborate with NP to strengthen democratic processes and accountability, and to help improve the safety, confidence and ability of Sri Lankans to address conflict in nonviolent ways.

Since 2006, the Sri Lankan government has again been focusing on a military solution to the country's political problems, finally abrogating the 2002 Ceasefire Agreement in January 2008. The Liberation Tigers of Tamil Eelam (LTTE – 'the Tamil Tigers'), who have been fighting for an independent homeland for the minority Tamils since 1983, have responded in kind against government security forces and against other Tamils who attempt to assert their independence from the LTTE. Innocent bystanders and civilians inevitably and repeatedly find themselves

Photograph 8.1   Women in Trincomalee, Sri Lanka, requested the presence of observers from Nonviolent Peaceforce at their sit-down protest. (NP)

in the wrong place at the wrong time. The deteriorating security situation has had a major impact on the civilian population in the north and east where NP focuses its peacekeepers, with daily military clashes and full-scale battles, massive displacement of civilians, and human rights abuses of all kinds throughout the country – most violations going unreported and uninvestigated.

People approach our field offices with a variety of problems and requests. For those we cannot help directly – such as a widow seeking government compensation for the death of her husband, or a family looking to be reunited with other relations who were separated when they fled the fighting in their village – we make referral calls or arrange meetings with other agencies or humanitarian organisations. For those we might be able to help more directly, we interview the family to get the basic details of their situation, learn what actions they have already taken, discuss options for next steps, and determine what, if any, contribution NPSL might be able to make to improve their safety. Because we seek always to help and support, it is the unpredictability of the work, the not-knowing where the work might lead us in a quickly changing environment, that challenges us every day.

In addition to work at the individual/family level, we also work at the community level and with all sectors of the society. These relationships need to be nurtured and maintained, so we also spend much of our time meeting and conversing with others, increasing our knowledge of the local stakeholders and the changing context, and building relationships of mutual trust that we can turn to in the future on behalf of the individuals and families who are suffering as a direct consequence of the violence.

Our work is often difficult to describe, and we still have a lot to learn about how to tell the story of NP without, on the one hand, further endangering those who trust us enough to engage with us and share their extreme vulnerability with us, and on the other hand, without raising our own profile to such an extent that we become perceived as an unacceptable liability to state or non-state actors, possibly leading to becoming targets ourselves or to non-renewal of our work permits and visas.

Our work in Sri Lanka is also slow work. It is premised on relationships of trust, trust that is gained slowly and after repeated interactions over time. Of necessity, the kind of project we are developing – and our greatest security as unarmed civilian peacekeepers – must come from our acceptance as non-partisan 'outsiders' who can demonstrate to all stakeholders, including by our longer-term 'embeddedness' in the life of the communities where we both live and work, that we are also somehow 'insiders', ordinary people who have a deep commitment to helping build lasting peace with justice for all citizens, from all ethnic and religious communities, from all social classes. And ultimately, not just in Sri Lanka, but in all places where violence still prevails.

What we in NP are living out, in the end, is a vision of the kind of world we want, not just for our own children and grandchildren, but for *all* children and grandchildren.

NP is a small but important part of transitioning to a world beyond war. As Gandhi reminded us: 'Whatever we do may seem insignificant, but it is most important that we do it.' Our goal is not to rid the world of conflict – that is neither possible nor perhaps even desirable – but to help demonstrate that there are better and more sustainable results for all parties to a conflict from pursuing nonviolent solutions to conflict.

Note

1. In the meantime, my husband pointed out I had over-stayed my original two-year commitment, so he retired from his job and joined me in Sri Lanka in 2005.

9

CROSS-BORDER NONVIOLENT ADVOCACY DURING THE SECOND PALESTINIAN *INTIFADA*: THE INTERNATIONAL SOLIDARITY MOVEMENT

*Véronique Dudouet**

This chapter analyses the activities of international volunteers working with Palestinians to empower them in their nonviolent struggle against the Israeli occupation. Since the outbreak of the second *intifada* in September 2000, there have been several intergovernmental attempts to deploy an international force of unarmed observers to interpose themselves between the Israeli army and Palestinian civilians during outbreaks of violence,[1] but they have been relentlessly vetoed at the Security Council by the USA. In the absence of inter-state initiative, 'transnational civil society' has filled the gap by sending delegations of international volunteers to the region.

Several different organisations are explicitly committed to nonviolent forms of intervention. The focus here is on the International Solidarity Movement (ISM), because it 'has emerged as the most visible face of international activism in Palestine', and is 'sufficiently effective to be the object of stepped up Israeli pressures' (Seitz 2003: 50).

According to the definition on its web page, ISM is

> a Palestinian-led movement committed to resisting the Israeli occupation of Palestinian land using nonviolent, direct-action methods and principles. Founded by a small group of [foreign and Palestinian] activists in August 2001, ISM aims to support and strengthen the Palestinian popular resistance by providing the Palestinian people with two resources, international protection and a voice with which to nonviolently resist an overwhelming military occupation force.

---

* This chapter is based on research for the author's Ph.D. at the Department of Peace Studies, Bradford University, and updated.

This description clarifies the links between foreign volunteers and the local population (international advocacy at the service of Palestinian activists), the goal of the movement (raising awareness globally, and ending the occupation locally), and its methods of engagement (nonviolent direct action).

This chapter examines how far ISM lives up to its principles of nonviolence and of serving, rather than influencing, local Palestinian communities. It then considers how far ISM has been successful in its main objectives of providing international protection to Palestinian civilians and nonviolent activists; raising global awareness; and empowering Palestinians. The evidence is based on my own experience with the ISM in 2003, complemented by interviews with its co-founders and documents retrieved from the organisation's website.[2]

ISM'S commitment to nonviolence and its limits

According to ISM's original mission statement,

> as enshrined in international law and UN resolutions, we recognise the Palestinian right to resist Israeli violence and occupation via legitimate armed struggle. However, we believe that nonviolence can be a powerful weapon in fighting oppression and we are committed to the principles of nonviolent resistance.

This sentence was withdrawn.[3] Currently the website states:

> The ISM maintains that all military tactics should be stopped by all sides in favour of nonviolent alternatives. ... The ISM seeks to bring about an end to violence by actively resisting the occupation through nonviolent means. The Israeli government has long worked to crush peaceful resistance, making it very difficult for Palestinians to act nonviolently on a large scale. We're working to develop an alternate way of resisting – nonviolently – that can be effective. (http://www.palsolidarity.org/main/about-ism/tough-questions [accessed 12 October 2008])

Two of the co-founders of the movement define nonviolence both negatively (exclusion of the use of verbal and physical abuse) and positively: it implies respect for everyone, including the opponent (Arraf and Shapiro 2003). Another co-founder adds the dimension of 'standing up for the powerless but not against the powerful', and the importance of establishing links with the opponent (Andoni 2003).

As a condition for joining ISM in Palestine, all new volunteers are required to commit to supporting only nonviolent resistance. However, owing to the particularly loose system of recruiting unscreened volunteers (who can enlist from anywhere in the world through the ISM website or local ISM groups), ideological ties between activists are inherently weak (Seitz 2003: 65). Some volunteers pursue nonviolence as a way of life, others are for Palestinian solidarity and opposing Israeli occupation, while others are from Jewish and even Zionist groups who are ashamed of Israeli policy. There are also peace and justice groups from Christian churches, who claim to be 'here to make peace', and anarchists or adherents of the anti-globalisation and anti-capitalist movements (Arraf and Shapiro 2003: 67–8).

During the two-day intensive training that new volunteers have to take on their arrival, a few hours are dedicated to the theory and practice of nonviolent intervention. Various rules are spelt out: positively, the need for communication, to behave openly and with respect for all people; negatively, don't touch or verbally abuse soldiers or settlers; don't use anything that could be seen as a weapon. Role-plays and practical exercises are used to prepare volunteers for legal, media and security issues they might encounter during their support activities. However, most training programmes only last for one weekend and there is not sufficient time to go deeply into the principles, strategy and dilemmas of nonviolent resistance or third-party intervention.

The few weeks I spent with ISM enabled me to verify that the principles of nonviolent intervention are clearly followed on the ground. One example demonstrates the impact that nonviolent action makes in the mind of the Israeli occupation forces. On 5 August 2003, I was one of 41 international volunteers arrested for 'obstructing the army' by refusing to leave a 'closed military area' in the village of Mas'ha.[4] We were all released the following day and praised for our 'passive resistance' except for one Italian volunteer who was expelled from the country for having resisted her arrest 'violently'.

ISM also embodies the principles of a nonviolent way of life in its decentralised decision-making process. At the time of my visit, the group had a consensus-based structure, with a core group that met once a month but with details left to local affinity groups.

The most challenging debates concerning nonviolent rules of engagement related to ISM's position on Palestinian stone-throwing. Officially, the organisation expressly forbids its volunteers from participating in such acts of symbolic violence, or acting as a human shield for someone throwing stones. However, it allows them to stay on in situations that evolve into stone-throwing against a heavily armed and armoured army (during demonstrations or invasions), with the view that international presence can help keep the Israeli retaliation a bit less disproportionate. Nevertheless, when such situations occur, the group often becomes divided over the appropriate response. I witnessed a confrontational demonstration against the Wall near Tulkarem, where six internationals were injured by rubber bullets while protecting stone-throwing teenagers, and at the time of my leaving the country, the debate was still continuing on this issue.

Are international volunteers at the service of Palestinian nonviolent activism?

What measures are implemented to ensure that external and internal groups work on the base of equality rather than subordination, so that foreign presence does not compete with or replace local action?

Its founders insist on defining the ISM as a 'joint Palestinian–international movement with a Palestinian leadership'. The decision to be a joint movement

---

Box 9.1   A Palestinian's comment on international solidarity

The first *intifada* of 1987 created a unique degree of international solidarity with the Palestinians. Since 2000 we have been living with the violence of the second uprising, and Palestinians have realised that we need international support and solidarity if we are to achieve independence.

International solidarity activists come from all over the world to witness our suffering and to participate with us in our nonviolent resistance to the occupation. They have also played an important humanitarian role and in relation to the mass media. They accompany us in our humanitarian work – on our health visits, with the ambulances and the mobile clinics to the villages isolated by the Israeli checkpoints. As workers in the health sector we can feel more secure with 'internationals' alongside us.

In the Jenin area there have been many nonviolent activities against the racist separation wall. Our solidarity friends have been at the fore, forming human shields, and several have been wounded and many arrested and deported. And here I want to pay tribute to Rachel Corrie and Tom Hurndall, the two International Solidarity Movement activists who fell in defence of peace and justice in Palestine. We should also acknowledge the role of the Israeli movements that oppose the occupation.

On the basis of my activities with solidarity groups I can make a number of observations:

1. It is necessary to improve the coordination mechanisms with local activist groups. Sometimes coordination has been carried out with people or groups not qualified to reflect a true image of the reality of the Palestinian struggle.
2. The internationals should not be blinded by the different political points of view within the Palestinian arena. They should preserve neutrality when dealing with the different factions.
3. It is necessary that every solidarity member visiting the occupied territories is fully informed and has a clear programme for the time period of their visit.
4. It is important to maintain communication with solidarity activists after they have departed in order to create an ongoing relationship and so that Palestinians can feel that there are people all around the world working in support of their just cause.

Omar D is a health worker living in the Jenin area of the Occupied West Bank.

has several implications. In terms of decision-making, the highly decentralised ISM relies on working groups in each area of operation, which are coordinated by a mix of local and foreign volunteers selected and trained by the central staff. In addition, to ensure that ISM does not compete with or replace internal initiatives, all activities are jointly organised with civil society NGOs or political parties, invited to take part in direct action as equal partners. ISM is open to collaboration with every local organisation that agrees to abide by the nonviolent rules of engagement. In order to maintain this inclusive line of operation, it has turned down offers of financial assistance from the Palestinian Authority or any other political party.

During their orientation and training weekend, ISM newcomers are repeatedly instructed to avoid making cultural, political or strategic judgements, or creating the impression that they are dictating to Palestinians. One ground rule is the ban on interfering in Palestinian domestic issues, no matter what the outsiders feel about who is right or wrong. All work must be done within the norms and traditions of Palestinian society.[5] Although the movement trains its volunteers, it avoids using the term 'training' in the community so as not to sound insulting to Palestinians. On the contrary, foreigners are 'here to learn, not to teach'. The then coordinator of ISM, the Palestinian activist Ghassan Andoni, also adds:

> we don't need people making proposals from abroad about how we should organise resistance. In a way, this is like colonialism. The Palestinian people can only accept those who are engaged in the resistance themselves and those who support approaches already existent in the society. (Interview with the author, 22 July 2003)

How are these principles understood by foreign activists, and are they applied on the ground? Every activity that I observed was preceded by consultation with locals, even such routine actions as a checkpoint watch. However, I noticed some variations in how relationships were built between a regional ISM team and the local population, according to the style of each individual ISM regional team. Moreover, my overall impression of the dynamics of international–Palestinian relationships in summer 2003 was that, rather than simply assisting local nonviolent activists, ISM often took over the planning of activities without waiting for Palestinian spontaneous initiatives. The timing of actions also indicated a relative dependency on foreigners: planned protests in the Occupied Palestinian Territories peak around Christmas and summer holidays, which is when most foreign volunteers are able to travel to Palestine.

At the time of my visit, Andoni also expressed his wish that in the near future, ISM would be able to shift from initiating action to supporting locally initiated massive popular resistance:

When Palestinians start participating en masse, they will be able to take real ownership of ISM, but at present, it is still a joint movement; and the moment you talk about joint international–Palestinian action, foreigners are always tempted to take the lead. ... [It is also] important for the ISM to support local action rather than initiate it, [for] ... international activists come and go, but indigenous people have to live through the consequences of the actions, and especially they are the ones to suffer retaliation from the Israeli army or administration.

Over five years later, however, there is evidence that Palestinians have taken the lead in several sustained nonviolent campaigns against the Wall (see below).

Assessing the effectiveness of ISM

Protecting Palestinians in war-zones, especially nonviolent activists

Protection is provided through the physical accompaniment of Palestinians endangered by frequent attacks from soldiers or settlers (including children on their way to school), or by acting as 'human shields' during demonstrations, offering an international presence, which often prevents local activists from being injured when they engage in nonviolent action on their own. When international volunteers do not succeed in preventing violence, they can at least act as 'witnesses' of occupation by publicising what they have seen.

Although the ISM specialises in direct action, it is also ready to perform humanitarian missions in times of crisis. For example, during Israel's Operation Defensive Shield in March–May 2002, when most Palestinian cities were reoccupied and placed under curfew, ISM shifted its focus to reactive missions, engaging in life-saving work. Its volunteers were the first foreigners to enter the massively bombarded Jenin refugee camp, and it is also widely known across the occupied territories for its forced marches through the sieges of Arafat's headquarters or Bethlehem's Church of Nativity. Seitz reports that many villagers from Yanoun, who had fled their homes under harassment by nearby settlers, returned to their land because they felt safer since the arrival of internationals (Seitz 2003: 64). Additional protection or interposition activities carried out by ISM volunteers include visiting houses occupied by the army to deliver food and medicine to families detained in their own houses, or 'home stay' – which consists in sleeping over at suicide bombers' family homes so that the houses won't be demolished in revenge (which under international law would constitute illegal collective punishment).

Some volunteers consider the campaign of repression of the ISM by the Israeli government as a testimony of its effectiveness. By Israel's own account, since Operation Defensive Shield, hundreds of foreign citizens have been turned back from entry points on suspicion of being linked with 'pro-Palestinian groups' and dozens more have been arrested and deported, on the charge of being 'provocateurs' or 'riot inciters'.

Negatively, it needs to be acknowledged that in a few cases the intervention of ISM volunteers has made things worse for the Palestinians they were trying to protect. Therefore an activity like ambulance accompaniment, which was practised a lot during the spring 2002 campaign, is now off the agenda because Palestinians felt that the response of the army was worse when internationals were present.[6] The tragic events of spring 2003, when two ISM volunteers were killed during their protection or interposition mission, have also proved that the function of providing a 'human shield' is becoming less relevant, since soldiers are no longer afraid of shooting at internationals, even at the expense of bad media publicity outside Israel.[7] In the aftermath of these events, the organisation nevertheless decided to carry on with its protective mission, despite the risks involved.

Perhaps the activities most sustainable in the long term, even if they do not bring as much media coverage, tend to be proactive and constructive rather than confrontational and disruptive. But the format of intervention adopted by the ISM is not adapted to such projects; the focus is on direct action with numbers maximised by recruiting short-term volunteers. Volunteers are required to participate in the ISM campaigns for a minimum of ten days, and the average time of stay is three weeks. Critics reproach the organisation for bringing in volunteers who do not know enough about the local context, and who leave the region without having learnt much about Palestinian culture. However, many volunteers move on from ISM to other projects, such as city twinning, social, youth or media projects, or the widely publicised Free Gaza campaign in August 2008.[8]

Other advocacy groups are more specialised in long-term projects that can be sustained once the internationals are gone, even if they do not bring as much media coverage. Both the International Women's Peace Service (IWPS) and the Christian Peacemaker Teams (CPT) have chosen to stay permanently in a particular area where local people have called on their help (IWPS in Hares, CPT in Hebron). These projects rely on a small number of highly trusted and well-trained activists coming for several months at a time. This enables them to develop long-term relationships with the local population and to work on well-prepared projects that really fit local needs and customs.

Rather than weakening the movement, this subdivision of solidarity work between different groups and networks, each with its own style and local contacts, enables a complementarity in action that can only benefit the development of nonviolent resistance in Israel-Palestine. Far from competing, these autonomous solidarity groups participate in each other's activities, and manage to avoid duplicate action through an appropriate geographical distribution. Most demonstrations I observed in summer 2003 were attended by members of different solidarity groups. And for most Palestinians, the plethora of international groups are lumped together under the catch-all '*ajanib*' (foreigners) rather than distinguished by the array of confusing acronyms in the field (Seitz 2003: 51).

Gaining global attention and promoting solidarity

An important success claimed by ISM is its media coverage. The organisation's media section attracts journalists to its demonstrations and sends reports to a worldwide audience. Volunteers are proud that the issue of the Wall became more prominent in the Israeli and international public arena after the intensive 2003 Freedom Summer campaign. Demonstrations were reported in major newspapers such as the *New York Times*, *Washington Post*, *Guardian* and *Le Monde*.

Part of this success is ascribable to the media and campaigning work by ISM regional teams. Indeed ISM claims that 'militant tourism' in Palestine is only one facet of its activities and at least half of what they do takes place in the volunteers' own countries. Developing international support for Palestinians through lobbying, educational and public awareness campaigns in the USA and Europe is crucial. ISM estimates that half of its several thousands of volunteers have come from the USA, a quarter of whom are of Jewish origin and can therefore offer an alternative voice to the influential pro-Israel lobby. However, local US campaigns to claim justice for Rachel Corrie, run over by a bulldozer when trying to protect a Palestinian home from demolition, have not had the same success as the parallel British campaign over Tom Hurndall: Israel prosecuted the IDF soldier who shot this British activist in the head while he was escorting Palestinian children out of the line of Israeli fire.

Recently ISM members in their home countries have also been engaging forcefully in debate in favour of international sanctions against Israeli occupation policies, for instance through an economic, sporting or cultural boycott. According to one of the co-founders of the organisation, the promotion of 'boycott, divestment sanctions' has become one of the main strategies of intervention (e-mail correspondence with Huwaida Arraf, June 2007).

Empowering Palestinians

From my observations during the ISM Freedom Summer 2003, individual actions rarely prevent Israelis from controlling the lives of Palestinians. When roadblocks or fences were dismantled during demonstrations, they were invariably rebuilt the day after, and very few cases have been recorded where the ISM successfully prevented a house from being destroyed. Nevertheless, the overall impact of such acts of nonviolent direct action is empowering for the Palestinians. A long-term ISM volunteer in Falmiya asked a local if he regretted the unsuccessful resistance to the Wall, which had brought a lot of extra repression on the villagers. On the contrary, he replied: the fact that people from all over the world came to stand

and resist with them helped them to maintain their own humanity and their belief in humanity (interview with Heidi Niggermann).

Since my last visit to the Occupied Territories, there has been a dramatic increase in popular resistance in Palestinian villages, illustrated especially by the so-called 'third *intifada* against the apartheid Wall'. In the village of Budrus, for instance, where several demonstrations managed to delay the building of the wall, local leadership has reversed the previous relationship between outside activists and Palestinians. A local resident recalled that:

> In the north, from Jenin until Budrus, there were Israeli and international demonstrators, supported by Palestinians. But here we think that is our problem and that we have to defend our land or do something, and the Israeli and international protesters are only supporting us. We are very grateful for their help, but the Palestinians have to make a stand. (Levy 2004)

Several of these grassroots campaigns have claimed legal victories, the Israeli Supreme Court ruling against the planned route of the security barrier in cases where the expropriation of Palestinian land could not be justified by the security needs of Israeli citizens and settlers (Galili 2004).[9]

It is difficult to measure the real impact of the ISM and other international groups on the increasing appeal of popular resistance across the Occupied

Photograph 9.1 Women have been especially prominent in the Palestinian nonviolent resistance in Budrus, which succeeded in changing the course of the Separation Wall. (Gary Field)

Territories. According to Arraf and Shapiro, 'at a minimum level, [the presence of the ISM on the ground] has greatly raised the morale of the Palestinians' (2003: 69), and in the opinion of the Mustafa Barghouti,[10] demonstrations led by the internationals have 'illustrated to the Palestinians the power of peaceful, nonviolent resistance to the occupation, and have perhaps empowered them to use these very methods' (2002).

What is certain is that the modest legal victories of civil resistance in villages threatened by the Wall have encouraged others to use the same techniques. A member of the local popular committee in Budrus reported that during his administrative detention, leaders from all the factions told him that the 'Budrus method is good' and that they had to reconsider their own methods (Rapaport 2005). Similar reports come from Bil'in, where observers have also noted the participation of Hamas officials in Friday demonstrations. Interviewed there by an Israeli journalist, the alleged Hamas leader in the West Bank declared, 'we have tried everything, and we will try this way too'. During the campaign for the February 2006 Palestinian elections, the Bil'in anti-Wall marches have even become an active arena of electioneering, as the contending parties all sent high-ranking candidates to march at the front – another sign of how much this village has become a symbol for all Palestinians. Bil'in organisers have also been invited by other villages to help them organise popular demonstrations, deemed successful because they 'attract media and foreign and Israeli supporters and reduce violence' (Daraghmeh 2005).

Local developments on the ground in the coming months will decisively influence the future expansion of this grassroots movement, and eventually whether its efficacy is acknowledged by both West Bank and Gaza Palestinian leaderships.

Notes

1. For instance, since 1994, a 'Temporary International Presence' operates in the highly divided city of Hebron in the West Bank. Composed of civil–military delegates from six European countries, this mission is very limited as it only has an observation mandate, reporting back to the delegates' respective countries and Israel on human rights and security issues (www.tiph.org).

2. In summer 2003, I spent several weeks as a participant observer with ISM, in the context of Ph.D. research fieldwork, following volunteers in their different areas of operation within the West Bank (Jenin, Tulkarem, Qalqilia and Nablus districts).

3. In the intense debate in the US press following the killing of the volunteer Rachel Corrie, this sentence was misused or misquoted by hostile journalists trying to depict the ISM as supporting Palestinian armed resistance.

4. In a collective effort of international (ISM and IWPS), Israeli (Anarchists Against the Wall and Gush Shalom) and Palestinian activists (local grassroots committee against the Wall and local ISM coordinators), the group was attempting to prevent the demolition of the segment of a house that stood in the way of the separation Wall

under construction. When released (on bail signed by an Israeli guarantor), we were forbidden from re-entering any Palestinian area for the rest of our stay.

5. This means, for example, that female volunteers need to abide by the local customs when it comes to the role of women in the public domain. In a predominantly Muslim society, it is also forbidden to consume alcohol.

6. The army used international accompaniment as an excuse to stop and delay ambulances under the pretext of 'illegally carrying non-official volunteers'.

7. Officially ISM rejects the term 'human shield' as it is associated with 'a special reference to civilians used by military or armed personnel for protection' (ISM press conference statement, 5 May 2003).

8. On 23 August 2008, 46 activists broke the Israeli-imposed blockade of the Gaza strip, entering by sea on the small boats *Free Gaza* and *Liberty*. The campaign was co-founded by ISM activists forbidden to return to Palestine by Israeli immigration authorities.

9. For example, in Budrus, in March 2004, after several months of popular struggle, the Wall was rerouted much closer to the Green Line, confiscating only 38 dunums of land (100 olive trees) instead of the 1,000 (3,000 olive trees) initially planned. In Azawiya, a ruling was issued on 25 June 2004 to halt the construction work in view of proofs of disproportionate use of force by Israeli armed forces, causing hundreds of injuries and leading to growing international concern.

10. Mustafa Barghouti, not to be confused with the imprisoned Marwan Barghouti, is a Ramallah doctor who helped initiate the independent democratic Al Mudabara coalition in 2002 to unite civil society bodies in active resistance to the occupation.

9A
THE WORK OF THE ECUMENICAL ACCOMPANIMENT PROGRAMME IN PALESTINE AND ISRAEL (EAPPI)

Ann Wright

The Ecumenical Accompaniment Programme in Palestine and Israel (EAPPI) is one of a number of civil society organisations that send international volunteers into the Occupied Palestinian Territories (OPTs). Its aim is to end the 40-year Israeli occupation.

In 2001, at the beginning of the second *intifada*, several resolutions were passed in the UN Security Council calling for the UN to send peacekeepers to the OPTs to protect the civilian population. All the resolutions were vetoed by the US. In response, the churches in Jerusalem called for civil society organisations worldwide to come to the OPTs. The World Council of Churches answered that call and set up the EAPPI to recruit and deploy volunteers. Since 2002, over 600 volunteers from

16 different countries, mostly from Europe and North America, but also Australia and South Africa, have joined the programme. EAPPI is administered in the UK and Eire by the Quakers but applicants of all faiths (or none) are welcome.

EAPPI adopts what it calls 'principled impartiality'. Its code of conduct states that

> we do not take sides in the conflict and do not discriminate against anyone, but we are not neutral in terms of principles of human rights and international humanitarian law; we stand with the poor, the oppressed, the marginalised and the dispossessed and aim to serve all parties in the conflict in a fair and unbiased way.

The premise is that the Occupation harms both occupied and occupier because:

- it causes Palestinian suffering and dispossesses and impoverishes them; and
- Palestinian resistance to the occupation has caused Israeli civilian suffering, intensifies the militarisation of Israeli society and brutalises the conscripts serving in the OPTs.

UK volunteers receive two weeks' training on the history of the conflict, the different actors involved and nonviolent strategies. This is complemented by a further week's local training in EAPPI's Jerusalem headquarters. Teams of three or four are then sent out to placements throughout the West Bank: Jerusalem, Bethlehem, Hebron, Tulkarem, Jayyous and Yanoun. Volunteers can no longer get into Gaza.

Volunteers follow the three-pronged EAPPI mandate of providing protection by presence, supporting Israeli and Palestinian peace activists in their nonviolent actions, and generating advocacy opportunities at home, although tasks do also vary according to the placement. Together with a Swiss parson turned activist and a young Norwegian town planner, I served from February to May 2006 in Tulkarem, a city of 120,000 people in the north-west of the West Bank.

When we arrived, Tulkarem was de facto a closed town with a collapsed economy: the separation barrier ran down one side, Israeli checkpoints blocked every road out of town, and soldiers controlled the gates in the barrier that ostensibly let farmers reach their land now on the Israeli side. Given this scenario our team concentrated mainly on the protection part of the mandate, something I was familiar with, having previously worked with Peace Brigades International who pioneered the protective accompaniment model.

Monitoring the checkpoints out of Tulkarem was grim. It was shocking to see how every aspect of Palestinian life (trying to get to work, to study, to hospital, to visit family or religious shrines) is controlled by the Israeli army. There are over

600 physical obstacles to movement on the West Bank, and when I was there it took about seven hours to travel from Tulkarem to Jerusalem, a distance of 50 miles. Those who manage to get exit permits face harassment and humiliation, with no guarantee their pass will take them through. We could do nothing about the orders the soldiers received, of course, but we were able to ascertain whether they were following orders rather than inflicting the 'mean soldier' type of abuse, and take it up with their commanders. We logged every serious incident.

The farmers in the villages round Tulkarem also faced increasing harassment in their struggle to get permits to farm their land: they could be refused 'for security reasons', and permits were often only given to the youngest and oldest in a family (the least able-bodied). And even with permits, the gates did not always open at the right times, sometimes not at all, produce was sometimes not allowed back in, tractors were impounded – a whole host of petty abuses were suffered under the catch-all of 'security'. Again, with persistent monitoring by our team and liaising with the Red Cross, the gate system could be made to function but the sheer precariousness of the farmers' existence took your breath away. They feared that in the long run this land would be stolen anyway.

Tulkarem did not have any large illegal Israeli settlements nearby so protecting Palestinian farmers from aggressive settlers, which is such an important part of the work of the EAPPI teams in Yanoun and Hebron, was not part of our brief. Nor did we have as much opportunity to work with Israeli peace activists as our Jerusalem and Bethlehem teams do: our main contact was with the extraordinary women of Machsom Watch whom we met at checkpoints where they come to monitor their own soldiers' behaviour. We also occasionally ventured further afield and joined Rabbis for Human Rights to help Palestinian farmers plant olive trees and plough and sow. We did, however, do a lot of solidarity work with Tulkarem women's and youth organisations, especially in the refugee camps, listening to their history and stories, and offering a pair of hands for anything that needed doing. We also monitored the passage of the families of the approximately 1,000 Tulkarem prisoners held in Israeli jails through the checkpoints into Israel (out of a total 12,000 Palestinian prisoners held).

Did we really do any good? It is hard to quantify. People in Tulkarem told us that checkpoint abuse decreased when we were there monitoring, that the flow of traffic was faster. (We did not, of course, see the extrajudicial killings and kidnappings that went on during the nightly Israeli incursions into the camps.) Farmers were also very appreciative and said our presence increased access. Also, because we were three of only five foreigners permanently in Tulkarem at that time and people felt so very abandoned, they did seem genuinely thankful that we'd come to see for ourselves how harsh their lives are.

And this ultimately is the point of EAPPI: to use the information gained for advocacy at home. Returned volunteers are contracted to do a certain number of speaking engagements, and EAPPI helps them prepare presentations for advocacy. Most volunteers do many more talks than required. Speaking from first-hand experience is very powerful. Not many people spend time on the West Bank and those who do are so shocked that they need no encouragement to tell what they have seen.

For my part, I was shocked at the way Palestinians are imprisoned in their own towns, their economy in tatters and with little prospects of work, their land criss-crossed with settler-only roads and half a million Israelis living in illegal settlements on their land. But I was also shocked to realise, despite being a 'political' person and reader of the broadsheets, how little I had previously understood about what was going on. I was shocked at how Israel gets away with violating all the clauses of the Fourth Geneva Convention, which sets out the rules governing protection of civilians under occupation. And I was above all shocked that the West has so purposefully ignored this gross injustice for so many years, and allowed Israel such impunity.

When our team left Tulkarem, the farmers wrote to thank us for our support and help. But it is us who should be thanking them. They truly opened our eyes to the upside-down reporting of this conflict.

9B
INTERNATIONAL WOMEN'S PEACE SERVICE IN PALESTINE

Angie Zelter

International Women's Peace Service – Palestine (IWPS) was founded in 2002, and began by establishing a presence in a rural village in the Salfit Governorate within Occupied Palestinian Territory. I initiated IWPS, but because I am no longer allowed to enter Palestine, I have ceased to be closely involved with it. Up-to-date information is given on our website (www.iwps.info).

IWPS was set up in order to:

- support nonviolent civil resistance by Palestinians and Israelis, and to create space for people to become more involved in resistance;
- monitor human rights abuses, provide accompaniment and intervene to nonviolently prevent human rights abuses;

- alert the world community to human rights abuses in the Salfit Governorate and to effect change in world opinion about the occupation; and also to
- provide an experiential model that can be used to create international women's peace teams in other areas.

The lessons we have learnt are:

Relatively few Palestinians have so far been able and willing to organise nonviolent resistance. A few resort to violent resistance feeling they have to fight, and the vast majority survive by keeping their heads down. Mohamed, a friend of mine in a Salfit village, explained why his village would not support a neighbouring village in nonviolent protest to protect their best land from the Wall Israel was building to divide Palestinians from Jewish settlers on the West Bank: 'We are a small village of only a few thousand people, we cannot afford to have anyone else killed.' But where Palestinians are taking nonviolent action, then internationals can and do support. This is our space, which can expand or contract depending on the quantity and quality of nonviolent resistance and on local factors.

The violence and control by the Israeli military makes it difficult to organise and sustain nonviolent civil resistance. The Israeli Defence Force (IDF) is expert at using tear gas, sound bombs, rubber bullets and live ammunition to break up demonstrations. They have even resorted to spraying sewage on villagers to stop them demonstrating against the Wall; they raid villages and towns and arrest anyone known to be organising the demonstrations; create closed military zones; and use administrative detentions to keep those arrested behind bars for years without charge or trial and at risk of torture. 'Internationals' are merely deported – it is the Palestinians who bear the consequences of any form of resistance.

The deportations, and refusing entry of many thousands of international volunteers into Israel/Palestine, is a deliberate policy by the Israeli authorities, who understand how important international support is for Palestinians. This policy interrupts continuity, making it harder to build and sustain relationships, and to gain a deep understanding and knowledge of local circumstances. When the frequent infrastructural damage to buildings, computers, libraries, resources generally are factored in then it is clear how difficult any kind of organised resistance is.

Poverty. The Israeli stranglehold on the Palestinian economy has turned a relatively self-sufficient community into a malnourished, dependent on food aid and desperately poor community. People's energies are sapped by the struggle to survive and feed their families. 'Internationals' are inundated with requests for money and resources for development, and the need for money skews and sours their relationships, and encourages in-fighting, corruption and fraud, as well as reducing the energy for nonviolent resistance.

There is no fair legal system. The Palestinians mostly do not even bother to try to get justice. Those 'internationals' who try to get the Israeli legal system to deal with crimes face intimidation, high legal costs and obstacles to getting to the court. For example, with the help of the British Consulate, I managed to bring to court a well-known violent settler from Hebron for assaulting me and destroying my camera, which held film of his teenage followers attacking an old Palestinian man who later died of his wounds. But first I was denied entry into Israel for the court case where I was appearing as a witness. Then I was imprisoned and deported from the Occupied Territory after the settler pleaded guilty to the trivial crime of destroying my camera. He was never questioned about why he had destroyed the evidence of a murder.

IWPS has tried in several cases to take evidence and institute legal proceedings against violent incidents they have witnessed themselves. They have taken to the Israeli police evidence in the form of photos and signed witness statements of shootings and woundings of Palestinian villagers by violent Israeli settlers. But none of these cases have been prosecuted through the courts, even when Israeli human rights groups have helped.

Factionalisation and difficulties in uniting in a national nonviolent movement. Confinement of the Palestinian population by the use of frequent curfews, road blocks, imprisonment and now the Wall has led to huge tensions within the villages and towns. There is much internal fighting, and often violent confrontations between different clans and different political factions. Some villages have a history of killing suspected collaborators. Although there is a great experience and wealth of examples of nonviolent resistance by Palestinians, there have been no effective calls for a national nonviolent struggle and little national leadership. In some extraordinary cases, good *local* leadership has emerged – for example, Abu Ahmad of Budrus, a village in the Ramallah District, managed to unite families and different factions in the Budrus Popular Committee against the Apartheid Wall and to stop work on the Wall several times (see Chapter 9 by Véronique Dudouet). The strong nonviolent resistance at Bil'in is another excellent example of sustained nonviolent resistance, which has resulted in the killings by Israeli forces of several Palestinian children.

But the Wall, though delayed, has been built.

Cultural insensitivities, lack of Arabic speakers, and tendency to interfere in local politics by 'internationals' are all problems that have emerged and have added to tensions. A well-known Palestinian Christian who leads a Palestinian nonviolent resistance movement says he values the work and solidarity presence of internationals but wishes they would only come for a few months at a time. 'Those who stay longer begin to think they understand everything, and start to interfere in local politics, making things much worse.' Groups like ISM may like to think that they are Palestinian-led, but they do often tend to initiate nonviolence campaigns and they have their own agendas.

For nonviolence to work I believe that there needs to be:

1. *A clear exposure of the crimes being committed by Israel.* The reality of the occupation is continually distorted by government officials (especially in the US and UK) and by Western media. The added complications of European guilt over the Holocaust, and the Israeli use of the anti-Semitism label, makes people scared to raise their voices over Israeli crimes. The 'organised' harassment of anyone who criticises Israel as being anti-Semitic is very hard to deal with.

I wrote an article for a local magazine in Aylsham, a small town in Norfolk, England, explaining in graphic terms what it would look like if all the things I had seen in Palestine were taking place locally in Aylsham. As a result this small magazine was inundated with hundreds of letters from angry Jewish people who accused me and the magazine of anti-Semitism and created such a furore that the editor decided he would never again print anything 'political'.

2. *A powerful outside international moral authority that can be a source of appeal, and can then put pressure on Israel to stop their war crimes and human rights abuses, their blatant ethnic cleansing and their theft and colonisation of Palestinian land and water resources.*

However, the major funder/backer of Israel is the USA and they have a strong geopolitical reason for backing Israel. Unfortunately, all the major states that could have some influence over Israel are committing their own war crimes in their various areas of strategic interest.

3. *International support for the nonviolence movement inside Palestine.* This is happening. When IWPS started work, we were the only international solidarity and nonviolence NGO based in a rural Palestinian village (most internationals were based in towns and only visited the villages briefly). We now have a series of village profiles and a record of the kinds of human rights violations visited upon the people. Our presence was important in helping provide sustained support and space for nonviolence, in encouraging women's involvement in the nonviolent resistance, and in helping to set up some of the anti-Wall protest camps that also brought Israeli and Palestinian movements together.

4. *Encouragement of the internal divisions in Israel.* There is a growing Israeli peace movement, including the Refuseniks to military service, Gush Shalom (Peace Bloc), the Israeli Committee Against House Demolitions and the Anarchists. Nevertheless too few Israelis actually know, understand or care about the reality of life in the Occupied Territories, and they are often too scared to even try to find out. A good example of Israeli nonviolence that

is having an impact is Machsom Watch – an Israeli-based organisation that organises monitors and intervenes at some of the major checkpoints. IWPS used to do quite a bit of checkpoint monitoring, but can now leave this work to the Israeli group. The monitoring provides a good learning experience for Israelis who can then use this understanding back inside Israel to break down the ignorance and encourage empathy.

So what is the role of the international peace and nonviolence movement in relation to Palestine and Israel?

Education and political lobbying at home

Maybe our most important role is witnessing, then writing and distributing reports, articles and presentations to counteract the US/UK media distortion. We will help more 'internationals' to experience and see for themselves what is going on and then, on getting home, to speak out about it, so that the mainstream view of the Israelis as being the victims of terrorism is countered by accurate reports of the state terrorism of the occupation. Direct experience helps in confronting lies and distortions. A group of returned IWPS volunteers is now engaged in regular lobbying of the UK Foreign Office and in letter-writing to the press and their MPs, as well as actions at the Israeli Embassy. The level of knowledge in the UK, Europe and in the USA is much higher than even a few years ago, and to some extent this is because of the quantity of volunteers who have gone over to Palestine and on their return have spoken at small local meetings.

Support for Palestinians and Israeli activists (other than monitoring and protective accompaniment)

An underestimated role for international volunteers is to empathise and listen – just being there and witnessing and hearing makes Palestinians feel less cut off from the outside world and brings hope. Similarly, interaction with Israeli activists also lessens their sense of isolation and supports them in their vital work.

Then there is a role in supporting nonviolent resistance: being a calm and steady presence, helping out with international media contacts, and discussing ideas and strategies, bringing a wealth of experience of struggles from all over the world. The women that IWPS brought over to Palestine were from South Africa, the Philippines, Colombia and India. They provided some useful insights for the women in Salfit.

And finally, there was – and maybe still is – a role for creating a safe space for Israeli/Palestinian dialogue and cooperation. Certainly, when we first arrived in Salfit there were few Israelis who felt able to go into the villages alone. We helped provide safe spaces where the two sides could meet more easily, and now we are often, happily, redundant.

10

VOICES IN THE WILDERNESS: CAMPAIGNING AGAINST SANCTIONS ON IRAQ, 1995–2005

Kathy Kelly and Milan Rai

From across the table in a US prison interview room, in between questions about Iraq, an agent of the Federal Bureau of Investigation remarked that he had interviewed hundreds of Iraqis in the USA. He had only ever heard positive comments about Voices in the Wilderness (VitW) and its campaign against the economic sanctions on Iraq.[1] VitW – both in the USA and in Britain – had as one of its key aims (prior to the anti-war mobilisation of 2002) conveying to people in Iraq the sense that they did not stand alone, that they had not been forgotten since comprehensive economic sanctions were imposed on their country in 1990, and that they were valued by many people in the two countries primarily responsible for their suffering. The testimony we received – from Iraqis abroad, from the FBI and from within Iraq itself – helps us to believe that we were at least partially successful in conveying this message to people within Iraq.

Dr Salih Ibrahim, an Iraqi doctor who has lived in the UK since the 1980s, observes: 'You mention the name of Kathy Kelly or Voices in the Wilderness in Iraq and you would be amazed how many Iraqi people knew about her and her group's work during the long murderous sanctions years.' In his view, many Iraqis looked on the VitW volunteers 'with lots of love and admiration for raising their voices against this crime against humanity'. VitW represented 'the living consciousness of the West'; they were 'voices of the voiceless Iraqis' and of anti-war people in Britain and the USA (personal communication, 6 March 2008).

VitW was founded (in 1995 in Chicago; in 1998 in London) not merely to express solidarity, but also to alter attitudes. It aimed to contribute to the shifting of public opinion in our countries (including within the peace movement); to counter ignorance and acceptance of government deceit with accurate evidence, and to replace shameful indifference with active concern. VitW's primary method was the delegation: we took over 70 delegations of ordinary people from our two countries to Iraq between 1996 and 2003 in open defiance of the UN Security Council sanctions. Doctors, nurses, students, boatbuilders, homemakers, priests and others went to see the effects of sanctions for themselves, and to deliver children's medicines and other humanitarian goods without seeking UN authorisation, thereby breaking the sanctions and risking years of imprisonment (maximum penalty: 12 years' imprisonment and $1 million in fines in the USA; five years' imprisonment in the UK). It was our experience that staggering statistics (for example, UNICEF's 1999 estimate that half a million Iraqi children under the age of five had died as a result of the abnormal conditions in Iraq) only became comprehensible to many people when they were married to particular stories of particular children inside Iraq, stories brought back with photographs and telling details by ordinary citizens with nothing to gain (and much to lose) from travelling to Iraq and relaying these tragedies.

In 1999, Archbishop Giuseppe Lazzarotto, the papal nuncio to Iraq, told a VitW delegation in Baghdad that he wished church leaders, particularly from the USA, but also from Europe, would visit. At that point, Bishop Thomas Gumbleton, auxiliary bishop of Detroit, had visited Iraq with VitW, and had spoken out strongly against the sanctions. The nuncio said he had told bishops in conversations in Rome that the only way to show solidarity and concern for the people of Iraq was to visit. 'Because once you come, your eyes look at it in a different way, I can assure you.' The nuncio, and numerous Iraqis who had offered hospitality and insight to VitW delegations, also charged each traveller with a mandate to build awareness within activist communities. There was a shared confidence that if people beyond Iraq understood the nightmare suffering endured by Iraqi civilians, the economic war of sanctions and siege would not withstand the light of day.

VitW was founded in December 1995 (mainly by radical Catholics) just as the international political logjam over Iraq began to move. 1996 was the year that the UN's 'oil-for-food' programme was signed (supplies actually began arriving in March 1997). VitW delegations – and fasts, petitions, postal sanctions-breaking and other forms of nonviolent civil disobedience – helped in the process of changing international and national attitudes towards Iraq, particularly after the inspection crisis of February 1998, when international media crews focused attention on the humanitarian crisis. Delegations gained coverage inside Iraq and in the region (encouraging Iraqis and others not to despair, and helping to mobilise pressure on the sanctions regime), and every delegate carried out media work in their own towns and regions, with, at the very least, op-eds and letters to the editor. Their testimony about what they had seen and heard eventually began to appear in newsletters and magazines circulated by larger peace groups. While most delegates managed to generate stories in their local media outlets, the national elite media in the UK and the USA generally ignored VitW activities.

This indifference did not prevent journalists from attempting to use VitW as a method of obtaining entry to Iraq. One freelance journalist, pitching his story to US National Public Radio, explained that he was having a hard time getting an Iraqi visa, but then came across VitW:

The group, while quite sincere, also served the Iraqi government's purposes, and as such had no trouble getting visas. They put me on their list and my visa magically appeared, but when I reached Baghdad in March 2000, I discovered that the authorities wouldn't allow me to leave the group. I found myself driving about Baghdad and the south, on an official tour of the horrors of the sanctions. (Lawrence 2008: 94–5)

In fact, VitW did have trouble getting visas, and often risked flying to Jordan with no visas issued, in the hope that, upon arrival, the Iraqi Embassy in Jordan would grant visas. As for the 'official tour' of the horrors of sanctions, VitW delegations were actually remarkable among groups visiting Iraq for their autonomy in determining their own itineraries. Intent on gaining a deepened understanding of the impact of economic sanctions, in summer 2000 a group of US VitW members lived for nine weeks in the poorest district of Basra. Several international media professionals working in Baghdad, including CNN's Jane Arraf, commented later that they didn't take VitW efforts very seriously before this Basra project. The willingness of team members to live with impoverished Basrans during the sweltering summer, when electricity and potable water were scarce, persuaded Arraf and others that VitW activists were genuinely and primarily concerned about Iraqi suffering.

In addition to media work around delegations, VitW also helped to defend the UNICEF estimate of Iraqi child deaths when it was published in August 1999 (a returning British delegation gained enormous coverage); contributed to John Pilger's ground-breaking ITV documentary 'Paying the Price' in 2000; and assisted UN Humanitarian Coordinators Denis Halliday and Hans von Sponeck with speaking tours after their resignations in protest at the sanctions in July 1998 and February 2000, respectively. These initiatives, and many other efforts by different groups and individuals, contributed to a growing sense of compassion for ordinary Iraqis living under sanctions. As a result of this work, for example, a US Ambassador to the UN in 2002, if asked about the hundreds of thousands of children killed in Iraq by the sanctions, could no longer simply say, 'The price is worth it', as had Madeleine Albright in 1996 (interviewed on CBS's '60 Minutes', 12 May 1996).

As well as delegations to Iraq, Voices in the Wilderness UK contributed analysis, producing briefings, lobbying materials and a regular newsletter (available from http://www.voicesuk.org). Believing that democracy is based on education, both VitW groups worked hard to educate the general public, loosening preconceived notions about Iraq and building greater empathy for Iraqi civilians. Working with the Cambridge-based Campaign Against Sanctions on Iraq (CASI – www.casi.org. uk), British VitW produced some of the most detailed and searching critiques of the sanctions. Based on a close scrutiny of UN documents, these analyses were circulated to activists and journalists around the world. VitW UK also organised conferences and regular national networking events that helped to build the personal relationships that were the bedrock of the anti-sanctions movement.

Changing attitudes, and educating journalists and the general public about Iraq, was not an end in itself. The ultimate aim of VitW in the years 1996–2002 was the lifting of comprehensive economic sanctions. There were significant – reluctant – shifts in policy in these years. In 1998, the limit on the level of Iraqi oil exports for oil-for-food was raised to $5.26 billion every six months; in December 1999, the ceiling on Iraqi oil exports was removed entirely, and the proportion of revenues directed to humanitarian spending increased from 66 to 72 per cent. On a smaller, but still important, scale, the UN Security Council allowed a wider range of goods to be bought under the oil-for-food programme, and accelerated the procedure for ordering goods by introducing the 'green list' of approved goods. So the national protests and the international pressure had an effect that was felt in the lives of hundreds of thousands of Iraqis. In March 2001, US Secretary of State Colin Powell testified before the Senate Foreign Relations Committee that the sanctions regime was 'collapsing' as countries began ignoring the UN-imposed restrictions. It is likely that, had it not been for the 9/11 attacks and the subsequent drive to war against Iraq, the sanctions would have suffered further revision and loosening, if not total collapse.

We will never know precisely what impact VitW had on policy-makers either in the USA or in Britain, but it is likely that the organisation had an influence out of all proportion to its small numbers and modest budget, which derived entirely from donations from the general public. The major item of VitW expenditure – delegations to Iraq – was largely a cost borne by the delegates themselves: each delegation member was asked to raise enough funds to pay for their own travel and to assist at least one experienced VitW traveller to accompany the delegation. VitW in Chicago operated for its entire existence out of Kathy Kelly's apartment, the second floor of a modest two-flat building in Chicago's Uptown neighbourhood. VitW UK worked out of a room in Milan Rai's home in London until it rented a desk in an office in Oxford owned by the Ethical Property Company in December 1999 (moving to another small office in central London owned by Peace News Trustees in August 2002). Activists working in other regions of Britain or the USA worked out of their homes, paying their own expenses and relying on grassroots organisations to host them at speaking events. At most, a few volunteers in Chicago were compensated with stipends to cover basic living expenses, never amounting to more than $250 per week.

Tom Roberts, managing editor of the US *National Catholic Reporter*, described his travel to Iraq with a VitW group largely comprised of Catholic Workers, who live a life of voluntary poverty serving the poor and marginalised, all of whom had to raise funds for their travel. 'The groups', he wrote, 'were surprised at the outpouring of support. Some were able to raise tens of thousands of dollars, far more than necessary, and donated the unused funds to VitW and to purchase medicine.' Roberts credited VitW (and other groups that sent delegations) with helping detect the hidden costs of the war and the sanctions:

> Overwhelmingly, what one sees in Iraq is a consequence of war – eight years of a bloody, costly war with its eastern neighbor, Iran, another 10 years of bombs and sanctions at the hands of the United States. But often the most dangerous wounds are the most difficult to detect. That is the case of the relatively hidden costs of the war and the sanctions: the continuing destruction of Iraqi culture that draws protests from North American religious groups such as the Quakers and Mennonites, as well as VitW and from Catholic leaders inside Iraq. (*National Catholic Reporter*, 21 May 1999)

VitW's impact derived to a large extent from its ability to reach out to, mobilise or assist other organisations and other sectors of civil society. VitW often functioned as a magnet, drawing larger and more capable organisations to consider how they might take action to end the economic sanctions. If a small core of activists on a shoestring budget, working out of their own homes, staying in one-star hotels while abroad and asking each traveller to be self-funded, could focus attention on economic warfare against Iraqi civilians, then surely the larger peace and justice organisations could follow suit, challenging the sanctions and educating their constituencies? Eventually, larger and more established peace movement organisations, such as the Fellowship of Reconciliation, Pax Christi, Christian Peacemaker Teams and Veterans for Peace began organising delegations to Iraq. VitW activists jointly led some of these delegations; VitW, as a policy, readily shared contact information and gave assistance in arranging logistics, obtaining visas and setting up meetings with UN agencies, media representatives and NGOs working in Iraq. When the New York-based International Action Center, led by former US Attorney General Ramsey Clark, proposed that 100 activists fly to Iraq for a January 2001 trip that would allow for barely four days inside Iraq, VitW gave its assistance though the logistical challenges seemed overwhelming. In retrospect, participants in that particular delegation played an indispensable role in building durable grassroots campaigns to end the economic sanctions.

While this chapter focuses on VitW's impact in relation to the anti-sanctions campaign, it is also true that, during 2002, the small grassroots anti-sanctions movement that VitW had helped to nurture grew into a massive grassroots anti-war movement. VitW's work had the unintended consequence of laying a basis in knowledge, understanding, organisation and experience for key parts of the

US and British anti-war movements. VitW's main contribution to the anti-war movement was probably the Iraq Peace Team – modelled on the Gulf Peace Team of 1991, that had brought many of the original VitW activists together (see Bhatia, Drèze and Kelly 2001).

Gene Stoltzfus, who helped found the Christian Peacemaker Teams (CPT) and who acted as Executive Director throughout the period when VitW sent delegations to Iraq, comments:

> In critical pre-war and war situations it is crucial that the peace movement has person(s) in place with competent eyes and ears to give updates, interpretation and warnings. ... [VitW] was the only international organisation with strong peace leanings and an action program to go along with nonviolent commitments to have a reliable track record in place and thereby created space for others who followed. ... Being present with all the senses and a critical mind provided energy and comment for the worldwide movement. (Personal communication, 5 May 2008)

There was another unintended consequence of VitW's campaigning – the impact on the people who participated in VitW. For many dozens of people, VitW was a life-changing experience, giving them skills, knowledge and confidence that they had never imagined possessing.

In evaluating any campaign, there are several dimensions that should be taken into account:

- its effectiveness and profile in the media;
- its ability to galvanise other elements of civil society into action;
- its effect on the general public (in terms of growing knowledge and changing attitudes);
- the group's effect on 'the activist scene', which lies on the border between 'the general public' and 'civil society'; and,
- finally and most importantly, the group's impact on policy-makers. It is policy change that affects the lives of those whose needs are at stake.

In the case of VitW, there was also a sixth dimension – of solidarity: of how well VitW conveyed to people in Iraq the sense that they had not been forgotten, as well as the extent to which its material assistance was of direct use to ordinary Iraqi people.

One could also add a seventh measure: how well a group uses the resources that it has available to it. In this text we have briefly tried to sketch out some answers to these questions.

Former UN Humanitarian Coordinator for Iraq Denis Halliday observes:

> I believe the important work and impact of VitW needs to be recorded. VitW must take credit for a realisation amongst member states, including those of the much corrupted

Security Council, that the deadly collective punishment of comprehensive sanctions is unacceptable and produces consequences incompatible with international law, including human rights. (Personal communication, 5 May 2008)

In 2004, the US government finally lifted economic sanctions against Iraq. In 2005, a federal judge imposed a $20,000 fine against VitW for bringing medicine to Iraq without a licence. 'Those who break an unjust law', wrote Judge Bates (quoting Martin Luther King's *Letter from a Birmingham Jail*), 'should do so openly, lovingly and with a willingness to pay the penalty.' US VitW activists publicly stated that if Judge Bates chose to put them in jail, they would go openly and lovingly, but they would not pay one dime of a penalty that might contribute towards prolonging war against Iraq. With the lifting of the sanctions, those working with VitW in the USA chose to bring that organisation to a close and to create a new organisation, Voices for Creative Nonviolence. In Britain, VitW UK continues to campaign against war and economic devastation.

Note

1. Kathy Kelly describes this interview, noting that she refused to answer any of the FBI agents' questions, in 'Change Agents', 19 May 2004, at http://www.commondreams. org/views04/0519-08.htm [accessed 13 October 2008].

Section III

Bases of Solidarity:
Shared Identities, Interests and Beliefs

EDITORIAL INTRODUCTION

'Global solidarity' represents an aspiration – an expression of our common humanity, a sense of connectedness across boundaries, of interdependence in struggling for life on this planet, of sharing causes and values. However, particular manifestations of solidarity are grounded in relationships and specific connections between groups. This section illustrates some of the bases of solidarity between campaigners across frontiers, whether derived from a sense of common identity (such as gender and ethnicity), common interests (for example, between workers or small farmers) or common moral and political beliefs (such as pacifism or socialism), or religious faith. These unifying factors may of course overlap.

The first example is the feminist peace network Women in Black, described by Cynthia Cockburn. Gender has been a particularly significant basis for transnational solidarity, with feminist networks against various forms of violence against and exploitation of women, and to promote empowerment and the assertion of women's rights. Women in Black also represents a long tradition of women working together against war. The second example too focuses on resistance to war and militarism, the role of pacifist organisations in supporting conscientious objectors facing government repression: in this case COs in Turkey today.

Sexual identity provides another basis for cross-border campaigning. Chesterfield Samba's analysis of lesbian, gay, bisexual and transsexual (LGBT) campaigning in Africa emphasises the need for a regional approach and forms of self-definition, especially since various politicians have denounced homosexuality as a 'Western import'.

As a result of earlier migration patterns and flows of refugees, people who identify with a particular national and cultural group are often scattered widely around the globe. Andrew Rigby examines the potential of national diasporas to support campaigns within their countries of origin, and the possible drawbacks of such support.

The global justice movement, that resists abuses of corporate power and governments pursuing neoliberal capitalist policies such as privatisation, is the most ambitious of today's movements in attempting a truly global reach. However, it can be argued that like peace, feminist and green movements it too often functions along a North–South axis. Stellan Vinthagen suggests both some of the strengths and some of the weaknesses of the World Social Forum as a meeting place and coordination point for this 'movement of movements'.

The global justice movement can be seen as a contemporary version of the earlier socialist internationals that avoids imposing a centralised discipline while embracing much greater diversity in order to reflect the role of local communities, women, indigenous peoples and peasant farmers as well as workers. Yet unionised workers can still play a pivotal role in resistance, nationally and transnationally. The brief account in this section of the South African workers' embargo on a Chinese arms shipment to the Zimbabwe government is an example of this potential.

The very term 'solidarity' drawn from the socialist tradition suggests an appeal to workers. Yet that idea of international 'fraternity' has rather lost its gloss, because of the bureaucratic and white, male-dominated nature of many trade unions and their defence of the interests of the Northern 'aristocracy of labour'. Nevertheless workers' solidarity remains a force, partly functioning through new and more horizontal networks, including employees at different points in a multinational corporation's global chain of production and distribution, but also involving established unions (Kidder 2002; Anner and Evans 2004). Many Northern trade union federations maintain an international department ready to cooperate in solidarity campaigns with workers in the global South.

Peasant farmers have played a key role in movement against multinationals and in resisting policies that promote or perpetuate poverty. They have also been especially successful in developing an ideal form of transnational solidarity through horizontal networking and parallel campaigns in the global South. Their network, Vía Campesina, originated in 1992, is not included in this section, but is significant enough to mention in this introductory comment. Originally a regional network, Vía Campesina remains strongest in Latin America, although in 2004 it gained a number of new African and Asian affiliates, and its global office is now in Indonesia (Borras, Edelman and Kay 2008; Desmarais 2007). Prominent affiliates include the Brazilian Landless Rural Workers Movement (Movimento dos Trabalhadores Rurais Sem Terra – MST), which for more than 20 years has been involved in grassroots direct action, such as land occupations, despite sometimes lethal repression. Vía Campesina also has strong links with various national groups of the anti-globalisation network ATTAC. Through its high-profile participation in international protests, as well as through organising parallel events to official intergovernmental meetings, Vía Campesina has succeeded in creating a platform for its critique of the 'neoliberal' approach favoured by the World Bank – 'Market-Led Agrarian Reforms' – opposition to genetic modification and in general to the kind of agriculture implicit in the activities of multinational corporations such as McDonald's. On the positive side, Vía Campesina also promotes native medicinal and crop plant varieties. Similar to some human rights groups, it has an 'emergency action network' to mobilise rapid and global protests when peasants are threatened with violent repression.

11

WOMEN IN BLACK: THE STONY PATH TO 'SOLIDARITY'

Cynthia Cockburn[1]

Among the many manifestations of opposition to war worldwide, Women in Black is a curious phenomenon. The name is well known, yet it has no address. The network is made up of hundreds of local groups in scores of countries, mostly choosing street visibility. While some are long-lived, some fade away to be replaced by others elsewhere, so that WiB is difficult to locate, bound and quantify. There is, however, a joyous mutual recognition. Last week (as I write) six women turned up at our London vigil, tourists from Ohio, USA, and with hugs all round, simply picked up our placards and leaflets and said 'We've come to stand with you for an hour before our theatre date.' They had taken the trouble to dress in black.

Among the many features of the movement that lack clarity is precisely whether we might call it an instance of 'global solidarity' between women. In this chapter I shall describe what the network does, its organisation (slight as this is), and some of the not-too-explicit principles that may lie behind its various practices. Then I shall return to the question whether 'solidarity' is a word that applies here.

From Jerusalem to the world

The movement began in Israel in response to the outbreak of the Palestinian *intifada* of 1987. A small group of Israeli Jewish women in Jerusalem were the first to go on the streets to support Palestinians' call to 'End the Occupation now'. Judy Blanc told me, 'the first thought was – let's do a *black* vigil'. They had in mind something like the Argentinian Madres of the Plaza de Mayo, or the South African women's Black Sash movement. Within weeks there were ten, then twenty, and soon many more 'Women in Black' vigil groups standing at prominent crossroads around Israel each Friday lunchtime, holding placards opposing the state's policy. In the north of Israel, where the concentration of Israeli Arab communities is greatest, Palestinian and Jewish women were standing together. At first it felt very bold, women putting their bodies into a public space. They were seen by, and provoked reactions from, many passers-by on foot and in vehicles, some of whom heckled and abused them, both in sexualised terms ('whores') and for their politics ('traitors'). Their policy was not to shout back, but to maintain silence and dignity.

In 1988 a group of women peace activists from various Italian cities came to Israel and held a peace camp, aiming to build relationships with Palestinian and Israeli women. Among those they met were Women in Black, who greatly impressed them. Returning home, the Italian women started a widespread network using the same name, *Donne in Nero*. Simultaneously in the USA (mainly) Jewish women were organising Women in Black vigilling groups aiming to influence local American Jewish communities against the policies of the Zionist state.

Photograph 11.1 Women for Peace, one of Belgrade Women in Black's posters. (Žene u Crnom)

The year 1991 brought events that shifted the focus of Women in Black activism away from Israel and prompted the spread of the WiB idea and name much further afield. In the Gulf War, Yasser Arafat emphatically aligned the Palestine Liberation Organisation with Saddam Hussein, to the dismay of many Israeli peace activists. This, and the progress promised by the 'Oslo' peace accords of 1993, caused the number and strength of Israeli WiB vigils to fall off sharply, a decline from which they would not recover till prompted by the renewal of Palestinian struggle in the 'al-Aqsa intifada' of 2000.

It was also in 1991, however, that civil war broke out in Yugoslavia. Many Italian *Donne in Nero* groups turned their attention to this disaster in a neighbour country. A group of Italian women visited Belgrade that year and were inspired by feminist activists fiercely resisting the patriarchal trio of nationalism, militarism and the resurgent Orthodox Church. Some of these Belgrade women decided to adopt the Italian women's name, which translated into Serbo-Croat as *Žene u Crnom protiv Rata*. They started to hold high-profile vigils opposing the Milošević regime. Women from many other countries organised moral and practical support for *ŽuC* in their anti-nationalist activities. A strong connection was soon built between *ŽuC*'s Staša Zajović, who speaks Spanish, and women in Spain, where there were soon many groups calling themselves *Mujeres de Negro*. Some women came to the movement from a background in feminist organisations, some from Spain's strong Conscientious Objection Movement. Defining themselves by three principles – being feminists, against war, and nonviolent – *Mujeres de Negro* developed contacts with women opposing ethnic cleansing in Bosnia, Croatia and Serbia.

By now the Soviet system was disintegrating, and the nature of the post-Cold War period was becoming clearer. The promised 'peace dividend' was nowhere in evidence. The Gulf War following Saddam Hussein's invasion of Kuwait, and economic sanctions imposed by the UN, directed peace activists' attention to Iraq. The genocide in Rwanda happened soon after the worst episodes of ethnic cleansing in the Balkans, and when a peace agreement was signed that brought ceasefire to Bosnia, the threat of violence in Kosovo still remained. Many women troubled by these events changed their group names, as we did in London, from some derivative of 'women against war' to, specifically, 'Women in Black'.

Some WiB groups, like the Belgrade and Spanish women, added the tag 'against war' to their name. But some have not wanted to rule out other purposes, including campaigning against violence against women. For instance, when, in 1992, the WiB idea was taken up by women in India, they were responding to the violence of Hindu fundamentalists against the Muslim minority, in which significant numbers of women were being raped and murdered. WiB in the city of Bangalore started to stand once a week, protesting this 'war against women', and other groups followed. The same year WiB began in the Philippines. In support of Lila Pilipina, an organisation of former 'comfort women', they gathered in front of the Japanese Embassy in Manila, dressed in black, demanding compensation for the crime of sexual slavery by the Japanese Army in the Second World War.

It was the Women in Black of India and the Asian Women's Human Rights Council who organised a thousands-strong vigil of women in Huairou, near Beijing, on 4 September 1995 at the moment of the Fourth UN World Conference on Women. Edith Rubinstein, from Belgium, tells me she wrote in her diary that day:

> It was around 4.30 in the afternoon. Women from everywhere were arriving. They were coming from Argentina, Brazil, India, Kashmir, Australia, the USA, Yugoslavia, from everywhere. The small posters and the oral communication had worked! We stayed an hour in silence, with a candle. After, we left the entrance to the global pavilion where we'd been standing, and started to walk to the main gate of the town, singing 'We shall overcome'. It was very impressive.

This first mass WiB vigil was calling for 'a world safer for women' and an end to wars and armed conflicts. Participants from all over the world took the WIB message home with them.

In the late 1990s the world watched the bombardment by the USA and allies of Sudan and Afghanistan, and the aerial attack on Belgrade and other Serbian cities. And then came 11 September 2001. Alongside massive protests by mixed groups in all countries, Women in Black stood for 'justice not vengeance', appalled by President Bush's revenge attack on Afghanistan and the subsequent extension of the 'war on terror' to the invasion of Iraq in 2003. So in a span of 15 years, WiB became a worldwide phenomenon.

Diversity and autonomy

We often describe Women in Black as 'less an organisation than a formula for action'. The formula of the classic and simple vigil, women only, in black, in silence, has one great strength. It is easy to mount such an event, not too threatening for first-timers to join, and is occasional – something you can pick up and put down. This is one of the reasons it is impossible to quantify Women in Black. A rough count made in 2006 tallied 360 groups calling themselves WiB, but many groups of quite other names 'do' Women in Black from time to time.

On the other hand, there are many permanent and strong WiB groups, and while some are dedicated to silence and stillness, others prefer action and drama. In London, while some of our vigillers like to remain just that, others take WiB banners to join women in nonviolent blockading of the Aldermaston nuclear weapons factory and the Trident nuclear submarine base in Scotland. Some of us designed a special mobile protest against the UK's promotion of the products of its weapons industry. We used children's windmills and toy guns, to counter the obscene notion of the London arms trade 'fair' with our own 'the merry-go-round of death'.

The theme of these many groups varies too, from 'stop war', to 'stop violence against women', 'stop homophobia' and (particularly after 9/11) resistance to racism, xenophobia and curtailment of human rights. This variety of focus and form is possible because of WiB's structurelessness. It has come about, rather than been ordained, that all WiB's groups are autonomous, answerable only to themselves and the intangible spirit of WiB. Anyone may set up a local group without reference to any authority. Any group may have its own website.

So what exactly does 'Women in Black' signify? The only definitive formulation, if indeed it is one, is contained in a few descriptive paragraphs on the international website (www.womeninblack.org). They have been through several drafts, and the statement has, so far as I know, never been 'agreed', simply 'not disagreed'. Who wrote it and when is not clear. I recognise some of my own words in it – but when did I write them, I wonder now, and by what authority are they (still) there? I am sure others feel the same about the bits they have variously contributed over time. Thus one can read that

> Women in Black … is a world-wide network of women committed to peace with justice and actively opposed to injustice, war, militarism and other forms of violence. As women experiencing these things in different ways in different regions of the world, we support each other's movements. An important focus is challenging the militarist policies of our own governments.

We can see that WiB has a philosophy concerning the gendered nature of violence.

> It is evident for instance that we have a feminist understanding: that male violence against women in domestic life and in the community, in times of peace and in times of war, are interrelated. Violence is used as a means of controlling women. In some regions, men who share this analysis support and help WiB, and WiB are supporting men who refuse to fight. Women-only peace activism does not suggest that women, any more than men, are 'natural born peace-makers'. But women often inhabit different cultures from men, and are disproportionately involved in caring work. We know what justice and oppression mean, because we experience them as women. Most women have a different experience of war from that of most men. All women in war fear rape. Women are the majority of refugees. A feminist view sees masculine cultures as specially prone to violence, and so feminist women tend to have a particular perspective on security and something unique to say about war.

Another paragraph suggests WiB's reasons for organising separately from the mainstream, mixed, anti-war and pro-peace organisations:

Women's voices are often drowned out in mixed actions of men and women. When we act alone what women say is really heard. Sometimes even peace demonstrations get violent, and as women alone we can choose forms of action we feel comfortable with, nonviolent and expressive.

Apart from these slender pronouncements, Women in Black's perspective (the website states) may be 'deduced from participants' actions and words'.

Minimal structure

The network has no constitution, no manifesto, no offices nor office-holders, and no membership – only participation. In this it differs markedly from the better known, much more formal and much older international network, the Women's International League for Peace and Freedom (WILPF), with its national structures, international office and representation at the United Nations. WiB has the advantage of spontaneity and creativity. Having no institutional form and no money, it is not a tempting object for infiltration – we cannot be suspected of being a 'front' for other forces. On the other hand, we cannot offer women activists the resources WILPF is able to provide for so many of us, including its invaluable website (www.peacewomen.org).

The movement has held together through the efforts of certain groups to organise periodic international 'encounters'. At first, while the Yugoslav wars still raged, these were held annually in Serbia, organised by ŽuC, bringing together women from all parts of the war-torn region as well as further afield. Latterly the encounters have become biennial and have been held in Brussels, Jerusalem, Marina di Massa in Italy, and in 2007 in the Spanish city of Valencia. If there is a decision-making process at all in the network, it is in the motions passed in the plenary sessions of these assemblies of 300 or 400 women.

At one of these encounters it was decided to set up a central website, and later a 'wib communications group' was formed, briefed to establish e-mail listings to disseminate information in Spanish and English, to which more recently have been added Italian and French. A current project is improving the design and function of the website – for which, for the first time in WiB's life, it was agreed to seek grant aid. Face-to-face relationships in WiB, assured by the big encounters and a great deal of individual travel, have given women a direct sense of shared values. They have also been the source of the network's liveliness and loves – for there is a huge amount of affection and warmth in it. On the other hand, the internet has become essential to the network's democratisation, spreading information wider, faster, more accurately and with more precision. Electronic networking has thrown up significant roles. The several women who devote a lot of their free time to translating and forwarding mail around the internet have come to have special value to the rest of us. Their work involves responsibility.

Lieve Snellings, who coordinates the English language e-list and translates its content between English and Flemish, feels at times she is called on to make difficult decisions for the network. At first anyone applying would be included in the mailing list without question. When concern was expressed about this at an encounter, it was decided that the list managers such as Lieve should screen those asking for admission. Now those who fail to respond satisfactorily are excluded from the e-list. No doubt similar decisions will have to be made when the international website develops the capacity to enable local groups to spontaneously put up their own 'page'. The question will arise: who is WiB and who is not? Exclusion seems hard. But the WiB 'brand' has already proved open to misuse by groups with different and even diametrically opposed agendas. WiB women in dangerous situations in police states or conflict zones are emphatic that their safety depends on knowing who is listening and communicating. Yet Lieve and the other list managers feel uneasy about the gatekeeper role they have to perform, without sufficient guidance or clearly delegated authority.

Is this solidarity?

So is Women in Black an instance of 'global solidarity'? Solidarity is certainly invoked casually among us, and the network includes many instances of practical friendship and support offered by groups in one region to those in another. The Spanish WIB groups, for instance, have been tireless in support of women in Colombia and other Latin American countries. Some groups in the USA have been unstinting in their efforts on behalf of women suffering femicide in northern Mexico. Yet, taking the network as a whole, it seems to me that 'solidarity' is agreed or agreeable only in the more limited sense of empathy with women suffering the effects of injustice or war, and an implicit partnership among women opposing the militarist thinking and war-prone policies of their 'own' governments.

'Global solidarity', like 'global sisterhood', is an optimistic notion that too easily overlooks differences in the positionality of individuals and groups in relation to power. Solidarity can only be securely established on the basis of respectful listening to differences of experience, acknowledgement of inequalities and wrongs, and careful, caring and explicit negotiation of shared values. The limited communication arrangements of Women in Black simply do not allow such finesse. Consequently, knotty political problems arise from time to time. Erella Shadmi has written poignantly of the marginalisation experienced by Misrahi (Middle Eastern) and working-class Jewish women during the 1990s in the predominantly Ashkenazi (white, European) groups of Women in Black in Israel (Shadmi 2000). The structurelessness characteristic of Women in Black results in lack of a process for discussing and resolving such problems – and not in Israel alone.

There has been painful disagreement too over the inclusion in the biennial encounters of certain groups of women whose autonomy some doubted, believing them to be associated with male-led organisations associated with armed factions. Occasionally we fall foul of the troublesome belief that 'the enemy of my enemy is bound to be my friend'. Thus there were differences in the network, for instance, over a motion to call on our governments to recognise Hamas as elected government of the Palestinian territories. Yes, Hamas are quite evidently anathema to the Israeli state and the US government. Yes, they were properly elected and the refusal to recognise them is costing ordinary Palestinians dearly. But some women wondered, should we, *as a movement*, be formally endorsing a political organisation that deprives women of their human rights? Lesbians for instance (and many WiB groups gain greatly from lesbian perspectives and energies) might find their lives in danger under such a regime.

At the same time it may be safe to say that there is 'universal' support in Women in Black for instances of women on different 'sides' in conflict working together across the divide to achieve peace and re-establish trust. *Žene u Crnom* in Belgrade have been exemplary in their efforts to bring together women of Serb, Croatian and Muslim background to talk through the issues of responsibility and guilt (very different things) for the crimes committed in those wars. Women from Belgrade, of Serb and other backgrounds, have prompted and participated in acts of commemoration at Srebrenica on the anniversary of the notorious massacre on 10 July 1995, of Bosnian Muslims by the Bosnian Serb army with the support of the Milošević regime. The act of reconnection has, what is more, included women from the Bosnian Serb community at neighbouring Bratunac who likewise had lost many relatives – at the hands of Bosnian Muslims.

The fact that this kind of painstaking and emotionally perilous work is widely respected in the international network makes me feel it might be safe to say that Women in Black does embody an aspiration to global solidarity, and even to global sisterhood. But it does so, I believe, with a certain healthy scepticism. Most of us would be aware that solidarity and sisterhood, given humankind's capacity for mutual oppression and fragmentation, may prove forever out of reach. Certainly they should never be proclaimed naively or rhetorically. They can only be worked towards through a careful 'transversal politics' that is alert to difference, exclusions and inequalities.

Note

1. I am a participant in the local Women in Black group in London, UK. In the manner that seems appropriate in the WiB network, I first asked, in my own group, and in the network via the international multi-language e-mail lists, whether there would be any objection to my contributing the chapter requested for this book. Subsequently I sent the draft around these lists, and did my best to accommodate suggestions before submitting it for publication. The ideas expressed here, however, should be seen as no more than my personal understanding of Women in Black.

12

TRANSNATIONAL SOLIDARITY AND WAR RESISTANCE: THE CASE OF TURKEY

Andreas Speck

Conscientious objectors to military service are often going against the tide in their country, especially when it is involved in some kind of war or where the military is a particularly dominant and esteemed institution – both of which are the case with Turkey. This chapter shows how, beginning with contacts with anti-militarists in other countries, Turkish objectors have found support from more mainstream human rights organisations, international NGOs and even some intergovernmental organs in criticising the practices of the Turkish state – Ed.

The Turkish war resisters are not a mass movement, but at most a 'movement in the making'. Their history goes back to 1990, when a small campaign against conscription included a public declaration of conscientious objection (CO). This led to the prosecution of the first objectors on the basis of Article 155, 'alienating the people from the military'. My personal involvement began in 1995.

A brief history

A first association to promote CO – the Savaş Karşıtları Derneği (War Resisters' Association, SKD) – was founded in Izmir at the end of 1992, trying to give some organisational base to the network of individuals. This was soon followed by a public declaration by six objectors in Izmir. A major event was the International Conscientious Objectors' Meeting (ICOM), which took place in Ören, Turkey, 10–17 July 1993. This meeting connected the Turkish groups with international antimilitarists, and – even 15 years later – serves as a point of reference and inspiration.

With even very limited organisational efforts came state repression: On 8 November 1993 the governor of Izmir disbanded the recently formed association

Izmir SKD, and its members were charged under Article 155 (see above). In May 1994, Istanbul SKD – founded in autumn 1993 – was disbanded after a press conference, which led to the arrest of Turkish COs and three visiting supporters from Germany. But in the early stages no one was actually charged or arrested because of their CO – the authorities preferred other charges, especially Article 155, to intimidate the movement.

These events in Istanbul set the stage for the next development. One of the Turkish COs arrested for the Istanbul press conference was Osman Murat Ülke (Ossi). Although in August 1995 he was finally acquitted of charges under Article 155, the court ordered him to be transferred to the recruitment office, where in turn he was ordered to report to his military unit within three days. Instead of doing so, he burned his call-up papers in a press conference in Izmir on 1 September 1995, and publicly declared his objection (*Peace News*, October 1995). This led to his arrest 13 months later, and a series of trials for 'disobeying orders'. He was sentenced to prison repeatedly, released, sent back to his unit, arrested, sentenced, and so on. Finally, he was released on 9 March 1999, but officially required to report to his unit. Ever since he has led a semi-legal life.

The time of Ossi's imprisonment marked a high point in international support by the network of War Resisters' International (WRI) and other organisations, especially Amnesty International. But it also stretched the capacities of the activists within Turkey, who had to provide support to Ossi, and organise a national and international campaign. They requested (and then had to host) international delegations to trials, they needed funding for lawyers and their visits to the prison and the trials, and so on. While in the beginning Ossi's arrest and imprisonment energised groups within Turkey, and solidarity committees sprang up in several cities, this was short-lived. After some months all the work fell on the old core of activists – a pattern that was repeated ten years later on the arrest of Mehmet Tarhan.

After Ossi's release, the movement went through a quiet phase. The Izmir activists – working informally, after their second association had also been banned following Ossi's arrest – were exhausted, and also shifted their focus, especially to nonviolence training.[1] Ossi himself decided that he did not want to risk arrest, and kept a low profile, which meant that the movement had lost its public face. At the same time, after his release the group discussed the gender dynamics of a male resister in prison requiring support, leading to the founding of an anti-militarist feminist collective in ISKD and a shift of focus away from CO and more towards nonviolence training.

Grassroots activities on CO and anti-militarism subsequently were mainly initiated by the Istanbul Anti-militarist Initiative (IAMI), a more loosely organised group. While there were a number of publicly declared COs, neither they nor the Turkish authorities seem to have been keen on a confrontation – no CO was arrested for a while.[2]

Activities increased from 2000 on, with new energy and new public declarations of CO. From 2004 on, the groups in Turkey have organised a Militourism Festival on or around 15 May (International CO Day), which offers some focus of activities for CO. However, it took the arrest of Mehmet Tarhan on 8 April 2005, and his subsequent trials, to spur a new wave of activism and international

Photograph 12.1 'Mehmet loves peace' – demonstration supporting Turkish conscientious objector Mehmet Tarhan. (Archives of War Resisters' International)

solidarity. Again, groups such as WRI and Amnesty International issued alerts, and raised public awareness abroad. Within Turkey, new activists joined solidarity committees for Mehmet Tarhan in several cities. The fact that Mehmet Tarhan is gay also broadened the audience, and led to LGBT groups joining solidarity actions for him.[3]

On 9 March 2006, Mehmet was released from prison, and now is in a situation similar to Ossi – being ordered to report to his unit, and therefore living a semi-legal life (*Peace News*, April 2006). His release followed two important legal victories: on 24 January 2006, the European Court of Human Rights in Strasbourg finally ruled in favour of Osman Murat Ülke, and in March, a second judgment of the European Court of Human Rights ruled in favour of members of the ISKD. In May 2008 the UN Working Group on Arbitrary Detention ruled that the repeated detentions of CO Halil Savda – at the time serving a fourth period of detention – violated Articles 9 and 18 of both the Universal Declaration of Human Rights and the International Covenant on Civil and Political Rights.

International support for the Turkish war resisters' movement

International support has been crucial for Turkish war resisters, but at times the situation has not been easy. In addition, the political focus of the groups providing support might have been different from the focus of the groups in Turkey, a situation that from time to time led to tensions.

Besides Amnesty International, which does not provide direct support to CO groups, but campaigns for release when COs are imprisoned – especially in the cases of Osman Murat Ülke and Mehmet Tarhan – international support was mainly provided by the following groups:

War Resisters' International (London office); focusing on CO, from Germany Connection eV and DFG-VK Hessen (Deutsche Friedensgesellschaft-Vereinigte KriegsdienstgegnerInnen, German Peace Society – United War Resisters); from the Netherlands, Stop de Oorlog (SOT); and from Spain, MOC (the CO Movement and the group Objeción Fiscal (war tax resistance)); and focusing mainly on nonviolence training, DFG-VK Nordrhein-Westfalen and Bewegungsstiftung (both Germany).

International support fell mainly into the following categories:

Emergency campaigning, including delegations and speaking tours

International campaigning for Turkish war resisters was often linked to state repression, including sending international delegations to trials. These delegations mainly served as a signal to the Turkish authorities and public that there is international support for the Turkish war resisters, and also tried to generate public awareness 'back home'.

Speaking tours abroad by Turkish activists played a similar role. In 1995, Ossi toured several European countries (Spain, France, Netherlands, Germany, Austria), laying the groundwork for later solidarity campaigns.

Movement-building support within Turkey

This is a broad category, and includes financial assistance to Turkish groups, as well as cooperation in organising seminars or events, mainly or partly serving the Turkish movement. This includes several trainings (nonviolence training, Movement Action Plan training – Patchwork 1988[4]), seminars (the WRI seminar and council meeting took place in Turkey in September 2001), and also long-term stays of foreign activists in Turkey, to work for and with the Turkish groups.[5]

Several problems can be associated with this kind of support:

- choosing to support one group and not another one can create tensions among Turkish groups;
- the criteria concerning who receives support might depend more on the agenda of the foreign supporter than on the Turkish situation;
- support can more easily be given to more formally organised groups than to more loosely organised initiatives. Thus, the Izmir SKD was the main recipient of foreign financial support, and as a result has been much better connected internationally;
- external support – financially or sending activists – can also create an artificial structure, which is not really sustained by support from within the country. The presence of foreign activists in Izmir probably prolonged the life of Izmir SKD;
- seminars or training sessions – even when co-organised with a Turkish group – were often based on the agenda of the foreign partner.

Building a link between groups in Turkey and the Turkish diaspora abroad

Connection eV in Germany and SOT in the Netherlands are heavily involved in working with groups of the Turkish diaspora, which became a source of tension and disagreement between groups in Turkey and international supporters. One of the main activities abroad is to promote public declarations of CO by Turkish citizens abroad (in fact most of these are people of Kurdish origin at different stages of their asylum application). Problems arise because making a CO declaration can be seen as strengthening an application for asylum, whereas groups inside Turkey fear that such declarations will not stand if the asylum application fails and the person is deported back to Turkey. Indeed, several rejected asylum seekers have returned and performed their military service.

An additional problem is that only very few Turkish diaspora activists do anything beyond their public declaration of CO.

Lobbying international institutions and legal support

The lobbying of international institutions – especially the Council of Europe and the different institutions of the European Union – has become more important following the decisions of the European Union to formally open membership talks with Turkey. It has been possible to build relationships with some members of the European Parliament, who supported Mehmet Tarhan while he was in prison and raised the issue with the European Commission. The European Parliament Peace Initiatives Intergroup organised a hearing on CO in Turkey in 2006.

International support helped bring the case of Osman Murat Ülke to the European Court of Human Rights (ECHR) in Strasbourg. While Turkish lawyers played an important role in preparing the case, it would have been much harder to bring it to the court without the cooperation of Kevin Boyle from the University of Essex.

Clarity of goals and differences: international/national

With the judgment of the ECHR the movement in Turkey enters a new phase. There is now pressure on Turkey to regulate the issue of CO according to the standards agreed in the European Union. This means basically a system of conscription with substitute 'civilian service' for COs. Groups that lobby for CO rights in the framework of human rights generally accept this, which can be a source of friction with anti-militarist movements of COs, such as the existing groups in Turkey. They define themselves as 'total objectors', meaning that they do not want a substitute service. However, they do want to legalise their situation and at the moment lack clarity collectively about how they would respond to a system requiring COs to do substitute service.

This can potentially be dangerous, because international groups have already started to act. For instance, the European Bureau for Conscientious Objection – a body that in its 20-year history has sometimes had a not unproblematic relationship with grassroots groups and especially total resisters – is lobbying European institutions to insist on European standards, which favour a substitute service. New actors might get involved – such as Turkish human rights groups or international human rights lobbyists – who simply follow the standard human rights approach without heeding the critique of anti-militarist objectors.

A conference held at Istanbul University in January 2007 and co-organised by the Istanbul branch of the Human Rights Association, Human Rights Watch, Amnesty International Turkey, EBCO, WRI and others highlighted some of these problems. While it was important in underlining the need for the recognition of CO in Turkey, it was mainly organised without the participation of the remaining CO activists in Turkey (with some exceptions), and did not manage to provide a stimulus for

Turkish CO groups. However, it did put the issue on the agenda of Turkish human rights organisations and – to some extent – progressive academia.[6],

Conclusions

The Turkish war resisters movement has come a long way since 1990. Achieving the recognition of the right to CO (as conventionally understood in a human rights framework) was never its main objective. International support was often crucial for the movement, especially in cases of imprisonment of activists, but also beyond, in providing inspiration, moral and practical support.

As a result of the combination of local, national and international efforts, but also of the wider political developments (such as EU membership talks), Turkey is now at a crucial point regarding the right to CO, which leaves the movement unprepared. In this crucial situation, despite the urgency to exploit the present 'window of opportunity', international supporters need to act with sensitivity to the needs and the state of discussion among Turkish groups if the generally positive cooperation is to continue.

Notes

1. In April 1996, a first nonviolent action training programme was held in Foca, near Izmir. This led to increased interest in nonviolence training. Some participants from Izmir became nonviolence trainers, building a core group of trainers within Turkey (*Probleme des Friedens*, 3/1997).
2. The brief arrests of COs Halil Savda in 2004 and Mehmet Bal in 2002 did not re-energise the movement. Both COs represented difficult cases, and were unable to provide identification for the CO movement.
3. The fact that Mehmet Tarhan is gay was a major factor in the involvement of Amnesty International (AI), which – having avoided gay issues until 1991 – now gives them higher priority than CO.
4. The Movement Action Plan, originated by the late Bill Moyer, offers a framework for organising and building social movements (Moyer et al. 2001).
5. In 1998, a German–Turkish activist worked with Izmir SKD as part of a programme of the German Shalom Diakonat. In 2000–01, two German activists organised their own stay in Izmir for 12 and 18 months, to work with the Izmir SKD.
6. The book of the conference is Özgür Heval Çinar and Coşkun Üsterci, eds., *Conscientious Objection: Resisting Militarized Society* (London: Zed Books, forthcoming, 2009).

13

SOLIDARITY BASED ON SEXUAL ORIENTATION: REGIONAL ORGANISING IN AFRICA

Chesterfield Samba

Same-gender sex acts are illegal in most countries of Africa, and several leaders of African governments have referred to homosexuality as a perversion imported from the West (see survey in Anyamele, Lwabaayi, Tuu-Van, and Binswanger 2005). President Robert Mugabe of Zimbabwe is the most prominent, although perhaps the most extreme is President Yahya Jammeh of Gambia who, in May 2008, called on homosexuals to leave the country or face beheading.

These are the headline items. Yet step by step a regional cooperation addressing issues of daily survival and basic rights is growing. The All-Africa symposium on HIV/AIDS and Human Rights in Johannesburg, February 2004, was a landmark for cooperation in Africa between Lesbian, Gay, Bisexual and Transsexual (LBGT) groups.[1] The eight-day symposium had 55 participants from 22 LGBT groups in 17 African countries and set up the most solid structures yet for LGBT organising in Africa.

The evolution of such cooperation has been fraught with problems – most obviously strong social disapproval. Even in the country with the world's most progressive constitution on sexual rights, South Africa, events still happen such as the February 2006 mob murder of Zoliswa Nikonya for being a lesbian. There are other problems, too: the demands of simply coping with poverty or the spread of HIV/AIDS; the striking differences between the social, cultural and economic contexts around Africa; the need for African forms of self-definition instead of uncritically adopting Western terms and in general the patterns of relationships with the West.

Dependence on the West

From many African countries, it is easier and cheaper to travel to Europe or the USA than to other parts of Africa. LGBT groups tend to look to the West for funding and support, often 'playing the victim' to attract resources. Some individuals have even established spurious organisations to obtain Western funding, while many people seeking asylum in the West – for understandable reasons – make exaggerated claims and so feed the myth that it is impossible to be gay or lesbian and live in Africa.

The evolving situation can be illustrated from the history of Gays and Lesbians of Zimbabwe (GALZ). This group was founded in 1990 and soon affiliated to the International Lesbian and Gay Association (ILGA) at a time when Amnesty International was about to extend its mandate to include gay rights (1991), before post-apartheid South Africa became the first country with a constitution supporting gay rights (1996), and before the major international funders of HIV/AIDS-related work decided to fund LGBT groups in Africa.

Western support was, of course, welcome, but carried the problem of reinforcing the attitude that homosexuality is a Western import, and sometimes was based on Western assumptions. For instance, in 1994, a US gay rights campaigner, William Courson, unilaterally filed a complaint to the African Commission for Human and People's Rights against Zimbabwe's discrimination against homosexuals. Ultimately GALZ convinced him to withdraw this, fearing that an unfavourable interpretation of the Africa Charter would worsen the situation. A more welcome form of solidarity – although also unilateral – came in 1999 when the British gay rights group Outrage! carried out a citizens' arrest of Robert Mugabe when he was on a private visit to London. Following this GALZ received many letters of support from Zimbabweans and appreciated its raised profile. At the same time GALZ requested that any group planning any similar stunt in future should inform them so that they could prepare the community for any potential backlash.

What became increasingly clear – to GALZ and to groups elsewhere in Africa – was that the transnational solidarity that would matter most would be cooperation with other groups in Africa.

The evolution of African LGBT cooperation

Although in 1992 the International Lesbian and Gay Association (ILGA) adopted a regional structure, the African region could not yet establish sustainable regional structures. Then the 1999 ILGA World Conference in South Africa offered a real opportunity. For the first time the African region was well represented. Zimbabwe sent 15 delegates, many South African groups were present, and there were delegations from numerous other African countries. The conference was hosted by the National Coalition for Gay and Lesbian Equality (now called the Lesbian and Gay Equality Project) and agreed to sponsor a desk to build up the African region and elected a prominent South African activist as co-secretary general of ILGA. But within months she left to take a job in Latin America and the office closed.

At the next ILGA conference (Italy 2000), Africa was again seriously underrepresented. At the 2001 conference in the USA, despite efforts to sponsor Africans, only South Africa, Uganda and Zimbabwe were represented. As these delegates decided they could not speak for the whole continent, no resolutions relating to Africa were presented. Furthermore, the two Africans voted on to the ILGA board as regional representatives sought asylum in the USA, one immediately after the conference and the other a year later.

Despite such discouraging experiences, the situation was ripening for the creation of the All-Africa Rights Initiative (AARI) at the level of organisational development within Africa and at the level of international funding. The urgent need for African coordination was highlighted by the crackdown on men who have sex with men (MSM) in Egypt in 2001. After arresting 50 men at a disco on a boat on the Nile, the Egyptian government launched a vilification campaign in state media and used informants to trap men using the internet into sending incriminating messages. As a result many more were arrested and tortured. Campaigns by groups such as Human Rights Watch and Amnesty International succeeded in getting the men released or retried, but there was no African regional response. In December 2001, a workshop in South Africa for African LGBT groups drafted a protest declaration but only those from South Africa, Namibia and Zimbabwe were willing to sign, and so it was abandoned. However, groups such as GALZ in Zimbabwe, the South Africa-based website Behind the Mask (http://www.mask.org.za) and later the Coalition of African Lesbians (CAL – initially called the African Lesbian Association) were ready to assume more responsibility in promoting regional coordination.

In 2000 GALZ was approached by HIVOS (the Dutch Humanist Institute for Development Cooperation). HIVOS views AIDS as a human rights issue linked to structural poverty and believes that strengthening LGBT groups is essential to combat HIV among people who engage in same-sex activity, whatever their sexual identity. Seeing GALZ as a useful example of LGBT organising in a hostile climate, HIVOS asked us to help train LGBT organisations it was supporting in East Africa, specifically Kenya, Uganda and Tanzania. The outcome was a seven-day training course in October 2000 in Zimbabwe.

Most of the East African groups had registered with their governments as AIDS service organisations. They focused on safe sex and general HIV/AIDS intervention for men and women, as well as seeking to address issues of poverty and access to resources. Instead of using the Western terms 'gay' and 'lesbian', or the terms for same sex-activity that exist in their own languages (terms that are usually offensive), they tend to use 'MSM' for men who have sex with men, and 'WSW' for women.

GALZ in its own work was keen to reach outside Harare and, in 2001 – inspired by the South India AIDS Programme – launched a national Affinity

Group programme, using the platform of HIV and AIDS to help groups organise around their sexuality and be self-reliant. This led in 2003 to GALZ drawing up two LGBT training manuals for Africa – one on mobilising in a hostile climate, the other on organisational development. These were to be followed up with a series of pan-African meetings to discuss training for newly formed groups and possible revision of the manuals. Initial plans were made to hold a first (English-speaking) All-Africa conference in Tanzania, and a Ugandan coordinator – Ronald Lwabaayi – appointed to organise it, but this was abandoned when the Tanzanian press began to whip up anti-gay feeling.

However, the website Behind the Mask was in a perfect position, with help from Ronald Lwabaayi, to host the All-Africa Symposium. Founded in 2000, Behind the Mask publishes news from throughout the continent and has built up a network of contacts – either groups or individuals – in 36 countries. E-mail and the internet have been vital tools for LGBT activism in Africa since the early 1990s, especially where independent media are weak or as prejudiced as the state media, and by 2004 it was possible to issue virtually all the invitations via e-mail.

The conference was well supported by international funders. In addition to HIVOS' continuing commitment, the World Bank and UNAIDS were now convinced that funds had to be channelled directly to LGBT groups, as homophobic attitudes meant that grants to governments were not being used effectively.[2]

In parallel, in 2003 there was good African representation at the 'Sex and Secrecy' conference organised in South Africa by the International Association for the Study of Sexuality, Culture and Society. The African lesbians present decided to form a separate association to ensure the visibility of lesbian and bisexual women within the broader (male-dominated) movement of LGBT groups in Africa. This became the Coalition of African Lesbians (CAL).

The 2004 symposium and aftermath

The All-Africa Symposium in February 2004 resulted in widespread agreement and organisational plans for the future. The participants formed Southern, East and West African regional 'alliances', each drawing up priorities for the next year. A strong steering committee was appointed to organise a second conference, to be held in West Africa, and with a special effort to draw in French- and Portuguese-speaking countries.

One theme was making a joint approach to the African Commission on Human and People's Rights, which would have much greater impact than isolated complaints from countries in South Africa and indicate to the African Union that there is a critical mass of oppressed people. With the support of the US-based International Gay and Lesbian Human Rights Commission (IGLHRC), strategy sessions and training were organised for activists from around Africa to decide which mechanisms of the African Charter might be most useful, and to see how to develop relationships with other human rights defenders who regularly attend the commission's sessions – both official, such as commissioners and special rapporteurs, and unofficial, such as the NGOs from different parts of Africa. As a result, in May 2006 a statement was issued at the NGO Forum of the African Commission about the detention of Cameroonian men and women on charges of homosexuality (full text at http://www.mask.org.za/article.php?cat=HumanR ightsMonitor&id=1059).

Originally, it was HIVOS' intention to continue to support the development of All-Africa Rights Initiative (AARI). It supported the meeting of Southern African partners in Johannesburg towards the end of the year to finalise the constitution and draft a proposal for consideration by HIVOS. Mention was also made of plans to hold a second all-Africa conference in Senegal in order to include Francophone Africa. However, changes in HIVOS staff and leadership problems in AARI eventually led to HIVOS rejecting the proposal in preference for working directly with groups in their home countries, in particular East Africa. Their fear was that AARI had the potential of turning into a super-NGO with a top-heavy administration that devoured resources but achieved little impact.

Nevertheless, although overtaken by events, AARI achieved a great deal. It brought together 22 groups representing 17 Anglophone countries, and many of these have stayed in contact. ILGA has made a concerted effort to support the presence of African representatives at its world conferences, as was clearly visible in Geneva in 2006. IGLHRC has since set up an office in South Africa and continues to coordinate important regional initiatives such as an African LGBT presence at the African Commission. It assists with developing strategies towards encouraging the incorporation of MSM and WSW in HIV and AIDS intervention work on the continent, and is helping with the development of frameworks to challenge homophobic legislation.

HIVOS' approach has also been vindicated. The inter-group fighting in Uganda has dissipated and a coalition, Sexual Minorities of Uganda (SMUG), has emerged as a strong and vibrant force, which successfully challenges the harassment of LGBT people by law-enforcement agents by appealing to the courts.

Conclusion

Much of the African LGBT discourse is centred on the hopeless situation facing LGBT people rather than highlighting any achievements or progress. Certainly some discussions in Africa are only in their infancy: around the right to choose one's sexual identity, the right to all safe and consensual sexual activity with other adults, and the right to bear children. Yet there is a growing confidence that through regional organising in Africa, backed by enlightened funders and access to the resources and expertise international defenders of LGBT rights, we can work for a different Africa. In the words of an African declaration to the 2006 ILGA World Conference:

> an Africa where colonial prejudices have disappeared along with colonial power ... an Africa where no one's health is held hostage to either money or morals ... an Africa where no one faces violence or abuse because of their gender identity or sexual orientation. (Full text online at http://www.ilga.org)

Notes

1. The conference considered adding an 'I' for Intersex to the LGBT acronym, but as nobody identifying as Intersex attended, this was left inconclusive.
2. In view of the critical references to the World Bank elsewhere in this book, tribute should be paid to the influence of an openly gay and openly HIV-positive senior advisor, Hans Binswanger, now retired.

14

DIASPORAS: POTENTIAL PARTNERS IN STRUGGLE

Andrew Rigby

The term 'diaspora' is commonly used to refer to members of a particular community, people or population group that are dispersed around the globe, geographically separated from their homeland. Diasporas can be divided into those created by forced migration and those arising out of voluntary migration (Cheran 2004: 4), but most migrants probably leave their homeland out of a combination of 'push' and 'pull' factors.

Why migrants leave may influence their political identity and how they perceive conflicts back home. For example, a group forced to leave by social divisions and violent conflict may carry these divisions with them into the diaspora; an extreme example is provided by the 1,300 Rwandans in the Netherlands in 2004, divided into 13 organisations representing diverse interests (Mohamoud 2007: 30). In contrast, economic migrants might retain a vision of their society prior to fragmentation. For example, the communities of Greek and Turkish Cypriots in London, whose businesses exist side by side, both want – despite differences of language and religion – to see the island of their origins reunified (Zunzer 2004: 31).

Diasporas are not homogeneous. Members may be divided not only by the caste or class, tribe or ethnicity, but residence in the host country creates divisions of language, culture and outlook between generations. As a result while the first generation may remain deeply involved in the politics of the country they left, the second generation may have little interest in such conflicts – as in the case of the Somali diaspora (Zunzer 2004: 33). In addition, members of the same broad diaspora groups can manifest contrasting political preferences and orientations. British Jews, for example, vary widely in their political reactions to the conflict between Israel and the Palestinians.

The willingness of members of a diaspora to engage with conflicts back home may also be influenced by the differing rights of citizenship and degrees of personal security in their host countries. Because Tamil migrants in Canada have citizenship rights not enjoyed by fellow Tamils in France, those in Canada tend to be more vocal and active in relation to the Sri Lankan conflicts than Tamils in France.

The actual and potential roles of members of diasporas in relation to conflicts and resistance movements in their home countries depend critically on communications. As a result of the twin 'revolutions' of cheaper long-distance travel and the burgeoning growth of the internet and other forms of electronic communication, contemporary members of diasporas can remain much more closely in touch with developments 'at home' than previous generations, and thereby play a more significant part than ever before in the struggles within their homeland. One example is the *Electronic Intifada* founded in 2001 to send out regular news items and reports from Palestine on the internet.

Main channels of diaspora engagement with homeland struggles

The rest of this chapter explores the four main ways in which members of diaspora communities can support resistance movements with which they identify:

- financial remittances and community development aid;
- providing political and strategic input to the resistance movement;
- preserving and promoting forms of cultural resistance;
- advocacy work in host countries.

Financial remittances and community development aid

Perhaps the most common manner in which diaspora members support struggles in their homeland is through the remittances sent home to support family, relatives and friends. Worldwide, the flow of remittances exceeds US$100 billion a year (Koppall at al. 2003: 59). In my research on the Palestinian *intifada* of 1987–91 I found that most Palestinian families were dependent to some degree upon the financial support of one or more family members living and working outside Palestine, very often in one of the Gulf states. Without this support Palestinians would not have been able to sustain their struggle for as long as they did. The stemming of the financial flow in 1991, after the Iraqi invasion of Kuwait, intensified the level of economic suffering in the West Bank and Gaza Strip and, along with a number of other factors, helped explain the decline in the commitment to unarmed resistance against the Israeli occupation (Rigby 1991: 16–17).

Apart from the financial aid from individuals to their own family networks, there is another category of financial aid provided by diaspora communities in support of resistance movements at home – the payment of unofficial taxes, tithes or contributions to organisations that use the funds to support the struggle, whether it be an armed or an unarmed movement. Just as Irish-Americans made donations to NORAID that were used to support the Republican movement in all its guises in Northern Ireland, so the Tamil Tigers (LTTE) have a number of 'front' organisations throughout the world that collect money, with some estimates putting the amount raised as equivalent to $100 per head of the worldwide Tamil diaspora (Cheran 2004: 10).

Agencies and individuals among diaspora communities also raise funds for relief, reconstruction and development projects for their people back home. The building of hospitals, schools and community centres, along with investment in local economic enterprises, can help provide the means to satisfy basic needs, which is a fundamental prerequisite of any sustained struggle, whether it be armed or unarmed. Moreover, to the extent that diaspora investment and aid can help people provide for their basic needs, it strengthens their steadfastness and their capacity to impose various forms of nonviolent sanctions involving types of social and economic boycott.

Providing political and strategic input to the resistance movement

Developments in communication technology, noted above, have enabled diaspora groups with access to new ideas and expertise to feed these into the resistance movement. One simple example is the manner in which certain diaspora groups have coordinated the translation of key texts on nonviolent resistance and made these available to compatriots active in the resistance. Gene Sharp's booklet *From Dictatorship to Democracy* (first published 1993) has now been published in over 30 languages, and Palestinians from the diaspora facilitated the translation of a number of Sharp's texts during the first *intifada*.

Members of the diaspora are also in a good position to transmit new ideas and practices that can enhance the political impact of the resistance movement and increase its legitimacy in the eyes of significant publics and decision-making circles throughout the international community. One example comes from the struggle of the Sahrawi people to end the Moroccan occupation of Western Sahara. According to Maria Stephan and Jacob Mundy:

> The local Sahrawi resistance is being supported by a strong transnational component led by members of the Sahrawi diaspora who are in daily communication with their compatriots using interactive internet chat rooms. This internet communication has helped promote unity, nonviolent discipline, and strategic coordination in the Sahrawi movement. (2006: 2)

Members of the diaspora with particular skills and expertise can also act in various types of consultancy and advisory roles on behalf of resistance movements. It was expatriates who drafted the documents that formed the basis for the peace dialogue between different Somali groups in Nairobi during 2003–04, and it was members of the Eritrean diaspora who helped draft the constitution after the 1993 separation from Ethiopia (Mohamoud 2007: 32–3).

Of course, tensions can arise between political leaders based in the diaspora and those remaining in the country of origin. During the Kosovo Albanian nonviolent resistance after 1990, the 'prime-minister-in-exile' Bujar Bukoshi was publicly critical of his colleague, 'president' Ibrahim Rugova Living in Prishtina (Clark 2000: 118). Moreover, there is always the possibility that advocates of nonviolent resistance in the diaspora can grow out of touch with the 'realities' experienced by those living in the midst of the struggle. Thus, someone from the Palestinian diaspora suggested, at a conference on nonviolent resistance held in Bethlehem in January 2006, that his compatriots burn down and destroy their refugee camps as a way of increasing the moral and political pressure on Israel to negotiate a peace agreement. Coming from someone living a comfortable middle-class lifestyle outside of occupied Palestine, this proposal was not well received (personal communication from Jørgen Johansen who was at the conference).

If diaspora groups can help strengthen the unity and coherence of a resistance movement, they can also foment divisions and factionalism, supporting local warlords rather than promoting nonviolent modes of struggle. Mohamed Guled, a Somali living in the Netherlands, reports:

> There are individuals among the Somali diaspora in the Netherlands who travel regularly to Somalia and Kenya carrying sometimes more than 10,000 Euros in cash which they give to the militia and faction leaders in order to buy favour. ... The financial support from the individuals and groups in the diaspora perpetuates the dominance of warlords, faction leaders and rebel groups in the political theatre and prevents the emergence of an alternative nonviolent civilian leadership in the homeland. (Mohamoud 2007: 28–9)

By contrast some diaspora groups can eschew partisan positions and work to promote some form of peace settlement. An example is the work of the Acholi community from Northern Uganda concentrated in London. They have been active in creating opportunity for conflict parties and interested intermediaries to engage in dialogue, for example by convening a meeting in London between representatives of civil society, the Ugandan government and the Lord's Resistance Army in 1997. Unfortunately the violence continued, despite their best efforts (Poblicks 2002: 62).

Preserving and promoting cultures of resistance

An important function of diaspora communities in relation to any type of resistance movement in their home country (armed or unarmed) is the preservation and celebration of cultural heritage. Perhaps the best example of this is the Dalai Lama who, along with his community of Tibetan exiles in Dharamsala in Northern India and elsewhere around the world, has succeeded in maintaining and promoting the religious rituals and cultural practices of traditional Tibet. This form of cultural resistance remains a counter to what some would term the 'cultural genocide' practised by China over past decades. It is also through the promotion of Tibetan Buddhist philosophy and rituals that the Tibetan exile movement seeks to raise awareness regarding the fate of their homeland. As Samdhonh Rinpoche, a key adviser to the Dalai Lama, explained:

> The Tibetan culture has spread in the West during the last 30 years in a very big way and that is a source of strength for us. Now we believe that Tibetan culture may not completely disappear from the surface of the earth very easily even if Tibet does not get autonomy in the near future. (McNair 2002: 6)

Diaspora groups can play a slightly different 'cultural' role by constituting an audience for artists from their home country and thereby enabling them and their work to appear in public. Invariably there is an overt political dimension to such events, seeking to influence wider publics by, for instance, showing Palestinian films, Kosovan drama troupes or Burmese crafts. An article 'Beyond protest rallies, what next for the diaspora?' (13 July 2005) urged Ethiopians abroad to organise 'socio-cultural events on a regular basis throughout the world to raise funds, to introduce the rich culture and tradition of Ethiopia to the international community and at the same time highlight the plight of the Ethiopian people under dictatorship and poverty' (www.ethiomedia.com/newpress). But beyond the particular political message of such events, there is the celebration of a culture that embodies and symbolises the traditions and the values that in some way might 'define' a people and the legitimacy of their struggle, and indicates that these traditions will endure.

Advocacy work in host countries

One of the key elements of any unarmed resistance strategy is to strengthen the movement's support base, while undermining the pillars upon which their opponent relies. This is an area in which diaspora groups can play a significant role, particularly with regard to raising the profile of the struggle in the international arena, highlighting its justness by comparison with the illegitimacy of the opponent's stance. To do this diaspora groups, like any other interest group, can pursue whatever advocacy activities are available within their host societies. In certain cases protest may extend to civil disobedience, for example, during visits by controversial political figures, by those migrants possessing full rights of citizenship in their societies of settlement.

There are three target groups for such advocacy work – the diaspora community itself, wider public opinion, and key decision-making circles in the society of settlement and beyond. Targeting the diaspora community is generally aimed at mobilising them in solidarity with the resistance movement. Wider publics are targeted with a view to raising awareness and thereby eliciting sympathy and support. The hope is to put pressure on politicians and others so that they will use their influence to work for a satisfactory outcome to the conflict. However, the available evidence seems to indicate that attempts to exert direct influence on politicians through mobilisation at elections is only effective in special circumstances. There are, for example, a couple of constituencies in Toronto where the proportion of Tamils in the electorate is sufficiently high to ensure the return of candidates who proclaim their concern about the plight of the Tamils. Likewise, in those constituencies in north London where there is a high proportion of members of the Cypriot diaspora, successful candidates tend to take a special interest in peace efforts to reunite the island (Cheran 2004: 10–11; Zunzer 2004: 32).

Diaspora groups often establish research and information agencies to produce policy documents and educational materials, and monitor developments in their homeland, in order to influence public opinion. Methods of campaigning can include the holding of memorial events, adoption of 'prisoners of conscience', organising conferences, issuing press statements and various forms of printed and electronic publications.

All such activities and initiatives have a broader purpose than advocacy. The holding of a cultural event to commemorate a particularly significant date in the history of the struggle can be seen as significant as a means of raising awareness among the diaspora community and wider publics, but they can also be important fund-raising events as well as a celebration of the symbols of resistance. Nadia Hijab has identified ways in which Palestinian institutions in the diaspora can link relief and rehabilitation with solidarity and advocacy. They can:

a)   Enable Palestinians to tell their own story and allow the international community to hear it first hand, so contributing to the growth of an international movement for Palestinian human rights;
b)   Provide protection for Palestinian resources and investments by mobilizing diaspora communities to help a school or provide free passage for goods and services;
c)   Increase the sources of assistance reaching the Palestinians to enable them to survive and endure until independence is achieved. (Hijab 2004: 7)

In the case of anti-corporate struggles, diaspora groups have achieved some successes. Alcan't in India – a group founded in Montreal in 2003 by expatriate Indians – mounted an effective campaign against Alcan's involvement in a bauxite mining project in Kashipur, Orissa, that would displace indigenous people. Together with the Polaris Institute, they produced a well-documented corporate profile of Alcan (http://www.alcantinindia.org/alcan%20profile.pdf). Alcan't's interventions in shareholders' meetings were not only well publicised, but in 2006 they succeeded in persuading more than a third of those voting to support a proposal for an impact assessment on the Kashipur project. In April 2007, Alcan ended its involvement in the Kashipur project by selling its 45 per cent share in Utkal Aluminia (www.minesandcommunities.org).

Conclusion

People are moved by stories, and enabling those engaged in unarmed resistance to tell their stories to others is a powerful resource for any movement. One of the strengths possessed by diaspora groups, when it comes to supporting movements for change in their countries of origin, is that they can tell their own stories, thereby personalising the grander narrative in a manner that can have the capacity to touch and to mobilise others.

Without blinding ourselves to the fact that diasporas can be as divided as their societies of origin, with further divisions superimposed from their societies of settlement, and that they can consequently foment divisions within resistance movements struggling for change, it should be clear that they also have tremendous assets and resources to be utilised in support of such movements. Those seeking to promote unarmed resistance movements as a means of transforming oppressive and violent circumstances should factor into their strategising the various diaspora communities around the world, not as external third parties but as potential partners in struggle.

15

GLOBAL MOVEMENTS AND LOCAL STRUGGLES: THE CASE OF WORLD SOCIAL FORUM

Stellan Vinthagen

The World Social Forum (WSF), which held its inaugural meeting at Porte Alegre, Brazil, in 2001, seeks to promote cooperation and coordination between the numerous and diverse groups campaigning to promote social justice and save the environment by resisting neoliberal economic policies and the power of multinational corporations. Through the 'IMF-riots' against Structural Adjustment Programmes in African and Asian countries in the 1980s and a succession of mobilisations in the 1990s – the Ogoni people's campaign against Shell Oil in the Niger Delta; movements of the landless such as Movimento sem Terra (MST) in Brazil; campaigns against mega-industrial projects such as the Narmada dams in India; campaigns against privatisation such as the city-wide general strike in Cochabamba, Bolivia in 2000 against water privatisation; consumer boycotts against sweatshops; campaigns against the policies of global financial institutions; various movements in cities and rural areas around the world exemplifying the Zapatista slogan 'making change without taking power' – a Global Justice Movement was rising (sometimes labelled Anti-Globalisation). It became newsworthy through the transnational demonstrations at the World Trade Organisation (WTO) summit in Seattle in 1999, by which time it succeeded in mobilising movements in the Western world who realised they had a common enemy: 'global exploitation'.

Since then the WSF has become the most significant meeting place for this 'movement of movements'. The WSF can claim that more than 1,000 organisations from over 120 countries have come together in the numerous workshops and seminars at WSF gatherings. A forum meeting in Florence also prompted transnational cooperation in mobilising between 10 and 30 million people to demonstrate on 15 February 2003 against the US war on Iraq. The WSF aspires to a new form of resistance politics, not based on 'new' left parties or popular armed struggle, but a kind of civil society based on 'nonviolent social resistance' (see the WSF charter at www.forumsocialmundial.org.br). But despite its potential, WSF also illustrates the problems of effective and mutual transnational cooperation, some of which are discussed in this chapter.

Photograph 15.1   'Save the Amazon' – a 'human banner' made by participants at the January 2009 World Social Forum in Belem, Brazil. (Lou Dematteis/Redux. Aerial Art by John Quigley/Spectral Q)

What is the world social forum movement offering?

Among the key documents outlining the WSF is first and foremost the founding document, the *Charter of Principles*: its opening paragraph describes the WSF as 'an open meeting place for reflective thinking ... by groups and movements of civil society ... committed to building a planetary society'.[1] The Charter goes on to emphasise plurality and open space while encouraging participation of some movements/organisations (for example, workers, indigenous groups, farmers, women and youth) and discouraging others (for example, neoliberals and fundamentalists), and actually excluding some (that is, non-civil groups).

WSF is trying to forge a space for a *new politics* through firstly rejecting two of the main strategies of earlier liberation attempts: the revolutionary army and the oppositional political party. Thus, guerrilla groups, as well as governments or political parties, are not allowed to send representatives. Secondly, WSF breaks so strongly with the idea of an avant-garde taking the lead of the struggle that they even reject joint resolutions. Since WSF neither has nor wants a formal political leadership or joint decision body, it refuses the typical 'conference declaration'. It is possible for alliances of movements or specific meetings at a forum to issue their declarations, but in their own names, as one of several declarations emanating from the forum. Some groups try to get around that. At the end of the forums the 'Assembly of Social Movements' stages a mass meeting and adopts a statement developed by some persons during the forum. This statement is sometimes treated as or mistaken for the statement of the forum. Prominent leaders of movements or intellectuals have on several occasions also issued political programmes for the WSF and the movement, stirring heated debates and accusations of trying to lead a movement that rejects global leadership (Sen et al. 2007).

WSF is not a global party or new international but an *open space* for cooperation, networking, co-learning, campaign-building, action-planning and dialogue between various groups, organisations and movements. An open space is an interactive collaborative learning structure in which self-organised activities are encouraged (Whitaker Ferreira 2006; Sen and Kumar 2003; see also http://www. openspaceforum.net). This space is administered by the International Secretariat in São Paolo together with the Organising Committee (which is based in Brazil but assists and integrates new countries that host the forum). Nowadays the International Council with its 100-plus members is the main decision-making body. But since WSF is an open space the council only decides on the place, time, organisation and funding of the forum – the content is constructed by the participants. Today the WSF is not only a massive yearly event somewhere in the Global South but a process of 50-plus forums a year, which are decentralised geographically, divided into specialised sectors or themes in which, for instance, mayors, judges, trade unions and parliamentarians meet at their own forums.

The global movement of movements facilitate transnational cooperation between local and regional movements in several ways. Fundamentally WSF makes new 'transnational advocacy networks' possible, networks that use new media and foster a 'boomerang-effect' (Keck and Sikkink 1998) of *moral and material pressures* on corporations and authoritarian regimes, thus facilitating the work and room of manoeuvre of local groups constrained by repressive regimes. New *international norms* or standards of behaviour are developed in alliance with progressive regimes, similar to the anti-personnel mines campaign; as well as new and civil society-based *governance structures*, such as Fair Trade. Policy suggestions become *accessible and understandable* by pooling of resources, information-sharing in distributed networks (mainly the internet), similar to the internet-based campaign that stopped the Multilateral Agreement on Investment (MAI).[2] Ultimately, the infrastructure of a global civil society is developed.

Participants decide themselves their level of engagement at forums. WSF offers, firstly, a space for *inspiration and info-exchange*. Secondly, it facilitates *contact-making* and networking. Thirdly, an option exists of *coordination*, to act in concert with each other. Without having to make decisions it becomes possible to act in awareness of the plans of other movements and organisations. Fourthly, and most ambitiously, WSF can be used as a space to *organise* together, to create new campaigns as well as plan and decide on joint actions.

In a more specific sense, WSF offers at least ten things for local struggles:

1. A *regular and open space* for presenting local struggles and analysis of oppression and solutions, as well an opportunity to find cooperation with others.

2. A *multi-level structure* for making discussions on multi-level connections between conflicts and social problems. By discussing, say, the privatisation of medical care in your home town at a local Social Forum, as well as a regional SF (for example, the European) and then WSF, it becomes possible to not only see the links between local privatisation and WTO rules but also to develop detailed knowledge and create links with other concerned groups on different levels.

3. Possibilities to *learn from experiences* of similar struggles and avoid making similar mistakes.

4. An opportunity to *influence global struggles*, agendas and coordination that might facilitate local development.

5. A place to *pick up action techniques and new organisational forms* from different groups.

6. Participating 'Watch-organisations' – such as corpwatch.org – that investigate and hunt the corporations and regimes that exploit and suppress people around the world, offer a *global bank of information and critical research methodology* to be used locally.

7. Facilitate transnational *support networks* for local resistance under strain, for example, for the landless workers' movement (MST) in Brazil and the indigenous resistance in Chiapas, Mexico.

8. A forum for *alternative media* distributing suppressed or marginalised information, for example, independent media centres (indymedia.org).

9. To formulate *global calls* together with other interested groups within certain theme-groups at WSF and through WSF reach a yet wider circle of organisations that might be interested to join.

10. To *coordinate actions* with the help of the 'Wall of Proposals' or '4th day of action proposals' in which *joint projects or actions* are announced.

Problems of WSF networking

All this sounds great, but the main empirical studies display that WSF actually has a serious social, global and democratic deficit (Santos 2006: 69–72). Furthermore it is obvious that WSF has a political weakness. Most depressing is maybe the fact that strategy-development and forum-development does not interest very many people at the WSF (Vinthagen 2007 on WSF Kenya).

The democratic deficit of WSF is displayed by a *lack of a formal leadership*. No one can represent the WSF as a unit but a de facto *informal leadership* of influential individuals (for example, Bernard Cassen, Francisco Whitaker Ferreira, Samir Amin) and leaders from influential organisations (for example, some French and Brazilian organisations such as French ATTAC, the Brazilian trade union CUT and MST) do exist. Further, the 'movement of movements' has a *media-appointed leadership* (for example, Arundhati Roy, Naomi Klein, Jose Bové, Vandana Shiva).

There is a *lack of geographical inclusion*. In each forum there are 50–80 countries that don't even have one participant attending. Generally Middle Eastern, Asian, African and Eastern European groups have weak representation.[3] This is still a serious problem despite the improvement since WSF moved to new host countries in 2004.

There is a *lack of social inclusion* of other groups than the typical participants of the educated, English speaking middle-class from Latin America, Europe, North America and India. In these investigations it becomes clear that WSF draws an *elite of the counter-hegemonic globalisation* emanating from middle-class sectors in their societies. Most participants have a college degree, are employed and organised (Santos 2006: 88–107, using surveys from WSF 2003 and 2005). And as many as 10 per cent have a Masters or PhD… which, by the way, makes WSF one of the major academic world gatherings (yearly 10,000 to 15,000 academics)! From the Mumbai SF 2004 the trend was broken and several thousand Dalits ('untouchables') took part. In Nairobi 2007 a big group of slum-dwellers also participated. This world tour of the WSF helps to increase the inclusion, as do differentiated fees for participants. Still, WSF as a global space can't avoid favouring the more *resource strong movements/groups* that can involve in the preparation of forums and participate regularly (because of the high costs of several intercontinental travels per year to preparatory meetings of WSF).

Besides these democratic, social and global deficits, there is a political deficit that is disappointing for those local groups who want help with their campaigns. WSF does facilitate discussions effectively but lacks a *structure that facilitates joint projects or campaigns* (Sen et al. 2007). Right now organisations and individuals present themselves at various workshops, bookstalls and seminars, creating a 'political market-place' (Vinthagen 2002). The respect of heterogeneity – of various approaches to the same problem or different choices of important issues – is big within WSF. But the structure is badly adopted to facilitate actions and lasting collaboration (although it of course occurs anyway). The attempt with a final 'day of action proposals', in which proposals are announced and those interested join, is an interesting experiment that might develop into an 'open space of action-facilitation' (Vinthagen 2007). A controversial debate is going on and factions are struggling both on the formal and informal level, a debate framed as one between WSF as an 'open space' or a 'movement' (with a political programme) (Sen et al. 2007). So far it seems like the support of open space is growing. But the battle is far from over, and sometimes it rises to the level of groups setting up minor counter or alternative forums to WSF.

Suggestions for increased support of local resistance

If we take both the possibilities and problems of WSF into account there still exist several ways in which local and regional movements can use this unique transnational forum structure to achieve at least a *more* effective and mutual local–global cooperation.[4]

Local groups can get together and pool resources with others in their field in order to send representatives that can tell about their work and facilitate support that increases the scope for local resistance. They can prepare manifestos and proposals (specific action and collaboration proposals) that would strengthen local work. Groups can make appointments with partners at Social Forums and have their own network meetings before, during or after a WSF (that is, less travel), as several international NGOs, unions and churches already do.

A key is international organisations (of environment, peace, trade, media, etc.) that gather local groups within a certain sector. They can act as brokers of WSF agendas and campaigns in the interest of local groups that are too small to make a difference. Many of them are able to join the International Council and influence the process and structure of WSF. Most importantly, they can function as a bridge between various local struggles, for example, bringing together locals struggling against transnational corporations, mining, deforestation, GMO, etc. by creating own or join existing thematic forums or assemblies within or separate to WSF (for example, Health, Housing or Anti-War), or by organising panels or joint sessions around vital issues bringing in ongoing local work.

Conclusion

Even though the global movement of movements and its World Social Forum structure is the best yet global cooperation between social movements, it is far from ideal. But it is what we have so far, and its development will depend on how we use it. In an effort to diminish unequal and ineffective forms of cooperation the WSF's own capacity to reform itself is key, together with the bridging role that different specialised international organisations can play between local organisations and WSF.

Since issues and struggles often are interlinked something similar to WSF would be necessary even if it didn't exist, and, WSF's focus on a new politics of heterogeneity, empowerment and cooperation is promising for the future of global resistance politics.

Notes

1. Together with a clarifying 'Note from the Organizing Committee on the principles that guide the WSF', see http://www.forumsocialmundial.org.br.
2. In the 1990s the Organisation for Economic Cooperation and Development was quietly negotiating a Multilateral Agreement on Investment to 'liberalise' the framework for international investment – that is, reduce the say of local communities. The proposals were leaked, scanned and posted on the internet. The project collapsed in 1998: in announcing its withdrawal from the MAI negotiations, the French government noted the new role of 'global civil society' in international economic negotiations.
3. The national forums in Lebanon, Egypt, Mozambique and Ethiopia are here important signs of the possible future change of WSF.
4. Of course, the WSF needs to reform itself as well – and WSF has shown a remarkable ability to do so before – but that discussion is too large for this chapter. See, for example, Santos 2006 or Vinthagen 2007; 2008.

16

WORKER SOLIDARITY AND CIVIL SOCIETY COOPERATION: BLOCKING THE CHINESE ARMS SHIPMENT TO ZIMBABWE, APRIL 2008

April Carter and Janet Cherry

Socialists once looked to worker cooperation across national frontiers as the primary means of promoting effective international resistance to economic and political exploitation and war. This vision has always been utopian – although there have certainly been important instances of trade union solidarity with workers on strike and those resisting oppression in other parts of the world. Given the decline of a homogeneous working class in the more developed countries, and the impact of today's neoliberal global capitalist economy, trade unionism has now been weakened in many countries as a force for radical change. Since the 1970s other social movements and civil society groups have become more prominent in transnational activism.

Nevertheless, organised workers can still be central to national opposition movements and initiate transnational solidarity. The trade unions in South Africa played an important role in the anti-apartheid struggle and constitute a key element in South African civil society today. The South African trade union federation COSATU has also become an active ally of the independent trade unions in Zimbabwe that are resisting Mugabe's oppression (see Section I, Chapter 3 by Janet Cherry). It is therefore not surprising that South African trade unionists were responsible for a dramatic act of international solidarity with their fellow unionists and the people of Zimbabwe.

South African dockers refuse to unload arms

When the Chinese ship, the *An Yue Jiang* (owned by the state-run shipping company), came into harbour in Durban, South Africa, in April 2008 to unload a shipment of arms that was to be transported overland to the Zimbabwe government, dockers in the Transport and Allied Workers' Union announced they would refuse to unload the ship. The Chinese government has given active support to the Mugabe regime, including supplying it with arms. The ship was reportedly carrying 'millions of rounds of assault rifle ammunition, mortar rounds and rocket-propelled grenades' (*Amnesty Magazine*, May/June 2008: 4). The dockers' action was immediately supported by the International Transport Workers' Federation.

Other civil society groups in South Africa were also active in opposing the arms shipment. Church, legal and human rights activists in the Justice Alliance of South Africa urgently sought a legal ban on the weapons reaching Zimbabwe via South African territory. Although the government declared that there was no embargo on Zimbabwe, the Durban High Court ruled that the arms should be held in secure storage by the sheriff of Durban until the case returned to court, when the judge 'must take judicial notice of the brutal military campaign of repression in Zimbabwe'. The ship then left the harbour without unloading its cargo, and continued round the coast of Africa looking for a friendlier port.

Initial reports suggested that the ship had not been able to unload the arms at any port in Southern Africa, and a Chinese Foreign Ministry official announced that the shipping company was recalling the ship to China. This announcement was contradicted by a report in *Jane's Defence Weekly* (27 April 2008) that the ship had docked at Luanda in Angola. There were also claims that the cargo had been unloaded in either the Democratic Republic of Congo or the Republic of Congo, and Zimbabwe's Information Minister claimed on 6 May that the arms had reached Zimbabwe. However, the Chinese Foreign Ministry denied all these claims, and stated on 26 May that the *An Yue Jiang* was on its way back to China with the arms. The International Transport Workers' Federation also rejected reports that the Zimbabwe government had received the arms.

Although some uncertainty remains about how successfully the arms shipment was blocked, the action by the South African dockers and other South African activists did mobilise both international and regional concern. The International Action Network on Small Arms (IANSA) offered immediate support, joining with African civil society bodies to urge Southern African countries to impose a total freeze on arms shipments to Zimbabwe to avoid plunging the country into deeper political violence. IANSA's Africa Co-ordinator, Joseph Dube, announced the launch of a campaign calling on the governments in the Southern African Development Community to 'declare an immediate moratorium on the transfer of all military, paramilitary and security equipment to Zimbabwe that can be used in internal repression' (Reuters, 5 June 2008).

Section IV

Controversies in Transnational Action

EDITORIAL INTRODUCTION

This section addresses two controversial accusations that have arisen specifically in response to 'electoral revolutions' in Serbia, Georgia and Ukraine: that outside funding – in particular Western funding – is used to manipulate 'pro-democracy movements', and that nonviolent action training is being used to support Western imperialism.

In the past decade, the US government has presented 'democracy promotion' as a priority of its foreign policy – to the point of justifying military invasion and occupation. For the Bush administration of 2000–08, 'democracy promotion' is equated with furthering US strategic objectives – concretely expanding market capitalism and military cooperation. Consequently, there has been a backlash, criticism pointing not only to the USA's own domestic 'democratic deficit', but also to the history of US foreign policies sabotaging democracy elsewhere. Some go further, suggesting that US support for 'people power' is little more than another strategy for 'regime change' and point to the strategic advantages gained by removing the USA's main opponent in the Balkans, Slobodan Milošević, and then installing governments in Georgia and the Ukraine more hostile to Russia, indeed with Ukraine's leaders keen to join NATO.

'Democracy promotion', however, cannot be reduced just to the policy of US governmental or quasi-governmental agencies. The advocacy of democratic values as a counter to abuses of power is widespread, embracing a range of intergovernmental, governmental and quasi-governmental bodies, plus a host of private foundations and citizens groups. The activities of democracy promotion are usually less likely to involve support for particular opposition campaigns than programmes to strengthen democratic processes – including election monitoring, education on international human rights law, journalist training and support for women's, youth and other civil society groups. While some programmes are a guise for governmental interference, not everything under this heading should be dismissed as being a front for power interests.

Jørgen Johansen reviews the range of funding needs and funding options for unarmed opposition movements, the problems of public legitimacy when a group is known to receive foreign funding and the problem of foreign influence if a group becomes dependent on this funding. While foreign assistance may be a factor in the success of a movement, he maintains that 'people power' depends essentially on what significant numbers of people are motivated to do on their own account.

The success of 'people power' in Serbia was celebrated by the documentary 'Bringing Down a Dictator' explaining how unarmed resistance worked in practice, and activists from Otpor began travelling to other countries to discuss their experiences. Various governments and sections of the Western left reacted against nonviolent action training and in particular the work of the Albert Einstein Institution (AEI) established by Gene Sharp and the International Center on Nonviolent Conflict (ICNC) established by Peter Ackerman and Jack DuVall.[1]

Ackerman, previously the main funder of the AEI and now the chair of Freedom House, distinguishes between the forms of power exercised by governmental foreign policy and that by nonviolent struggle. He argues that foreign policy exercises 'hard power' (military force, economic sanctions) or 'soft power' (incentives to cooperate, cultural exchanges), but that there is a third type of power – the civilian-based power seen in nonviolent struggle:

> The difference between civilian-based power and hard and soft power is that civilian-based power is indigenous. It is not something controlled or imposed by great powers on others; civilian-based power is local, and it springs from the concerted, collective, strategic, nonviolent actions of large groups of people within a country or conflict. (Ackerman 2004)

The internet attacks do not see unarmed resistance in this light and rather improbably present the ageing Gene Sharp and the penurious AEI as 'the main handler of these coups on the street side' (Mowat 2005).[2] They pay little attention to the contents of the materials and resources produced by either the AEI or ICNC, never discussing the analyses of social struggles in the main books promoted by both bodies (Sharp 1973 and 2005; Ackerman and DuVall 2000; Schock 2005).

However, these attacks do touch on one serious issue for those who – like Sharp and Ackerman – advocate the techniques of unarmed resistance mainly on the base of their effectiveness. This concerns the use of unarmed techniques for unjust ends. Sharp and Ackerman have consciously separated study of the technique of nonviolent conflict from the values and social critique represented by Gandhi or radical pacifists. For them, nonviolent action is a tool for people of various ideologies and political alignments in resisting oppression and authoritarianism.

George Lakey is a veteran US nonviolence trainer who shares this attitude but has been active in civil rights, peace, anti-capitalist and gay movements in his own country for more than 40 years. He also has led nonviolence training workshops in many countries. He suggests some useful questions for trainers in reflecting on who they work with and how. He then goes on to challenge the 'disempowering' assumptions about social movements made by the internet critics of nonviolence training.

Notes

1. The charges emanate primarily from three sources on the internet, with articles being repeatedly reposted, cited and debated in various blogs. Meyssan 2005 first appeared on www.voltaire.net. The site www.global research.ca, established by Michel Chossudovsky, published Mowat 2005, and followed with articles by site associates, Stephen Gowans and F. William Engdahl. The third main source has been solidarity activists with the Bolivaran revolution in Venezuela, such as Eva Golinger and George Ciccariello Maher, whose articles have been posted on sites such as www.venezuelanalysis.com, www.greenleft.org. au and www.counterpunch.org. Two latecomers to the debate have been Adam Larson of the Guerrillas without Guns blogspot (specialising in the former Soviet Union) and the Australian Michael Barker who is researching US-based 'democracy promotion' foundations, writing on various sites, including www.monthlyreview.org and www. greenleft.org.au. Both the AEI (www.aeinstein.org) and the ICNC (www.nonviolent-conflict.org) have replied to various comments, as has Stephen Zunes personally (2008a, 2008b) on the *Foreign Policy in Focus* site, www.fpif.org and elsewhere.

2. In the days when the Albert Einstein Institution was better funded, it maintained a 'fellows programme' awarding research grants for scholarship on nonviolent struggle. I was one of the last to benefit from this excellent scheme as financial problems caused it to be suspended in 2000.

17

EXTERNAL FINANCING OF OPPOSITION MOVEMENTS

Jørgen Johansen

This chapter analyses the financial influences on nonviolent movements that have the explicit goal either of replacing the political leadership or the changing nature of a regime within a state. The movements covered here are those relying primarily on a nonviolent strategy, and not the use of arms and other lethal means – although some have occasionally resorted to violence. The success or failure of such movements depends on many factors, but financing is one variable that adds to the complexity of conflicts.

There have long been debates about the implications of movements receiving funds directly or indirectly from foreign governments, or from other international sources. But since 2000 there has been criticism of official Western support for opposition movements in Serbia and in former Soviet republics, not only from governments opposed to Western encroachments and fearing internal oppositions, but also on the Western left. The new moves to counter terrorism after September 2001 have also made many states more suspicious of opposition groups, and giving money has become more complicated.

This chapter begins with a brief examination of some of the recent nonviolent movements demanding a change of government after rigged elections, and some governmental reactions. It then explores the broader issues of who the international donors are, and the problems and implications of giving and receiving donations.

Nonviolent movements in less democratic states since 2000

This chapter focuses on nonviolent movements striving to remove regimes in less democratic states, although references will also be made to less 'revolutionary' movements. Many of the arguments for these cases will probably be valid also for other organised actors in the social–political domain.

The movement in Serbia succeeded in toppling Milošević in October 2000, after mass demonstrations filled the capital, occupying the TV building and parliament in protest against rigged elections. Nonviolent resistance had begun in 1996–97 with sustained protests against election rigging, and although NATO bombing in 1999 weakened opposition to Milošević, the earlier experience became a base for a new and better-organised movement. Members of the Serbian student group Otpor, which itself received some Western aid, have since led workshops in other countries and had other contacts with the 'Rose Revolution' in Georgia in 2003, the 'Orange Revolution' in the Ukraine in 2004 and the more complex 'Tulip Revolution' in Kyrgyzstan in 2005. The opposition in Serbia received support from Western governments and institutions from late 1996, as did the later movements against authoritarian regimes in the former Soviet Union. But the amount as well as the importance of the external support are contested.

The reaction of the governments being challenged was to attack foreign funding and the *bona fides* of the protest movements. Milošević in Serbia, Shevardnadze in Georgia and Yanukovych in the Ukraine all labelled the opposition 'terrorists', and cited foreign donors as 'evidence' of the movements' unpatriotic and illegal nature.

President Putin of Russia said in July 2005:

> I am categorically against the foreign financing of [NGOs'] political activities in Russia. … We understand that he who pays the piper calls the tune, … Not a single self-respecting country will allow that, and neither shall we. … Let us solve our internal problems ourselves. (Reuters, 20 July 2005)

Putin therefore introduced legislation demanding the reregistration of all Russian NGOs, and a crucial question in reregistering is whether or not they get foreign financial support.

As well as Russia, governments in neighbouring countries such as Belarus, Azerbaijan, Kazakhstan and Uzbekistan have increased pressure on and control of NGOs. In Belarus almost a hundred NGOs were forced to close in 2003–04 (Silitski 2006). In other parts of the world, governments have also reacted against foreign, especially Western, funding of social movements and opposition groups. Chinese Premier Hu Jintao issued a report to the Communist Party Central Committee in May 2005, outlining policies to 'crush US attempts to start a colour revolution in China'. Zimbabwe adopted new policies cracking down on NGOs, which are seen as vectors of peaceful revolution, and Eritrea introduced a new law in May 2005 sharply limiting the role of civil society bodies (Åslund and McFaul 2006).

Who are the donors?

Movements need money, and most of them are short of funds for posters and stickers, for communication and public events, and for offices and salaries. When organisations, networks and movements organising large-scale nonviolent actions receive money from donors from abroad, this is likely to be used as an argument against the movement: it is often easier to criticise the sources of funding rather than tackle the real threat, the goals and policies of a movement. Any state governed by an undemocratic regime will use every available argument to reduce the popularity of an oppositional movement: for example, claims about 'state sovereignty' and 'unpatriotic' citizens. The USA – the dominant donor to oppositional movements globally – itself shares this fear of foreign influence in domestic politics and has laws forbidding foreign financial support to US politicians.

When critics use foreign financial support as an argument against a movement it seems that they differentiate on the basis of both who receives the money and who the donors are. Not only social movements, but states too receive financial support. As shown in Table 17.1, we can imagine a number of different approaches here. The first division is between the donors and the recipients. Within the recipients I have divided states from 'civil society' – a problematic term as there is no consensus on what to include in 'civil society': some would include most of the actors who are not part of the direct power-structure within the state apparatus, even embracing 'political parties not in power', as well as 'business communities' and 'media'. There are numerous examples of all of these entities receiving support from foreign donors. Table 17.1 mainly focuses on the donors and the diversity among them.

Table 17.1 Mapping financial support

		Donors						
	Domestic		Diaspora	Foreign donors				Large private and 'independent' donors from the country itself or foreign origin
				Civil society	Development agencies	A state or private organisations close to a state		
	The movement itself	Other domestic supporters				'Switzerland'	'USA'	
Recipients — Civil society								
Recipients — State								

The first division is between domestic and foreign donors. Within the domestic we can distinguish between the movement itself and other supporters. The movement can collect money from its own ranks (membership fees, donations), the public, or even as a more or less voluntary informal taxation. Other domestic sources can be rich individuals or organisations, who donate money because they support the movement and its goals. Diaspora groups constitute a distinct category, and have been vital for the economic base of several movements (see Andrew Rigby in Section III, Chapter 14). There have also been examples of movements that manage their finances via illegal trade, robbery or bribes; but this is more common when there is a mixture of armed and unarmed strategy.

States donate money in several ways. State-run development agencies have a long tradition of supporting civil society organisations in other countries. The Swedish International Development Agency (SIDA), the UK Department for International Development (DfID), and similar organisations give large amounts to movements in many authoritarian and semi-democratic states worldwide. Part of that support is labelled 'democracy promotion'. This includes funds, but also takes the form of 'capacity-building', which can include material support, such as equipment, and various forms of training. Even if development agencies rarely act in contradiction to the present policy of their government, direct financial support from governments is often regarded in a different light to that channelled via development agencies. State-financed foundations and trusts are also major donors to groups, networks and movements abroad. Many of them run covert operations abroad and their activities may not be known until years later.

Foreign donors also include civil society organisations that collect money to show solidarity, or because they share the aims of the movement. In the 1990s, peace groups and NGOs in the Balkans received financial support from sister organisations in other countries. To collect money to support sister organisations abroad is still important for movements such as trade unions, religious communities and solidarity organisations that have a long tradition of such activities.

If the donation is overt, the political motivation will normally be more suspect when it comes directly from a government. A donation direct from a state is not only a financial contribution, but also a political signal of support, recognition and acknowledgement. It will also be judged differently if the country in question is Switzerland, say, rather than the USA. Large countries with a belligerent and active foreign policy tend to be regarded with more mistrust than small countries with a long tradition of neutrality.

On the international scene, various donors act more or less independently of any government. For example, the support given by George Soros, and his Open Society foundations to organisations in the Balkans, Eastern and Central Europe has been enormous in the last three decades. In Georgia he supported the opposition in 2003 and then paid large amounts to the Saakashvili government after the success of the 'Rose Revolution'.

In addition there are a number of international governmental organisations that support oppositional movements, as well as newly established states, either directly or by transferring funds from other sources. The European Union, International Monetary Fund, World Bank, League of Arab States, Socialist International and Commonwealth of Nations all have a funding role.

Each category of donor will be regarded differently by recipients, as well as the power-holders in the respective state. And within each category the judgement will differ based on the history and interests of the donor, the present context and political situation in which the recipient works. The legacies of the Cold War, and of other historical events, are still factors in many of these conflicts.

What are the problems?

Support for revolutionary oppositional movements has always been difficult and often illegal. Since 11 September 2001 especially, the transfer of money has been problematic. On the pretext of restricting financial support to alleged 'terrorists', states have created an atmosphere suspicious of foreign support to political movements. As part of the 'war on terrorism', UN Security Council Resolution 1373 asked states to include laws on 'terrorism' in their criminal codes. A major part of this new legislation deals with financial support and international transfer of money. The definitions of 'terrorist' and 'terror organisation' are loose, and have been used by a number of states to include peaceful groups from civil society. Human rights organisations, peace groups, solidarity movements and nonviolent revolutionary movements are among those who have faced difficulties with state repression.

During the Cold War, the issue of external support surfaced in European peace movements. The movements in question in the 1970s and 1980s had a limited focus and goal: to prevent more nuclear weapons being placed on European soil. Allegations of financial support from Soviet bloc sources were used to discredit them, although in most countries groups receiving such funds tended to be sidelined during the mass mobilisations of the 1980s. In several European countries, individuals and groups with close relations to the Soviet-funded World Peace Council were regarded as security threats and were under secret police surveillance. Public investigations in Denmark, Norway and Sweden have revealed that the secret agencies of these states were following closely the links, including funding, to other states. The exaggerated fears the special police forces expressed in their internal documents were less a serious assessment of the movements than a justification for maintaining or raising secret police budgets.

Many opposition movements receive money from abroad, and it is in most cases those holding state power at the time who argue against it. But there are an increasing number of cases where critiques have come from civic organisations, analysts and the media, criticising the influence of external donors on movement agendas and in some cases, such as George Soros, commenting on how and where they acquire their capital.

In Scandinavian countries most civil society actors today tend to depend more on governmental funds than do movements in other countries. Such funding obviously does influence their activities, but to what extent is an open question. An internal debate on this takes place periodically, but no consensus has yet been reached.

Implications of different types of donations

Receipt of external money is used to question the legitimacy of movements. This discussion is not new and can be traced back to the decolonisation process in Africa. When liberation movements got financial support from foreign sources (for example, SIDA channelled the equivalent of US\$ 24 million to several liberation movements in Southern Africa between 1969 and 1995) (Sellström 2002: 900–1), a number of international and national actors protested. This, they said, was a form of interference in another country's internal affairs, a violation of the sovereignty of the state. Some labelled the liberation movements as 'terrorists' and argued that all forms of support should be condemned. It is difficult to imagine what would be the consequences if it was made public that European states today in secret were giving financial support to organisations listed as 'terrorist' by the US State Department, the UN or the EU.

Of course, there is power in giving away money. There will always be a relationship of dependence when large sums are transferred. But this should not be exaggerated. The fact that someone receives money does not necessarily result in the contributor deciding on and controlling the agenda of the beneficiary. The relationship is more complex than that of domination and subordination. It is partly a question of the size of the sums. Large sums from one or just a few donors will create greater dependency than many small sums from a high number of donors. In the case of the 'Orange Revolution' in Ukraine, Pora claimed to have received no more than \$130,000 from foreign sources – the Canadian International Development Agency, the US-based Freedom House, and the German Marshall Fund of the United States – a small amount compared with the €5 million they claimed to have received in donations 'in kind' from local sources (Wilson 2005: 186).[1] To what degree foreign support later influenced the agenda of Pora is difficult to judge, but it is clear that foreign money did not and never can inspire the growth of a movement such as Pora.

As with other sorts of development aid, there are two main categories: funding for specific projects; and core funding (general support to be used as the recipients decide). Project funding gives the donors more power as recipients are tempted to design their applications according to donor priorities rather than pursuing their own agenda. However, this form of 'control' over the activities of the recipients is the responsibility of both donors and recipients.

The importance of external financial aid varies with the type of movement. Some nonviolent movements emerge relatively spontaneously with little time for planning and preparation. Maybe the most extreme example was the 1989 overthrow of the regime in East Germany. Few among the opposition had prepared for the opening up of the Berlin Wall and the takeover of the state, and had had little 'need' for money for training and organising. For others there is a much more gradual build-up. The opposition groups in Serbia were involved in preparations over three years from 1997 to 2000, and their preparations included strategic planning, organising and training. This approach is obviously more expensive.

Money may help expand civil society activity, but at the same time it can divide and foment conflicts. In countries like Palestine, Cyprus and Colombia large civil societies have been built with a high degree of foreign money. Competition between NGOs to gain access to the sources of funding has, however, had a negative impact on movement unity and cooperation. Quite how much damage to a movement such conflicts cause is still to be investigated.

Financial support is the most controversial but far from the only form of assistance to movements. Moral support and political attention are of fundamental importance for suppressed oppositional movements. Experience, skills, practical training, access to networks and literature are all integral and necessary ingredients for a successful campaign. Such work has been made much easier and cheaper through new technology. The web has made it partly possible to communicate, disseminate and train people without face-to-face meetings and without extensive travel. Activists worldwide learn, get inspired and build networks to an extent never possible in the last century. To be connected to 'the rest of the world' means a lot for the local activists' self-image, perspective, energy and strength. Therefore governments in Burma, China, Zimbabwe, Belarus, Eritrea and other places have done their utmost to limit access to the web, closed down cellular networks and refused visas for people who want to travel in or out of the country. Financial support can only to a limited degree help to overcome such obstacles.

Conclusion

The importance of financial support varies much from case to case. No nonviolent opposition movement is completely in the hands of donors, and some do not even need it. Even in those cases where foreign financial support has been crucial, it has not been sufficient by itself to bring about success. The key is always a movement's base in its own society.

Donors that have given vital support to one movement might also have caused damage in another situation. The point is not to judge a donor on the basis of a single case, but to identify trends, being aware that there are always exceptions. Good fund-raising handbooks advise those seeking funds that they need to educate their donors – to teach them about the situation and the issues. This is also true in the world of social movements.

Note

1. Most of the $65 million the US State Department is said to have allocated to 'democracy promotion' in the Ukraine in 2003 and 2004 is justified in terms of support of democratic 'process' rather than particular candidates or movements. As Wilson points out, referring to the implict support for the 'Orange' cause of some US-funded websites, the line between process and candidates cannot always be drawn (Wilson 2005: 189).

18

NONVIOLENCE TRAINING AND CHARGES OF WESTERN IMPERIALISM: A GUIDE FOR WORRIED ACTIVISTS

George Lakey

The ugly spectre of imperialism has been raised by some left-wing critics, who argue that certain groups offering training in nonviolent resistance are in league with Western power-holders, and promoting hidden agendas. There's nothing new about right-wingers attacking social movements for getting outside assistance ('outside agitators!'). But when critics on the left join in, a reply is needed.

This chapter explores key issues from the standpoint of someone who has provided training to a wide variety of campaigns using nonviolent action, ever since Martin Oppenheimer and I joined the US civil rights protests and wrote *A Manual for Direct Action* (Quadrangle Press, 1965) as a service to that movement. Over the years I've worked in over 30 countries, often returning to train trainers, so that the movements there would have their own training capacity. The focus of the workshops varied, from team-building and leadership development to the dynamics of nonviolent action.

This chapter does two things that might be helpful to worried activists. I'll share in a personal way some standards we use at Training for Change. Secondly, rather than address charges made mainly on the internet against particular individuals and organisations, I will comment on the experience of social movements and the need for allies, to suggest that critics who stress the role of hidden agendas in external training in nonviolent action misread history as conspiracy theory.[1] I conclude with some reflections on the changing nature of nonviolent struggle today.

Assisting grassroots empowerment: criteria

The first and fundamental question for trainers to ask is whether the organisation or campaign inviting help is genuinely working for justice, peace and/or environmental sustainability. Then there are a number of criteria that trainers should apply to themselves.

Do I know that my struggle is interconnected with theirs?
'If you have come to help me, you are wasting your time. But if you are coming because your liberation is bound up with mine, then let us work together.' – Aboriginal activists group, Queensland, 1970s[2]

Am I accountable to the people who invite me?
I make it easy for the inviters *not* to invite me back, because I'm aware that cultural norms of hospitality and obligation can make it difficult to say that I'm no longer needed. For example, when in both Thailand and Russia we made ten trips, it was always clear that the inviter was in charge of whether we would be invited back.

Am I fighting on my own front, as well as working with others?
The struggle for change at home is where I know most and where I am most responsible. It grounds me. If I put all my attention on other cultures, other countries, I run the risk of losing my authenticity.

If I sense political ambiguity, do I 'push the envelope'?
I once assisted some grassroots trainers to do a workshop in Central Asia and felt uneasy about the fiscal sponsorship. I therefore introduced an exercise that brought the workshop participants into a major debate about the validity of capitalism. The sponsor was furious and I wasn't invited back, so the test worked; the sponsor's hidden agenda really was to facilitate capitalist development rather than to empower groups to make thoughtful choices about options.

Do I assist a group that is unaware of its oppressive patterns like sexism, classism, racism, homophobia?
It depends. I've given a workshop to an anarchist group ruled by a covert patriarch, for example, knowing that there is no such thing as a completely liberated group, and that particular group wanted to launch a worthy campaign. If their campaign succeeded, there would be a modest increment of justice even though internal democratisation was still badly needed!

I have many considerations, but my bottom line for a 'no' is this: *will my training empower this group systematically to hurt others, or put in place policies that will hurt others?* The answer to that question leaves room for honest disagreement, of course. In Venezuela, for example, I would offer trainings to some groups but not others. A capitalist group that wants to overthrow Bolivarian socialism would put in place policies that would increase the oppression of the poor; I therefore have no wish to empower that group through training.

Am I aware of my rank?
I'm often given rank as Westerner, expert/writer-of-books, white person, older man. Rank cannot be wished away, it is in the eyes of the beholders. Therefore I acknowledge it and use it to support others, by affirming their intelligence and, rather than giving answers to their questions, explore the issues in such a way that *they* discover the answer that's right for their situation.

Am I aware of my history?
A realistic way to show my awareness of rank is to know the history of the USA (which is *my* history) and to take responsibility for it. I am particularly responsive to invitations from overseas countries where my country has intervened disastrously; it seems a simple act of responsibility to do my small part in trying to clean up the mess.

Each time I've led workshops in Cambodia, for example, I wait until the appropriate moment – when the container is strong, when I have rapport with the participants – to stand before the group and make a formal apology to them for the US role in the horror that unfolded in their land.

Do I use an alternative to the Western mainstream model of education?
The mainstream Western educational model is teacher-centred, lecture-based and supports domination. Even when the content promotes defiance, the pedagogical medium is paternalistic.

I use a different model, Direct Education, based on Paolo Freire's popular education, and consistent with dialogical styles with roots in ancient Buddhism and classical Greece. At Training for Change we've added modern insights into how adults accelerate their learning and in some ways gone beyond popular education, to become more empowering. By avoiding the hegemonic educational style of the West, we open the door to liberatory work on a fundamental level.

Am I committed to capacity-building?
As soon as I work with a new host a couple of times and see that they are pleased with the results of direct education, I ask if they would like to build their own capacity to do that kind of training. Only when training is in the hands of local movements can it reach its full potential as a formative part of the struggle for justice.

Evaluating charges from the critics: guidelines

Criticism has spread on the internet that nonviolence training has been brought into the service of US imperialism. This began when US-based 'democracy promotion' agencies funded trainings for activists first from Serbia and then the 'colour revolutions' in countries neighbouring Russia. Trainers associated with the Albert Einstein Institution, the International Center on Nonviolent Conflict (ICNC) or the Serbian group CANVAS (one of the groups that grew out of Otpor) have subsequently been criticised for giving workshops in Burma, Venezuela and Zimbabwe.[3]

Many of the attacks on trainers have been made on the internet, where it is harder to sort out the validity of the charges of 'nonviolent imperialism' than in a face-to-face debate. How does the activist distinguish possible truth from conjecture? In a world where many things are not what they seem, maybe 'nonviolence' is a clever spin used to hide elite manipulation of the masses?

Rather than directly discussing the charges against trainers, I suggest some questions as guidelines for reading the articles already posted online and those that will undoubtedly follow.

1. Do the critics understand what their target is engaged in?

The trainers being attacked have repeatedly explained that they research and teach 'nonviolent *action*': a technique for waging conflict in which the protagonists use methods of protest, noncooperation and intervention without the use or threat of injurious force. They maintain that strategic choices about means (for example, armed struggle versus nonviolent struggle) should be made by the people on the ground who have chosen their goals and are willing to suffer to achieve them.

Does anyone believe it would be better if grassroots movements *wouldn't* explore their options before choosing? Or is the critic more afraid – as are those who have defended Milošević in Serbia and Mugabe in Zimbabwe – that *the people might succeed?*

2. Where is the hard evidence?

It is much easier to make a groundless charge against someone than it is for the target to defend her or himself against it. Activist cultures that give credence to such charges unconsciously support the power-holders, through forcing activists to chew up their time and energy defending themselves unnecessarily. Therefore we activists need to become more tough-minded toward the critics, based on the kind of evidence they bring forward to support their charges against other activists.

Is there any evidence that the trainers attacked are sharing their knowledge only with pro-US government social movements and withholding it from anti-US government social movements?

Instead of hard evidence, the internet attacks rely on guilt-by-association. The false charge that the Albert Einstein Institution is CIA-funded is particularly ludicrous as it coincided with a financial crisis that almost forced the institution to close.

3. Does the critic know how social movements work?

Historically social movement theory grew from mob and crowd studies (Le Bon 1896).[4] Mobs and crowds are highly suggestible, therefore can be manipulated by outsiders. If that's an accurate model of social movements, then look for manipulators! The critics need to examine themselves to see if they are holding that model.

Social researchers long ago put that original social movement model in the dustbin. Activists with in-depth experience of more than one movement are happy that sociologists are catching up with the reality they know; a successful social movement is actually very complex.

Take, for example, the need for allies. Successful activists know they need allies to win anything substantial. An ally is, by definition, someone who doesn't agree with everything we stand for, but agrees with part. Activists can choose purity ('We true believers will struggle by ourselves'), or we can choose change ('Let's invite others in who can buy part of our programme').

If Martin Luther King Jr had been obsessed with purity I suppose he might have tried to keep out of the US civil rights movement: (a) people who had ever associated with racist institutions or to racist figures, (b) Communists who didn't accept principled nonviolent philosophy, or (c) individuals like labour leaders who had gone along with the AFL-CIO collusion with the CIA in global labour politics.

Thoughtful commentators should know that the optimal size and spread of a movement coalition is the product of many judgments, including historical context, the relative strength and unity of elites, the ascendancy/decline of oppositional movements, the amount of internal resources within the movement, the nature of the goals, and so on.

The critics attacking movements using nonviolent struggle don't appear to understand the need for allies. When they observe allies (that is, people/forces with additional agendas) they seem to assume it's terrible (instead of necessary), and they assume that certain allies control the movement.

This point may be clearer if we again use the example of the US civil rights movement. In those days we got used to being attacked by the centre/right for being a tool of Soviet foreign policy. Were there Communists in our movement? Of course. Was the movement consistent with Soviet goals? Certainly. Was the movement, therefore, a tool of the Soviet Union? Ridiculous.[5]

Note the disrespect inherent in this attack: it had to be 'outside agitators' and 'Moscow gold' that drove the civil rights movement, not the intelligence, hard work and sacrifice of African Americans. I experience the same disrespect today from those who write off the work and sacrifice of grassroots movements, by inviting their readers to believe young people in Serbia or anywhere else aren't bright or passionate enough to make change without alleged puppet masters of the National Endowment for Democracy et al. stirring them up.[6]

Knowing what real movement work is like gives the critic perspective and sharper observations. A critic with the sensibility of a movement activist might ask useful questions: for example, 'Is there ongoing *dependency* on particular allies?' Observing a movement's temporary alliance and then making the insulting assumptions noted above – the case of Otpor getting funds from a US agency, for example – is of no use to an activist. On the other hand, raising a question about a *dependency relationship* forming with an ally can actually be useful.

In my experience effective grassroots organisers working with oppressed groups see threats and opportunities as choices about limitations rather than choices about purity. If we take a grant from X foundation, will it limit us, and how? If we don't and we can't hire the staff needed to do this anti-corporate campaign, will that limit us and how?

I'll give an example in the new field of nonviolent struggle called third party nonviolent intervention, one version of which is 'unarmed bodyguards'. The technique was pioneered by Peace Brigades International in 1980s Guatemala and El Salvador, where US-backed dictatorships were slaughtering people's movements. The technique opened the political space a bit, giving more local activists the chance to stay alive while fighting for justice.

With the growth of third party nonviolent intervention in the 1990s, a well-researched training curriculum was needed. We in Training for Change had the expertise to create such a curriculum. The opportunity arose to get a grant for this from the Congress-funded US Institute of Peace. After careful discussion, we decided to apply for the grant, knowing (a) this was a one-time only deal, (b) there was no chance of our becoming dependent on the USIP, and (c) there were no strings attached as to creation or use of the curriculum.[7]

4. Is the critic in touch with global shifts in consciousness about resistance and struggle?
Left-leaning critics of training in nonviolent action are mainly those who study US strategies for dominance. Empire-bashing is good, but more pressing to many activists is: what can we *do* about it?

The old story of oppressed peoples is that grassroots movements often do rebel, resist and organise reform movements to give themselves some space and some relief. For thousands of years they've done that violently, and they've also frequently done that nonviolently. Although historians have mostly been more interested in the violent tactics than the nonviolent ones, the old story of people power is slowly being recovered.

That's the old story. The new story is that cultural changes are happening in many parts of the world that acknowledge – *explicitly* – the power of nonviolent struggle. The changes show up in language, among other places. In workshops in Cambodia and elsewhere I find participants coining new words to describe this technique that is so different from their old words connoting 'harmony' or 'humble petition'.

The conscious availability of '*militancia pacifica*' or 'people power' means that increasing numbers see new options for nonviolent strategy. We have seen the US-backed Shah of Iran, the US-backed Marcos in the Philippines and the US-installed General Pinochet in Chile defeated by nonviolent direct action.[8]

Such a cultural change means more action – for more goals. Any of us is free to disagree with the goals that nonviolent tactics may be put to; we may not like the white segregationists who launched school boycotts to maintain racism or the anti-choice activists who picket abortion clinics. Nevertheless, would anyone on the left prefer 'the good old days' when struggle was assumed to require that we inflict death and mutilation?

A fair question for the critics is: how can you give your support to increasing the availability of nonviolent struggle options, and still express your cautions and worries about, for example, choices of allies and possibilities of dependency – issues every movement faces whether nonviolent or violent?

5. Is the critic fear-based, or does s/he believe in the power of the people?
Reading the various critics on the internet I realise that their writing would be more compelling if I were terrified. I could resonate with the critic if I believed that the US Empire and its axis of evil has nearly won, that the agents of empire are *everywhere*, manipulating *everything*, with endless resources.

Fortunately, the persistent grassroots movements of the world are not fear-based. They suffer, they act and they have hope. They make allies because they're not driven by fear. Effective movement leaders know that expansion and grassroots power do not come from fear but come from boldness and risk-taking. When they see cracks in the wall, they widen the cracks rather than obsess that the cracks may narrow again.

In my personal experience, progressive movements' most useful resource for empowerment comes not from those who are overawed from studying the CIA but from those who are *in awe of* people power, those who learn patiently from movements that use it, and those who pass that knowledge along.

Notes

1. Those attacked for education about nonviolent struggle and who I know are: Gene Sharp (Albert Einstein Institution), Stephen Zunes, Jack DuVall and Peter Ackerman, all of the International Center on Nonviolent Conflict – ICNC), Col. Robert Helvey (US Army, ret.), Ivan Marovic of CANVAS and the Serbian Otpor movement of 2000.

2. This quote is frequently attributed to Lila Watson, but she requests that the collective origin of the quote be honoured. See http://northlandposter.com/blog/2006/12/18/ lila-watson-if-you-have-come-to-help-me-you-are-wasting-your-time-but-if-you-have-come-because-your-liberation-is-bound-up-with-mine-then-let-us-work-together/

3. See note 1 in the Section IV introduction for details on the internet debate.

4. See Gustav Le Bon, *The Crowd: A Study of the Popular Mind*, 1896.

5. The mirror image of this right-wing 'logic' is now popular among these left-wing critics. 'Are there people associated with this movement who might be sympathetic to the USA? Yes. Would the success of this movement be in US interests (in at least some way)? Yes. Well, then, the movement must be controlled by the USA.'

6. 'Colonel [Robert] Helvey and his colleagues have created a series of youth movements. ...' (Mowat 2005).

7. Daniel Hunter and George Lakey, *Opening Space for Democracy: Third Party Nonviolent Intervention – Curriculum and Trainer's Manual* (Philadelphia: Training for Change, 2004), available from TrainingforChange.org; part of the book is online as a pdf.

8. In the case of Marcos, the USA helped him leave once he had been defeated; in the case of Pinochet, the USA ceased backing him before the 1988 plebiscite.

AFTERWORD
THE CHAIN OF NONVIOLENCE

Howard Clark

'Global solidarity' lends itself to inspiring rhetoric: from the *Communist Manifesto*'s 'workers of the world unite, you have nothing to lose but your chains', through Virginia Woolf's 'As a woman I want no country. As a woman my country is the whole world' (*Three Guineas*) to Teilhard de Chardin's 'The Age of Nations is past. The task before us now, if we would not perish, is to shake off our ancient prejudices, and to build the Earth' (*Building the Earth*) – and beyond.

Such rhetoric has its place. This book, however, has been more concerned to ground the discussion in the experience of unarmed resistance, such as those in Section I, and in particular forms of solidarity. Section II looks at methods of physical nonviolent intervention, accompaniment and physically crossing boundaries to defy an unjust blockade. Section III explores specific examples of labour, feminist and anti-war transnational solidarity. It also considers how in some circumstances national or ethnic identification can provide important cross-border support for struggles within a particular country, and analyses the potential of the World Social Forum – a creation of the 'global justice movement'.

Many books on transnational activism emphasise the element of *leverage* – that local movements look for transnational allies to gain leverage on their opponents, be they regimes, corporations or representatives of oppressive traditions. Some resistance campaigns – for example, the student-led resistance to Milošević in Serbia analysed in Section I – have involved such leverage from transnational civil society organisations, international governmental organisations or some national governments. But as the chapter itself and Section IV of this book indicate, such external support can create its own problems. In general the contributors here tend to go beyond the perspective of leverage and look at solidarity fulfilling a range of purposes. For them – whether they are from local movements or from transnational organisations – it is crucial that the initiative remains with the local movement.

The discussion on protective accompaniment in Section II sets the role of the transnational accompaniers in a context of seeking specific and limited leverage.

The work of nonviolent escorts, such as those organised by Peace Brigades International (PBI), has been vital in the emergence and the operation of a number of groups, in the face of threats from armed forces – be they official government forces, or unofficial death squads and paramilitaries. However, PBI express this role in terms of 'expanding the space for local actors': accompaniment and all that implies is a form of leverage for this limited and subsidiary objective rather than for the ultimate goals the local activists want to reach.

For many recent movements, the primary perspective for activists is less of acquiring the leverage to gain concessions than to strengthen their own sense of empowerment. In Colombia, civil resistance takes the form of communities opting for peace and defying the armed actors – transnational support in this has been vital but Mauricio García-Duran emphasises its constructive role in supporting grassroots peace programmes rather than its leverage. Chesterfield Samba from Zimbabwe is particularly forthright that lesbians and gays in Africa have more to gain from steady and self-defined assertiveness than 'playing the victim'. He also emphasises that the solidarity that matters most for lesbians and gays in Africa is not what is offered from those with more financial resources and power in the global North, but rather between African groups, networking, learning from each other and ultimately combining to influence African institutions. Likewise Janet Cherry's chapter on Zimbabwe emphasises the role of community-based organisations in building up a sense of empowerment, and again the solidarity that can make most difference will not come from the West or global North but from neighbours.

Sometimes 'leverage' can seem a very distant goal, and the role of transnational networking and solidarity is limited to encouragement, moral support, keeping the flame burning, rather than achieving change. It is at this point useful to consider Johan Galtung's concept of 'the great chain of nonviolence', which does not detract from networking as worthwhile in itself yet offers hope of connecting it with leverage (Galtung 1989).

Unarmed movements achieve direct leverage either because of the strength of their message or because their withdrawal of cooperation undermines (or threatens to undermine) the power-holder concerned. There are also other sources of indirect influence, including the strategic concept of a 'chain of nonviolence'. The idea is that when an oppressed community cannot directly influence power-holders in a situation, they begin link-by-link to construct a chain of nonviolence by approaching those people they can reach, planning that each link will in turn connect with others until the chain extends to people closer to the power structures and even to decision-makers themselves. Galtung formulated this concept in the Israeli–Palestine context where, historically, the Palestinian–Israeli dialogue began with Palestinians meeting 'anti-Zionist' Israeli Jews – people generally considered politically 'marginal' in their own society. However, dialogue with anti-Zionists could lead to dialogue with 'non-Zionists', eventually connecting with more mainstream peace groups not opposed to Zionism per se but at least opposed to the Occupation. Thence links could be made to policy-makers in the major political parties and decision-makers. The chain is not necessarily direct – some links can be made by international intermediaries, and the links are built out of whatever is shared, whether that is music, football or archaeology.

Galtung tends to describe the process in terms of 'social distance'. When there is too great a social distance between adversaries for them to communicate, then there is a need for intermediaries. If one population is systematically dehumanising another, they are preparing the terrain for atrocities and not for a peace process. The chain of nonviolence aims to reverse this dehumanisation and create conditions for a more peaceful outcome.

Ralph Summy (1994) subsequently used the 'chain of nonviolence' concept to extend a central tenet of the theory of nonviolent action: that power-over depends on the cooperation of those ruled. Advocates of strategic nonviolence, however, face the problem that there are circumstances in which an oppressive power-holder is *not* directly dependent on the cooperation of a subject population. Summy suggests that in this case people should build 'a chain of nonviolence' aiming ultimately to connect with those on whom the power-holder *does* depend, affecting their loyalty and willingness to carry out orders.

The tendency to focus on leverage when writing about transnational activism is one example of focusing too much at the instrumental level. Particular functions of solidarity may be important – including exchange of various types of information, perhaps transfer of skills or support in 'capacity-building' – but for many networks they are secondary to the value of contact and making relationships. This is highlighted in Cynthia Cockburn's contribution on Women in Black – a network of mutual support and of respectful listening. Relationships of solidarity, rather than precise goals to be achieved by common campaigns, are at the centre of this. The face-to-face connection offers a different point of reference, a way of filtering the vast amounts of information now available, a motivation for shedding preconceptions and finding orientations for action.

Looking at networks such as Women in Black or my own political 'home' for the past two decades, War Resisters' International (WRI), offers a different perception of transnational activism than concentrating on professionalised NGOs or short-lived mass campaigns. Involvement in these long-term networks is usually an addition to – often an outgrowth of – the local activity of its participants. Generally the activists are people who are somehow trying to fit the transnational into their local work – be that responding to a global threat, countering the global impact of policies pursued by the power-holders in their own society or sometimes drawing inspiration from the activities of movements elsewhere. And sometimes they are people who are urgently looking for international support to help them find the answer to some of the issues they are facing or for specific solidarity when war resistance brings repression on them. Andreas Speck's contribution on support for Turkish war resisters is a recent example of a recurrent phenomenon.

Simple networking – that is, making and maintaining webs of connections – is a vital and perpetual activity in movement-building. Moses Mazgaonkar, writing on India, emphasises this from the grassroots point of view in terms of analysing 'success' in a more nuanced way than 'victory' or 'defeat'. At the transnational level, long-standing networks such as WRI continue to play a critical role in bringing into existence specific short-term projects or campaigns and transnational coalitions because they can provide useful connections and also carry a history of activism, and in the case of WRI participatory democratic and consensual ways of working.

Stellan Vinthagen believes that such long-standing transnational coordinations could meet some of the problems of the World Social Forum (WSF), the meeting place for movements thrown up by the global justice movement. He sees WSF's value as a site for interaction across movements as well as across other boundaries and praises its efforts to be more 'horizontal' and less hierarchical than previous anti-capitalist coordinations (from the First International onwards). Nevertheless, he concludes that it will not fulfil its potential unless it can address certain issues of internal democracy and in particular the dominant participation of a self-selected elite. To this end, he urges an expanded role for other international 'sectoral' networks (environment, peace, etc.) inside the Forum.

Conclusion

To mobilise transnational solidarity, movements are often tempted to concentrate on the negative, the threat, the vulnerability of a community, the suffering of the victims. As observed in the Introduction, and by particular contributors, this can be at the expense of cultivating local empowerment. To speak of solidarity in a framework of resistance marks a shift from solidarity not only on the basis of what is being *done to* people or communities but also responding to what they themselves are doing to overcome that. A local movement, instead of viewing transnational solidarity as some sort of *deus ex machina* that rescues a lost situation and imposes a 'solution', treats it as an additional factor to be included in their strategy, strengthening their counter-power against domination and oppression, and respecting their say in what the future should be. Transnational activists working in solidarity in this framework will then focus more on supporting the processes of empowerment at work as local resistance grows as well as contributing to the movement's international leverage.

In this situation, for the actors concerned – both the local movement and those in other countries – the central element of transnational solidarity is likely to be their own relationships, that is, their common commitment, their mutual understanding and the quality of their cooperation.

Box A.1   Read on!

In 2006, April Carter, Michael Randle and I prepared a bibliography entitled *People Power and Protest Since 1945: A Bibliography of Nonviolent Action* (London: Housmans). It includes a section on international nonviolent intervention. It is selective, and limited to about 1,000 entries. Already, since publication, more than 200 more have been added to the online update at www.civilresistance.info/bibliography.

Fortunately, there are always new examples of unarmed resistance to various types of injustice and against various threats to human survival, and new material being written about them, making sense of what happened and offering lessons.

In August 2008, as I was writing the Introduction, I learnt that the first two boats carrying humanitarian aid to Gaza had successfully docked. They presented the Israeli blockaders with the dilemma: let us through and break the blockade, or stop us and face international condemnation – and this time got through. Around the same time, the wall-to-wall media coverage of the 2008 Olympics in China was interrupted by the actions of foreign Free Tibet protesters in Beijing, as earlier was the carrying of the Olympic torch from Greece to China.

I hope that the experiences discussed and issues raised in this book will inform future analysis of new episodes of unarmed resistance and transnational solidarity. With my colleagues April Carter and Michael Randle, I will do my best to keep the reader up to date on such analyses through the ongoing bibliography at http://www.civilresistance.info/bibliography.

WORKS CITED

Ackerman, P. (2004) 'Between hard and soft power: The rise of civilian-based struggle and democratic change', online at http://www.state.gov/s/p/of/proc/34285.htm [accessed 23 October 2008]

Ackerman, P. and DuVall, J. (2000) *A Force More Powerful: A Century of Nonviolent Conflict* [New York and Basingstoke: Palgrave]

Ackerman, P. and Kruegler, C. (1993) *Strategic Nonviolent Conflict: The Dynamics of People Power in the Twentieth Century* (Westport, CT: Praeger)

A Human Security Doctrine for Europe (2004) The Barcelona Report of the Study Group on Europe's Security Capabilities (Barcelona)

Akay, E. (2003) *A Call to End Corruption* (Minneapolis: New Tactics in Human Rights Project), online at http://newtactics.org/ACalltoEndCorruption [accessed 13 October 2008]

Albó, X. (1993) 'Violencia cultural en los Países Andinos', in McGregor, F., ed., *Violencia en la Región Andina* (Lima: APEP)

Alternative Defence Commission (1983) *Defence Without the Bomb* (London: Taylor & Francis)

ALTSEAN [Alternative ASEAN Network on Burma] (2007) Saffron Revolution Update, 15 October, online at http://www.altsean.org/Research/Saffron%20Revolution/SRHome.php [accessed 12 October 2008]

Anderson, M.B. (2003) *Confronting War: Critical Lessons for Peace Practitioners* (Cambridge, MA: Collaborative for Development Action)

Andoni, G. (2003) 'Rachel', *The Electronic Intifada*, 25 March 2003, online at http://electronicintifada.net/v2/article1293.shtml [accessed 13 October 2008]

Ang, C.G. (1998) *Aung San Suu Kyi: Towards a New Freedom* (Sydney: Prentice Hall)

Anner, M. and Evans, P. (2004) 'Building bridges across a double divide: Alliances between US and Latin American labour and NGOs', in Leather, A. and Eade, D., eds., *Development NGOs and Labour Unions: Terms of Engagement*, Development in Practice Readers (West Hartford, CT: Kumarian)

Anyamele, C., Lwabaayi, R., Tuu-Van, N. and Bingswanger, H. (2005) *Sexual Minorities, Violence and AIDS in Africa*, African Working Paper Series No. 84 (Washington, DC: World Bank), online at http://worldbank.org/afr/wps/wp84.pdf [accessed 15 October 2008]

Aris, M., ed. (1995) *Aung San Suu Kyi: Freedom from Fear and Other Writings* (Harmondsworth: Penguin)

Armbruster-Sandoval, R. (2005a) 'Workers of the world unite? The contemporary anti-sweatshop movement and the struggle for social justice in the Americas', *Work and Occupations*, Vol. 32, No. 4

—— (2005b) *Globalization and Cross-border Labor Solidarity in the Americas: The Anti-Sweatshop Movement and the Struggle for Social Justice* (London and New York: Routledge)

Arraf, H. and Shapiro, A. (2003) 'The uprising for freedom is an international struggle', in Stohlman, N. and Aladin, L., eds., *Live from Palestine: International and Palestinian Direct Action against the Israeli Occupation* (Cambridge, MA: South End Press), pp. 67–75

Arrowsmith, P. (1972) *To Asia in Peace: The Story of a Non-Violent Action Mission to Indo-China* (London: Sidgwick & Jackson)

Åslund, A. and McFaul, M., eds. (2006) *Revolution in Orange: The Origins of Ukraine's Democratic Breakthrough* (Washington, DC: Carnegie Endowment)

Barghouti, M. (2002) 'Palestine: The amazing power of people', *Al-Ahram Weekly Online*, 10–16 January 2002, http://weekly.ahram.org.eg/2002/568/op11.htm [accessed 13 October 2008]

—— (2005) 'Palestinian defiance', *New Left Review*, No. 32, March–April

Barker, M. (2007) 'A force more powerful: Promoting "democracy" through civil disobedience', *State of Nature*, Winter 2007, online at http://www.stateofnature.org/forceMorePowerful.html [accessed 14 October 2008]

Bhatia, B., Drèze, J. and Kelly, K. (2001) *War and Peace in the Gulf: Testimonies of the Gulf Peace Team* (Nottingham: Spokesman Books)

Boothe, I. and Smithey, L.A. (2007) 'Privilege, empowerment, and non-violent intervention', *Peace and Change*, Vol. 32, No. 1, January

Borras Jr, S.M., Edelman, M. and Kay, C. (2008) *Transnational Agrarian Movements: Confronting Globalization* (Oxford: Wiley Blackwell)

Burrowes, R. (2000) 'The Persian Gulf War and the Gulf Peace Team', in Moser-Puangsuwan and Weber (2000)

Carter, A. (1977) 'The Sahara Protest Team', in Hare and Blumberg (1977) and Moser-Puangsuwan and Weber (2000)

Carter, A., Clark, H. and Randle, M. (2006) *People and Power Protest since 1945: A Bibliography of Nonviolent Action* (London: Housmans)

Cheran, R. (2004) *Diaspora Circulation and Transnationalism as Agents for Change in the Post-conflict Zones of Sri Lanka* (Berlin: Berghof Foundation)

Ciccariello Maher, G. and Golinger, E. (2008) 'Making excuses for empire: Reply to defenders of the AEI [Albert Einstein Institution]', Venezuelanalysis.com, 4 August 2008, online at http://www.venezuelanalysis.com/print/3690 [accessed 14 October 2008]

Clark, H. (2000) *Civil Resistance in Kosovo* (London: Pluto)

Cockburn, C. (2007) *From Where We Stand: War, Women's Activism and Feminist Analysis* (London and New York: Zed Books)

Collectif (2001) *Israel/Palestine: Des Femmes contre la Guerre* (Paris: Editions Dagorno)

Commission on Human Security (2003) *Human Security Now* (New York)

Daraghmeh, M. (2005) 'The new Gandhists – Belaen: Nonviolent successful experience' (Search for Common Ground: *CGNews*), online at http://www.commongroundnews.org/article.php?mode=8&id=794 [accessed 13 October 2008]

Democratic Voice of Burma (2007) *Activists March against Fuel Rise*, 20 August

Desmarais, A.A. (2007) *La Vía Campesina: Globalization and the Power of Peasants* (London: Pluto)

Dominguez, E. and Quintero, C. (2008) 'Apoyo transnacional-activismo local: Fortalezas y debilidades en la resistencia laboral y de género. Los casos del Comité Fronterizo de Obreras (CFO) en Piedras Negras y Factor X en Tijuana, B.C.', in *Género y globalización en América Latina. Décimo aniversario de la Red Haina (1996–2006)* (Göteborg: School of Global Studies), online at www.globalstudies.gu.se/iberoamericanstudies/samverkan/ haina [accessed 12 October 2008]

Donnelly, E.A. (2002) 'Proclaiming Jubilee: The Debt and Structural Adjustment Network' in Khagram, Riker and Sikkink (2002)

Dudouet, V. (2008) *Nonviolent Resistance and Conflict Transformation in Power Asymmetries* (Berlin: Berghof)

Ebert, Theodor (1981) *Gewaltfreier Aufstand. Alternative zum Bürgerkrieg* (Waldkirchen: Waldkircher Verlagsgesellschaft)

Eguren, L.E. (2005) *Protection Manual for Human Rights Defenders* (Brussels/Dublin: PBI European Office/Front Line)

Forbrig, J. and Demeš, P., eds. (2007) *Reclaiming Democracy: Civil Society and Electoral Change in Central and Eastern Europe* (Washington, DC: The German Marshall Fund of the United States)

Foster, L. (1999) 'Contribution to the Conference, Monitoring Peace in Bougainville', Australia National University, online at http://rspas.anu.edu.au/melanesia/documents/ bougainville/PDF/foster.pdf [accessed 15 October 2008]

Furnari, Ellen (2006) 'The Nonviolent Peaceforce in Sri Lanka: Methods and impact (September 2003–January 2006)', *Intervention*, Vol. 4, No. 3

Galili, L. (2004) 'Fence and defense', *Ha'aretz*, 21 March

Galtung, J. (1976) 'Three approaches to peace: Peacekeeping, peacemaking and peacebuilding', in Galtung, J., ed., *Peace, War and Defence – Essays in Peace Research,* Vol. II (Copenhagen: Christian Ejlers)

—— (1989) *Nonviolence and Israel/Palestine* (Honolulu, HI: University of Hawaii Institute for Peace)

García-Durán, M., ed. (2004) *Alternatives to War: Colombia's Peace Processes*, Accord 14 (London: Conciliation Resources)

—— (2006) *Movilización por la Paz en Colombia 1978–2003* (Bogotá: CINEP/Colciencias/ UNDP)

Gobernadores Indígenas de Urabá (1997) 'Proclama por la paz: La Paz es compromiso de todos', in Ramírez, J., ed., *Neutralidad y Vida – Un camino para hacer y vivir la paz* (Medellín: Consejería Indígena de la Gobernación de Antioquia/Alcaldía de Mutatá/Viva la Ciudadanía)

Greenpeace webpage, http://www.greenpeace.org/international/about/history [accessed 9 October 2008]

Griffin-Nolan, E. (1991) *Witness for Peace: A Story of Resistance* (Louisville, KY: Westminster/John Knox Press)

Hare, P. and Blumberg, H., eds. (1977) *Liberation Without Violence: A Third-Party Approach* (London: Rex Collings)

Helvey, R.L. (2004) *On Strategic Nonviolent Conflict: Thinking about Fundamentals* (Boston, MA: Albert Einstein Institution), online at http://www.aeinstein.org/organization/ org/OSNC.pdf

Hernández, E. (2004) *Resistencia civil artesana de paz – Experiencias indígenas, afrodescendientes y campesinas* (Bogotá: Editorial Pontificia Universidad Javeriana/Suipcol)

Hijab, N. (2004) 'The role of Palestinian diaspora institutions in mobilizing the international community', *Economic and Social Commission for Western Asia*, online at http://se2. isn.ch/serviceengine/FileContent?serviceID=RESSpecNet&fileid=9547FA70-9754-7CA8-184A-79C83C0A6DB0&lng=en [accessed 12 October 2008]

Hillen, J. (2000) *Blue Helmets: The Strategy of UN Military Operations* (Washington, DC: Brasseys)

Human Rights Watch (2005) *'Bullets Were Falling Like Rain': The Andijan Massacre, May 13, 2005* (New York: Human Rights Watch)

Hunter, D. and Lakey, G. (2004) *Opening Space for Democracy: Third-Party Nonviolent Intervention – Curriculum and Trainer's Manual* (Philadelphia: Training for Change), part online at www.trainingforchange.org

Ilić, V. (2001) *Otpor – In or Beyond Politics*, Helsinki Files No. 5, Helsinki Committee for Human Rights in Serbia, Belgrade, 2001; English version online at http://www.helsinki.org.yu/publications.html [accessed 13 October 2008]

International Crisis Group (2008) 'Nepal's new political landscape', *Asia Report*, No. 156, 3 July 2008, online at http://www.crisisgroup.org

Johnston, H. (2005) 'Talking the walk: Speech acts and resistance in authoritarian regimes', in Davenport, C., Johnston, H. and Mueller, C., eds., *Repression and Mobilization* (Minneapolis: University of Minnesota Press)

Karliner, J. (2001) *A Brief History of Greenwash*, online at http://www.corpwatch.org/article.php?id=243 [accessed 13 October 2008]

Keck, M. and Sikkink, K. (1998) *Activists Beyond Borders: Advocacy Networks in International Politics* (Ithaca, NY: Cornell University Press)

Kelly, K. (2005) *Other Lands Have Dreams: From Baghdad to Pekin Prison* (Petrolia, CA: CounterPunch)

Kember, N. (2007) *Hostage in Iraq* (London: Darton, Longman & Todd)

Khagram, S., Riker, J.V. and Sikkink, K., eds. (2002) *Restructuring World Politics: Transnational Social Movements, Networks, and Norms* (Minneapolis: University of Minnesota Press)

Kidder, T. (2002) 'Networks in transnational labor organizing', in Khagram, Riker and Sikkink (2002)

Kinane, E. (2003) 'Cry for justice', in Moser-Puangsuwan and Weber (2003)

Koppall, C. et al. (2003) *Preventing the Next Wave of Conflict: Understanding Non-traditional Threats to Global Security* (Washington, DC: Woodrow Wilson International Centre for Scholars)

Kothari, S. (2002) 'Globalization, global alliances, and the Narmada movement', in Khagram, Riker and Sikkink (2002)

Kreager, P. (1995) 'Aung San Suu Kyi and the peaceful struggle for human rights in Burma', in Aris (1995)

Lakey, G. (1987) *Powerful Peacemaking: A Strategy for a Living Revolution* (Philadelphia, PA: New Society Publishers)

Lawrence, Q. (2008) *Invisible Nation: How the Kurds' Quest for Statehood is Shaping Iraq and the Middle East* (New York: Walker Books)

Lederach, J.P. (2005) *The Moral Imagination – The Art and Soul of Building Peace* (New York: Oxford University Press)

León, J. (2004) *No Somos Machos, Pero Somos Muchos – Cinco crónicas de resistencia civil en Colombia* (Bogotá: Editorial Norma)

Levy, G. (2004) 'The peaceful way works best', *Ha'aretz*, 11 February

Lintner, B. (1989) *Outrage: Burma's Struggle for Democracy* (Hong Kong: Review Publishing; 1990 edn: London and Bangkok: White Lotus)

—— (2007) 'Burma's warrior kings and the generation of 8.8.88', *Global Asia*, Vol. 2, No. 2, Fall

Lofland, J. (1993) *Polite Protesters – The American Peace Movement of the 1980s* (Syracuse, NY: Syracuse University Press)

Mahony, L., ed. (2004) *Side by Side: Protecting and Encouraging Threatened Activists with Unarmed International Accompaniment* (Minneapolis: Center for Victims of Torture)

—— (2006) *Proactive Presence: Field Strategies for Civilian Protection* (Geneva: Henry Dunant Centre for Humanitarian Dialogue), online at http://www.hdcentre.org/Proactive+Presence

Mahony, L. and Eguren, L.E. (1997) *Unarmed Bodyguards: International Accompaniment for the Protection of Human Rights* (West Hartford, CT: Kumarian)

Malone, A. (2008) 'Day of the generals and the wife', *Weekend Post*, 12 July

Martin, B. (2005) 'How nonviolence works', *Borderlands e-journal*, Vol. 4, No. 3

—— (2007) *Justice Ignited: The Dynamics of Backfire* (Lanham, MD: Rowman & Littlefield)

Massey, D. (2000) 'Entanglements of power: Reflections', in Sharp, J.P., Routledge, P., Philo, C. and Paddison, R., eds., *Entanglements of Power: Geographies of Domination and Resistance* (London and New York: Routledge)

McAdam, D., Tarrow, S. and Tilly, C. (2001) *Dynamics of Contention* (Cambridge: Cambridge University Press)

McDonald, G. (1997) *Peacebuilding from Below – Alternative Perspectives on Colombia's Peace Process* (London: Catholic Institute for International Relations)

McNair, A. (2002) 'Tibetan nonviolence movement revitalizes', *Peace Magazine*, October–December

Meyssan, T. (2005) 'Albert Einstein Institution: nonviolence according to the CIA', *Voltaire*, 4 January 2005, online at http://www.voltairenet.org/article30032.html#nh7 [accessed 23 October 2008]

Miall, H., Ramsbotham, O. and Woodhouse, T. (1999) *Contemporary Conflict Resolution: The Prevention, Management and Transformation of Deadly Conflicts* (Cambridge: Polity Press)

Mohamoud, A. (2007) *Mobilising African Diaspora for the Promotion of Peace in Africa* (Amsterdam: African Diaspora Centre)

Moody, R. (2007) *Rocks and Hard Places: The Globalization of Mining* (London: Zed Books)

Moser-Puangsuwan, Y. and Weber, T. (2000) *Nonviolent Intervention Across Borders: A Recurrent Vision* (Honolulu, HI: Spark M. Matsunaga Institute for Peace)

Moser-Puangsuwan, Y., Andrieux, A. and Sarosi, D. (2005) *Speaking Truth to Power: The Methods of Nonviolent Social Struggle in Burma* (Bangkok: Nonviolence International), online at http://www.nonviolenceinternational.net

Mowat, J. (2005) 'Coup d'état in disguise: Washington's New World Order "democratization" template', *Centre for Research on Globalisation*, 9 February 2005, online at http://www.globalresearch.ca/articles/MOW502A.html [accessed 23 October 2008]

Moyer, B., with McAllister, J., Finley, M.L. and Sofier, S. (2001) *Doing Democracy: The MAP Model for Organizing Social Movements* (Gabriola Island, BC: New Society Publishers)

Müller, B. (2006) *The Balkan Peace Team 1994–2001: Non-violent Intervention in Crisis Areas with the Deployment of Volunteer Teams* (Stuttgart: Ibidem-Verlag)

Mushaben, J.M. (1986) 'Grassroots and Gewaltfreie Aktionen: A study of mass mobilization strategies in the West German Peace Movement', *Journal of Peace Research*, Vol. 23, No. 2, June

Nyamhangambiri, S. (2008) 'Deal gives Mugabe too much power: ZCTU', ZimOnline, 30 September

Oppenheimer, M. and Lakey, G. (1965) *A Manual for Direct Action* (Chicago: Quadrangle Press)

Pagnucco, R. and McCarthy, J. (1999) 'Advocating nonviolent direct action in Latin America: The antecedents and emergence of SERPAJ', in Zunes, S., Kurtz, L.R. and Asher, S.B., eds., *Nonviolent Social Movements: A Geographical Perspective* (Oxford: Blackwell)

Patchwork (1998) *A Movement Action Plan for Turkey. Documentation*, online at http://www.andreasspeck.info?q=en/node/32 [accessed 12 October 2008]

Peretti, J. and Micheletti, M. (2003) 'The Nike Sweatshop Email: Political consumerism, Internet, and culture jamming', in Micheletti, M., Follesdal, A. and Stolle, D., eds., *Politics, Products, and Markets: Exploring Political Consumerism Past and Present* (New Brunswick: Transaction Press)

Poblicks, N.C. (2002) 'Kacoke Madit: A diaspora role in promoting peace', in Lucima, O., ed., *Protracted Conflict, Elusive Peace: Initiatives to End the Violence in Northern Uganda* (London: Conciliation Resources)

Prasad, D. (2005) *War is a Crime Against Humanity: The Story of War Resisters' International* (London: War Resisters' International)

Probleme des Friedens. (1997) 'Aufstehen gegen Kulturen der Gewalt. Beispiel Türkei', *Probleme des Friedens*, No 3

Rai, M. (2003) *Regime Unchanged: Why the War in Iraq Changed Nothing* (London: Pluto)

Rajshekhar (2006) *Myanmar's Nationalist Movement (1906–1948) and India* (New Delhi: South Asia Publishers)

Randle, M. (1994) *Civil Resistance* (London: Fontana)

—— (2004) *Jubilee 2000: The Challenge of Coalition Campaigning* (Coventry: Centre for Forgiveness and Reconciliation [now Centre for Peace and Reconciliation Studies])

Rapaport, M. (2005) 'Gandhi Redux', *Ha'aretz*, 10 June

Rigby, A. (1991) *Living the Intifada* (London: Zed Books)

Ritchie, M. (2002) 'A practitioner's perspective', in Khagram, Riker and Sikkink (2002)

Roberts, A. and Garton Ash, T. (2009) *Civil Resistance and Power Politics: The Experience of Nonviolent Action from Gandhi to the Present* (Oxford: Oxford University Press)

Rose, C. (2005) *How to Win Campaigns: 100 Steps to Success* (London: Earthscan)

Routledge, P. (1997) 'A spatiality of resistances', in Pile, S. and Keith, M., eds., *Geographies of Resistance* (London: Routledge)

Sandoval, L.I. (2004) *La Paz en Movimiento 1993–2003: Realidades y Horizontes* (Bogotá: Instituto María Cano [ISMAC]), 2 vols

Santos, B. de S. (2006) *The Rise of the Global Left: The World Social Forum and Beyond* (London: Zed Books)

Schell, J. (2003) *The Unconquerable World: Power, Nonviolence and the Will of the People* (New York: Metropolitan Books)

Schirch, L. (1995) *Keeping the Peace: Exploring Civilian Alternatives in Conflict Prevention* (Uppsala: Life and Peace Institute)

Schock, K. (2005) *Unarmed Insurrections: People Power Movements in Non-Democracies* (Minneapolis: University of Minnesota Press)

Schweitzer, C. (2000) 'Mir Sada: The story of a nonviolent intervention that failed', in Moser-Puangsuwan and Weber (2000)

—— (2005), 'An experiment at mixing roles: The Balkan Peace Team in Croatia and Serbia/ Kosovo', in *People Building Peace* (Utrecht: European Centre for Conflict Prevention), II, pp. 369–75

Schweitzer, C. and Clark, H. (2002) *Balkan Peace Team – International e.V.. A Final Internal Assessment of its Functioning and Activities* (Minden: Bund für Soziale Verteidigung, Hintergrund- und Diskussionspapier No. 11)

Schweitzer, C., Howard, D., Junge, M., Levine, C., Stieren, C. and Wallis, T. (2001) *Nonviolent Peaceforce Feasibility Study* (Hamburg/St Paul: Nonviolent Peaceforce), online at http://www.nonviolentpeaceforce.org/en/feasibilitystudy [accessed 12 October 2008]

Scott, J.C. (1985) *Weapons of the Weak: Everyday Forms of Peasant Resistance* (New Haven, CT: Yale University Press)

—— (1990) *Domination and the Arts of Resistance: Hidden Transcripts* (New Haven, CT: Yale University Press)

Seidman, G. (2007) *Beyond the Boycott: Labor Rights, Human Rights and Transnational Activism* (New York: Russell Sage Foundation)

Seitz, C. (2003) 'ISM at the crossroads: The evolution of the International Solidarity Movement', *Journal of Palestine Studies*, Vol. 32, No. 4

Sellström, T. (2002) *Sweden and National Liberation in Southern Africa*, Vol. II: *Solidarity and Assistance 1970–1994* (Uppsala: Nordiska Afrikainstitutet)

Sen, J. and Kumar, M., eds., 2003, *Are Other Worlds Possible? The Open Space Reader on the World Social Forum and its Engagement with Empire*, Vol. 1 (New Delhi: The Open Space Series)

Sen, J., Kumar, M., Bond, M. and Waterman, P., eds. (2007) *A Political Programme for the World Social Forum?* (New Delhi and Durban: CACIM and CCS)

Shadmi, E. (2000) 'Between resistance and compliance, feminism and nationalism: Women in Black in Israel', *Women's Studies International Forum*, Vol. 23, No. 1

Shankman, S. (2008) 'Zimbabweans take to blogging, cellphone texting to pass on news', *The Herald*, 22 July

Sharp, G. (1973) *The Politics of Nonviolent Action* (Boston, MA: Porter Sargent)

—— (1985) *Making Europe Unconquerable* (Cambridge, MA: Ballinger)

—— (1993 [2003]) *From Dictatorship to Democracy* (Boston, MA: Albert Einstein Institution)

—— (2005) *Waging Nonviolent Struggle: 20th Century Practice and 21st Century Potential* (Boston, MA: Porter Sargent)

Sikkink, K. (1993) 'Human rights, principled issue-networks and sovereignty in Latin America', *International Organization*, Vol. 47, No. 3

Silitski, V. (2006) *Contagion Deterred: Preeemptive Authoritarianism in the Former Soviet Union (the case of Belarus)* (Stanford, CA: Stanford University Centre on Democracy, Development and the Rule of Law Working Papers No. 66)

Slater, D. (1997) 'Spatial politics/social movements', in Pile, S. and Keith, M., eds., *Geographies of Resistance* (London: Routledge)

Slim, H. and Eguren, L.E. (2004) *Humanitarian Protection: A Guidance Booklet*, Pilot Version (London: ALNAP [Active Learning Network for Accountability and Performance in Humanitarian Action])

Solnit, D., ed. (2004) *Globalize Liberation: How to Uproot the System and Build a Better World* (San Francisco, CA: City Lights)

Stephan, M. and Mundy, J. (2006) 'A battlefield transformed: From guerrilla resistance to mass nonviolent struggle in the Western Sahara', *Journal of Military and Strategic Studies*, Vol. 8, No. 3, Spring

Stolle, D. and Micheletti, M. (2005) 'The expansion of political action repertoires: Theoretical reflections on results from the Nike Email Exchange Internet Campaign', paper for the 101st Annual Meeting of the American Political Science Association

Summy, R. (1994) 'Nonviolence and the case of the extremely ruthless opponent', *Pacifica Review*, Vol. 6, No. 1 [*Pacifica Review* is now published as *Global Change, Peace and Security*; also available in Kumar, M. and Low, P., eds., *Legacy and Future of Nonviolence* (New Delhi: Gandhi Peace Foundation, 1996)]

Tarrow, S. (2005) *The New Transnational Activism* (Cambridge: Cambridge University Press)

Thalhammer, K.E., O'Loughlin, P.L., Glazer, M.P., Glazer, P.M., McFarland, S., Shepela, S.T. and Stoltfuz, N. (2007), *Courageous Resistance: The Power of Ordinary People* (Basingstoke and New York: Palgrave Macmillan)

Timberg, C. (2008) 'Inside Mugabe's violent crackdown: Notes, witnesses detail how campaign was conceived and executed by leader, aides', *Washington Post Foreign Services*, 5 July

Vanaik, A. (2008) 'New Himalayan republic', *New Left Review*, No. 49, Jan./Feb.

Villarreal, N. and Ríos, M.A. (2006) *Cartografía de la Esperanza – Iniciativas de resistencia pacífica de las mujeres* (Bogotá: Corporación Ecomujer)

Vinthagen, Stellan (2002) 'Motståndets globalisering' [The globalisation of resistance], in Löfgren, M. and Vatankhah, M., eds., *Vad hände med Sverige i Göteborg?*(Stockholm: Ordfront Förlag)

—— (2007) 'WSF Kenya: Another WSF is possible!', War Resisters' International, online at http://wri-irg.org/news/2007/wsf-vinthagen-en.htm [accessed 13 October 2008]

—— (2008) 'Is the World Social Forum a democratic global civil society?', *Societies without Borders*, Vol. 3, No. 1

War Resisters' International (2005) *Mehmet Loves Barış Documentation: Conscientious Objection in Turkey* (London: War Resisters' International), online at http://www.wri-irg.org/pdf/turkey05-en.pdf [accessed 12 October 2008]

Weber, T. (1996) *Gandhi's Peace Army: The Shanti Sena and Unarmed Peacekeeping* (Syracuse, NY: Syracuse University Press)

—— (2003) 'Nonviolence is who?: Gene Sharp and Gandhi', *Peace and Change*, Vol. 28, No. 2

Whitaker Ferreira, F. (2006) *Towards a New Politics: What Future for the World Social Forum?* (New Delhi: Vasudhaiva Kutumbakam)

Williams, J. (2008) 'Freedom in a fortnight: A view from the trenches', Women of Zimbabwe Arise communication, 24 July (online at several pages)

Wilson, A. (2005) *Ukraine's Orange Revolution* (New Haven, CT: Yale University Press)

Women in Black (various dates from 1994) Successive issues of *Women and Peace*. (Belgrade: Žene u Crnom, 11 Jug Bogdanova)

World Rainforest Movement (2008) *FSC [Forestry Stewardship Council] certification of tree plantations needs to be stopped*, online at http://www.wrm.org.uy/actors/FSC/WRM_Briefing.pdf [accessed 12 November 2008]

Yates, A. and Chester, L. (2006) *The Troublemaker: Michael Scott and his Lonely Struggle against Injustice* (London: Aurum)

Zelter, A. (2008) *Faslane 365: A Year of Anti-Nuclear Blockades* (Edinburgh: Luath Press)

Zunes, S. (2008a) 'Nonviolent action and pro-democracy struggles', *Foreign Policy in Focus*, 24 January 2008, online at http://www.fpif.org/fpiftxt/4923 [accessed 14 October 2008]

—— (2008b) 'Sharp attack unwarranted', *Foreign Policy in Focus*, 27 June 2008, online at http://www.fpif.org/fpiftxt/4923 [accessed 14 October 2008]

Zunzer, W. (2004) *Diaspora Communities and Civil Conflict Transformation* (Berlin: Berghof)

NOTES ON CONTRIBUTORS

Nenad Belčević is Training Coordinator of the Centar za Nenasilni Otpor (Centre for Nonviolent Resistance), Belgrade. From 1999 to 2002 he worked in Otpor, first as a member of the Press Service team and later as a trainer.

April Carter is an Honorary Research Fellow at the Centre for Peace and Reconciliation Studies, Coventry University. Her most recent books are *The Political Theory of Global Citizenship* (London: Routledge, 2001) and *Direct Action and Democracy Today* (Cambridge: Polity, 2005). She also compiled (with Howard Clark and Michael Randle) *People Power and Protest Since 1945: A Bibliography of Nonviolent Action* (London: Housmans, 2006).

Janet Cherry is a lecturer in Development Studies at the Nelson Mandela Metropolitan University in Port Elizabeth, South Africa. She is a human rights activist, and a trainer with the Centre for Applied Nonviolent Action and Strategies (CANVAS).

Howard Clark is an English nonviolent activist and independent peace researcher who now lives in Madrid. He has worked for *Peace News* and War Resisters' International, and since 2008 has been chair of War Resisters' International. A research fellow of the Centre for Peace and Reconciliation Studies, Coventry University, he has been responsible for the Centre's project on Unarmed Resistance: The Transnational Factor. He is author of *Civil Resistance in Kosovo* (London: Pluto, 2000) and co-author with April Carter and Michael Randle of *People Power and Protest Since 1945: A Bibliography of Nonviolent Action* (London: Housmans 2006), which is updated online at www.civilresistance.info/bibliography/update.

Cynthia Cockburn, a feminist researcher and writer, is Visiting Professor in the Department of Sociology at City University London. She is active in the anti-militarist network, Women in Black. Her latest book is *From Where We Stand: War, Women's Activism and Feminist Analysis* (London: Zed Books, 2007). Her current research project is on how mixed anti-war groups handle the theme of gender.

Véronique Dudouet has been a researcher at the Berghof Research Centre for Constructive Conflict Management, Berlin since 2005, concentrating on the areas of conflict transformation theory, civil society organisations and resistance/liberation movements in transition from war to politics. Her latest publication is *Nonviolent Resistance and Conflict Transformation in Power Asymmetries* (Berlin: Berghof, 2008). She has been involved in peace and nonviolent movements since her childhood (which she spent in the Communautés de l'Arche in France).

Luis Enrique Eguren is a physician in the Canary Islands, also working as a consultant, trainer and researcher on issues of protection. First volunteering with PBI in El Salvador in 1988, he has subsequently worked with PBI in Sri Lanka and Colombia as well as on shorter missions with PBI and other NGOs. Co-author with Liam Mahony of *Unarmed Bodyguards: International Accompaniment for the Protection of Human Rights* (West Hartford, CT: Kumarian, 1997), his other publications include *Protection Manual for Human Rights Defenders* (Brussels/Dublin: PBI European Office/Front Line, 2005).

Ivana Franović is a Belgrade peace activist and feminist, working with the Centar za Nenasilnu Akciju – Beograd (Belgrade Centre for Nonviolent Action) since 1998. She is co-editor of *I Can't Feel Well If My Neighbour Does Not* (Belgrade: Centar za Nenasilnu Akciju, forthcoming).

Mauricio García-Duran SJ is director of the Centro de Investigación y Educación Popular (CINEP, the Centre for Research and Popular Education) in Bogotá. He has worked on programmes with the displaced population for CINEP and the Jesuit Refugee Service, including with peace communities in the Bajo Atrato. He edited *Alternatives to War: Colombia's Peace Processes* (London: Conciliation Resources – Accord 14, 2004) and his Ph.D. thesis has been published as *Movilización por la Paz en Colombia 1978–2003* (Bogotá: CINEP/Colciencias/UNDP, 2006).

Jørgen Johansen is a Scandinavian scholar, activist, journalist and trainer of nonviolence. Active since 1970 in social movements focused on peace, nonviolence, ecology and solidarity, he was chairperson of War Resisters' International from 1991 to 1998. He now mainly dedicates himself to peace research and education, especially connected with the Transcend Peace University, the European Peace University and the Centre for Peace and Reconciliation Studies, Coventry University.

Kathy Kelly was the founder and a coordinator of Voices in the Wilderness (US) from 1995 to 2005. She is author of *Other Lands Have Dreams: From Baghdad to Pekin Prison* (Petrolia, CA: CounterPunch, 2005) and co-author (with Bela Bhatia and Jean Drèze) of *War and Peace in the Gulf: Testimonies of the Gulf Peace Team* (Nottingham: Spokesman Books, 2001).

George Lakey – the founding director of Training for Change – is currently the Eugene M. Lang Visiting Professor for Issues in Social Change at Swarthmore College, Pennsylvania. He's been an activist for half a century and presently lives in the anarchist neighbourhood of West Philadelphia. He is author of *Strategy for a Living Revolution*, updated in David Solnit (ed.), *Globalize Liberation* (San Francisco: City Lights, 2004); the article is available at www.TrainingforChange.org, along with field reports, descriptions of training activities, articles, essays, books and events.

Brian Martin is Professor of Social Sciences in the School of Science, Technology and Society at the University of Wollongong, Australia. He has written widely on nonviolence and suppression of dissent, including his contributions via Schweik Action Wollongongon. His most recent book is *Justice Ignited: The Dynamics of Backfire* (Lanham, MA: Rowman and Littlefield, 2007) and a full range of articles can be found on his web page, http://www.uow.edu.au/arts/sts/bmartin/pubs.

Moses (Anand) Mazgaonkar, based in Gujarat, is part of the Gandhian movement, currently working on environmental and economic policy issues, on land rights for tribal/ indigenous people and against displacement arising from 'development projects'. He is one of the national convenors of the National Alliance of People's Movements, an alliance of farmworkers, fisherpeople, displaced people, trades unions and other groups.

Yeshua Moser-Puangsuwan coordinates research on Non-State Armed Groups for the International Campaign to Ban Landmines annual Landmine Monitor report. From 2005/06 he was the course coordinator for Peace, Conflict & Human Rights at the Mahidol University Graduate Studies Faculty. He sits on the International Council of the nongovernmental organisation Nonviolence International and is a consultant for the International Peace Bureau in Geneva.

Danijela Nenadić is Programme Coordinator of the Centar za Nenasilni Otpor (Centre for Nonviolent Resistance), Belgrade, and a correspondent for Osservatorio sui Balcani.

Milan Rai was the founder and a coordinator of Voices in the Wilderness (UK) from 1998 to 2003 and since 2007 has been editor of *Peace News*. His books include *Regime Unchanged: Why the War on Iraq Changed Nothing* (London: Pluto, 2003).

Andrew Rigby is Professor of Peace Studies and founding director of the Centre for Peace and Reconciliation Studies at Coventry University where he teaches an MA course and runs other programmes. His past research includes studies on nonviolent and unarmed movements in India and Palestine, including his book *Living the Intifada* (London: Zed Books, 1991). Currently his main research is on processes of reconciliation after violence.

Chesterfield Samba is the operations manager for Gays and Lesbians of Zimbabwe, http:// www.galz.co.zw, and lives in Harare. He also works with other organisations dealing with victims of violence and torture and is a member of the international Council of War Resisters' International.

Christine Schweitzer has been active in the peace and nonviolence movements both as a volunteer and staff member. Since 2001 she has been working with the Institute for Peace Work and Nonviolent Conflict Transformation (www.ifgk.de), and until 2008 was first Research Director and then Programme Director for Nonviolent Peaceforce. Currently she is finishing a Ph.D. thesis on 'Strategies of Intervention in Protracted Violent Conflicts by Civil Society Actors'.

Andreas Speck coordinates the Right to Refuse to Kill Programme of War Resisters' International. He has been editor of the German nonviolent anarchist magazine *Graswurzel Revolution*. Detailed information on CO issues in Turkey and other countries can be found on the WRI website, http://www.wri-irg.org.

Stellan Vinthagen is a Senior Lecturer at the School of Global Studies' Department of Peace and Development Research, Göteborg University, Sweden. He is co-founder of the Resistance Studies Network (www.padrigu.gu.se/rsn/default.html), a member of the peace and development scholar network Transcend (www.transcend.org), and a council member of War Resisters' International. For more than two decades he has also been a movement activist and teacher in conflict transformation and civil disobedience; most recently, he was arrested in Scotland for a nonviolent direct disarmament action against the Trident nuclear submarine.

Rita Webb is programme officer for Nonviolent Peaceforce Sri Lanka.

Louise Winstanley has continued working in solidarity with Colombian human rights defenders since returning to Britain, and also campaigns against the monoculture of African palm plantations in Colombia.

Ann Wright, since retiring, has dedicated herself to human rights work and now lectures on the theory and practice of civilian peacekeeping: who does it, where, and how it works. She illustrates her presentation with examples from two field projects she has been on: PBI in Colombia and EAPPI on the West Bank. For a detailed account of her work in Tulkarem, see www.palestinejournals.co.uk, or contact her at anawright@hotmail.com.

Angie Zelter is a long-time nonviolent activist, perhaps best known for Ploughshares actions (in the 1990s against Hawk planes due to be sent to Indonesia and thence East Timor, more recently against the Trident nuclear missile programme). She has also taken nonviolent direct action on other ecological and human rights issues. Her most recent book is *Faslane 365: A Year of Anti-Nuclear Blockades* (Edinburgh: Luath Press, 2008).

INDEX